AGRICULTURE

IN THE

TROPICS

AGRICULTURE

IN THE

TROPICS

AN ELEMENTARY TREATISE

BY

J. C. WILLIS, M.A., Sc.D., F.R.S.

European Correspondent, late Director of the Botanic Gardens, Rio de
Janeiro; formerly Director of the Royal Botanic Gardens, Ceylon,
Organising Vice-President, Ceylon Agricultural Society, and
Editor of *The Tropical Agriculturist*

THIRD EDITION, REVISED

Cambridge :
at the University Press
1922

CAMBRIDGE UNIVERSITY PRESS
Cambridge, New York, Melbourne, Madrid, Cape Town,
Singapore, São Paulo, Delhi, Tokyo, Mexico City

Cambridge University Press
The Edinburgh Building, Cambridge CB2 8RU, UK

Published in the United States of America by Cambridge University Press, New York

www.cambridge.org
Information on this title: www.cambridge.org/9781107600201

First edition 1909
Second edition, Revised 1914
Third edition 1922
First paperback edition 2011

A catalogue record for this publication is available from the British Library

ISBN 978-1-107-60020-1 Paperback

PREFACE TO THE FIRST EDITION

DURING the last twenty-five years a great deal of attention has been drawn to agriculture in the tropics, as to other subjects connected with the same regions of the world. Not only do people travel more in the tropical regions, not only has there been great rivalry between the nations of the North in acquiring and developing colonies there, but also such agricultural phenomena as the collapse of coffee planting and the rise of cinchona, cacao, and tea in Ceylon, the depression of sugar in the West Indies and the formation of an Imperial Department of Agriculture to deal with the situation, the recent rise of rubber planting in Ceylon, the Federated Malay States, Mexico, and other tropical countries, and the depression in cotton, followed by the formation of the British Cotton Growing Association, and the extension of the cultivation of this crop in the West Indies and the British African colonies, have all in themselves excited very general interest. This has shown itself, among other things, in the formation of departments of agriculture in most of the colonies of the tropics.

The danger is now that we may try to go too rapidly, without a proper thinking out of the subject. There being no general work upon tropical agriculture other than those dealing with the technical side of the subject, such as Semler's great volumes upon *Tropische Agrikultur*, Mollison's *Textbook of Indian Agriculture*, and Nicholls' smaller but useful *Tropical Agriculture*, I have endeavoured to supply this want in the present work, and to place before the public, as clearly as may be, something of the underlying " political " and theoretical side of the subject, setting forth what such agriculture really is, the conditions under which it is carried on, its successes and disasters and their causes, the great revolution that is being effected by western influences, and other general principles underlying the whole subject, in whatever country it may be carried on. Under each product, also, I have tried to suggest promising lines for improvement.

No attempt has been made to write a book for the practical man to use in connection with his actual field work. The effort has been to produce a work that may be helpful and thought-stimulating for the student, the administrator, or the traveller. Those who read it must kindly remember, therefore, that it is a pioneer and strictly elementary work, capable of vast improvement after the subject has been properly discussed.

Agriculture in the tropics is wider and more varied in range than in the north, and we cannot doubt that there will be more and more rapid progress, and that the cooler countries will come to depend more and more upon the warmer zones for their supplies of food and other things. The white powers now control the bulk of the tropics, and are rapidly opening up Africa and south-eastern Asia. It is consequently of great importance that the peoples of the north should understand the general position with regard to agriculture there, and be able to direct matters to the best advantage, both of themselves and of the governed peoples.

The tropics cover so enormous an area that it is obvious that I can only write of much of it from reading, though the general principles set forth will apply to all countries. My own experience is mainly confined to Asia, in Ceylon, India, Java, and the Federated Malay States. On the agriculture of the last named I have written a comprehensive report, which often forms the basis of the present work, and I am much indebted to the Government of that dependency for allowing the use of it. I have also visited the American tropics, but have not been in tropical Africa, though the heads (to be) of many African departments of agriculture have come to Ceylon for part of their training.

It is a pleasure also to acknowledge the kindly encouragement and help of many friends, among whom I would specially mention Mr O. P. Austin, Chief of the Bureau of Statistics of the United States Treasury Department, Dr Melchior Treub, Director of Agriculture in the Dutch East Indies, Mr Francis Darwin, late Foreign Secretary of the Royal Society, Mr I. H. Burkill, Reporter on Economic Products to the Government of India, Mr G. W. Sturgess, Government Veterinary Surgeon, Ceylon, Mr E. E. Green, Entomologist, Mr M. Kelway Bamber, Chemist, and Mr T. Petch, Mycologist, of my own department, and last, but not least, my wife. I am also much beholden for loan of blocks for illustration to the Government of Ceylon, to the Kolonial Wirthschaftliche Komitee of Berlin, to Sir Daniel Morris of the West Indian Agricultural Department, and others. I am much indebted for help to Mr A. E. Shipley.

JOHN C. WILLIS.

Peradeniya, Ceylon,
December 21, 1908.

PREFACE TO THE SECOND EDITION

DURING the last few years the various countries of the tropics have been more occupied in establishing departments of agriculture than in considering the principles of the subject, and there has been so little profitable discussion that I have found but few alterations needed in this edition. In especial, I have adhered more strictly to the geographical definition of the tropics, excluding for instance North India.

The chief criticisms made have been to the effect that India is badly misrepresented. If so, I can but apologise, but as regards indebtedness of the peasantry may refer to Sir Andrew Fraser's recent book, where it is given at a truly astounding figure, or point to the success of the Cooperative Credit Societies, whose adoption I have preached for the last twelve years. No one can set up India as a model of agricultural efficiency or progress; she suffers now from the ruthless destruction of her natural capital that went on in former ages, and groans under a hot sun and badly distributed rainfall.

I have rewritten the chapter on rubber, which well illustrates the complex nature of the problems which lie before those interested in agricultural progress.

I am also accused of favouring the capitalist; if the book gives that impression it must be for want of clear expression, for its main thesis is the equal encouragement of both capitalist and peasant, but that they being at different stages of progress need different treatment.

For the last two years I have resided in Brazil, and am pleased to find that nothing in the agriculture of this country requires a revision of the main propositions of the book. Brazil, in my opinion, should be the great agricultural country of the tropics at some future time, provided her natural capital can be saved from exhaustion, as it has been exhausted in most eastern countries.

The chief alterations will be found on pp. 5, 10, 12, 64, 65, 120, 136, 148, 154, 160, 213.

J. C. W.

May 1914.

CONTENTS

PART I

THE PRELIMINARIES TO AGRICULTURE

PART II

THE PRINCIPAL CULTIVATIONS OF THE TROPICS

PART III

AGRICULTURE IN THE TROPICS (GENERAL)

PART IV

AGRICULTURAL ORGANISATION AND POLICY

LIST OF ILLUSTRATIONS

INTRODUCTION

THE tropics include an immense area of land in every continent but Europe. Their agriculture, however, was until lately only of serious importance to the world at large in Southern Asia, Brazil, Mexico, Central America and the West Indies, West Africa, North Australia, and a few groups of islands in the Pacific. The following rough figures, giving in round numbers the value or bulk of the chief exports from some of the principal exporting countries, will give some idea of the enormous trade that now goes on, and which is increasing year by year.

INDIA, 1919—20.

Cotton (raw)	£39,069,000
,, (manufactured)	18,935,000
Grains, pulse, and flour	10,097,000
Hides and skins	15,604,000
Jute (raw)	16,466,000
,, (manufactured)	33,344,000
Lac	4,843,000
Seeds (oils, etc.)...	17,506,000
Tea	13,710,000

CEYLON, 1919.

Tea	Rs116,500,000
Rubber	132,100,000
Coconut products	86,500,000
Cinnamon	3,700,000
Cacao	3,100,000
Areca nuts	3,000,000
Citronella oil	900,000
Cardamoms	900,000
Tobacco	600,000

Rs15 = £1

JAVA, 1918.

	metric tons
Sugar	1,574,201
Copra	68,578
Rubber	44,096
Tea	30,452
Cassava products	28,129
Pepper	25,899
Fibres (except kapok)	19,696
Kapok	9,253
Tobacco	8,050
Coffee	7,357
Quinine bark	2,440
Nutmegs	2,338
Coca	662
Coconut oil (1000 litres)	33,237

INDO-CHINA, 1917.

Rice	1,366,748
Maize	12,425

PHILIPPINE ISLANDS, 1917—18.

Abaca or Manila hemp	$54,493,970
Sugar	13,304,770
Copra	9,527,241
Cigars	5,708,718
Other tobacco and cigarettes	5,059,655

GOLD COAST, 1919.

Cocoa	176,000 tons
Palm Kernels	9,986
Kola nuts	7,143

FEDERATED MALAY STATES, 1919.

Rubber	106,453 tons
Copra	26,650

FIJI, 1920.

Sugar	73,000 tons

BAHAMAS, 1919—20.

Sisal hemp	6,341,000 lbs.

BARBADOS, 1918.

Sugar	57,000 tons
Cotton	188,000 lbs.

CUBA, 1920.

Sugar (estimated)	3,650,000 tons

JAMAICA, 1919.

Cocoa	£286,000
Coconuts	285,000
Coffee	356,000
Fruit (chiefly bananas)	1,141,000
Pimento	184,000
Rum	924,000
Sugar	1,317,000

TRINIDAD, 1918.

Sugar	35,104 tons
Rum	145,035 galls.
Cocoa	26,178 tons

BRITISH GUIANA, 1919.

Sugar	93,902 tons

BRAZIL, 1920.

Coffee (bags of 60 kilos each)	11,524,000
Sugar	109,140 tons
Maté	90,686
Chilled meat	60,897
Cocoa	54,418
Hides	37,265
Tobacco	31,469
Cotton	24,696
Rubber	23,586

When we look over this and similar lists, and realise that the tropics supply us with all our cinchona bark (for quinine), cinnamon, coconuts, coconut oil, copra, coir, coffee, gutta-percha, jute, palm-oil, rice (with the exception of a little in the Southern United States), rubber, sago, spices, sugar (except the beet sugar of the continent), tea, tapioca, and many other things, the vast importance of agriculture in the tropics, and of its proper conservation, improvement and extension, will be understood. The area occupied by the cultivation of the export products is perhaps 50 million acres and that spent in maintaining the actual people of the tropics is perhaps about another 275 millions. Even at this rate not more than half the available land is used, and not only so, but much of it is very inefficiently used, while intensive agriculture, as practised in Europe or America, is almost unknown, except among European planters. Could the yield of cereals in India, for example, be increased by a mere bushel an acre, a vast difference would for a time be made in the economic prosperity of that country. This, however, is more easily said than done.

The agriculture conducted by Europeans in the tropics is more efficient than that of the natives of the country. This may be roughly illustrated by the case of Ceylon, where the exports of "European" produce are to those of "native" produce as 3 to 1, while the area cultivated by the former, and the population supported by it, are only as 1 to 5, the population being equally dense in either case, or denser on the European estates.

Before agriculture upon any but the very smallest scale or basis can be carried on in a country, there must be in that country satisfactory conditions as regards certain indispensable preliminaries.

Land must be available at a moderate cost. The price of land will naturally vary with its advantages as regards nearness to market, good or bad transport facilities, good or bad climate, and many other things, but "moderate" in the sense used here will of course take note of all these things.

Roads or other means of transport must be in good order, to bring material to the plantation and to take the produce away. Without good means of transport, it is idle to expect any serious agricultural industries to be carried on, for sale or export of the produce.

Capital, to some extent at least, must be forthcoming. Even those undertakings which soonest give a return, such as cotton, whose crop can be picked in six months, need a certain amount of capital to tide over the period of waiting; without this only the very smallest enterprises can be carried on, and even these will often be in an unhealthy condition, their crops being mortgaged to money-lenders.

Labour must also be available, if any but very small enterprises are to go on. A man and his family cannot obviously till more than a few acres at most, and for anything more extensive—and efficiency in agriculture largely goes with the larger enterprises—we must have hired labour. This difficulty is one of the greatest that confront anyone proposing to start agricultural enterprises in the tropics. In India, Ceylon, the Malay States, Java, and some of the West Indian islands, labour is comparatively plentiful, but elsewhere it is usually difficult to obtain.

In the first part of this book, we propose to discuss, in brief, these necessary preliminaries to agriculture. In the second we shall consider the principal cultivated crops of the tropics in a general way, with a view partly to making suggestions for their improvement. In the third part we shall go on to consider village and capitalist agriculture respectively, with the directions in which improvement seems most possible, and in the concluding part of the work shall discuss agricultural policy, and the organisation of a department of agriculture, a thing which has now become a necessity in most tropical countries.

PART I

THE PRELIMINARIES TO AGRICULTURE

CHAPTER I

LAND AND SOIL

LAND in the tropics may be of many types, but the two chief kinds are forest and grass lands, and it is as a rule only on the former (or what has been so) that there is much agriculture. Speaking broadly, the greater part of the land near to the sea is, or has been (as apparently in India), covered with forest, which in general marks the districts of good and well-distributed rainfall. In the interior of tropical Africa, and in parts of South America, what the Americans term *savannahs*, i.e. open park-like grass lands, with patches of forest here and there, prevail.

Forest land is preferred for agriculture, not only on account of its (usually) better rainfall, but also on account of its richer soil, due to the humus, or decaying organic matter, contained in it. The forest is felled, and burnt off in the drier weather of the year. As a rule the timber does not pay to work, and is completely burnt, enough only being kept for houses, factories, etc. The crops are put out among the stumps, which in a few years are completely removed by decay and white ants.

A very favourite method of cultivation, among natives in the east at any rate, is what is called in Ceylon *chena*, in Malaya *ladang*, in India *jhuming*, etc. The forest, or rather the trees in it below a certain girth, is felled and burnt, and various cereals or other crops are sown upon the land in the rains. On a rich, newly cleared land, these give a very large return for a minimum of work, and this method of cultivation is in consequence highly popular, until the country becomes too thickly peopled to admit of it. After one to three crops the land is abandoned, and grows up in scrubby jungle, and may be again chena-ed after 8—50 years. Vast areas of good forest land have been ruined in southern Asia by this destructive practice, and in most countries chena permits for crown land are only issued now under stress of very hard times and failure of the regular crops.

Land in the tropics may be held in a variety of ways. For instance, in Ceylon the tenure is fully freehold, and the owner of land leaves it to his children, the men taking it in equal shares, as in France. By this means, emigration even to new districts in the same country is rendered difficult, and there is little chance of anyone showing any agricultural enterprise, unless he be a comparatively large holder of land. The ordinary villager owns a mere trifle of land, as a rule barely sufficient for his own support and that of his family. In this way, the land becomes very "ancestral," and the same family may go on in the same place for an almost unlimited number of generations. When the area is small, the ownership is commonly joint and this still further retards agricultural progress, for all the owners must consent before any change can be introduced.

While in Ceylon the holder of land pays no tax to the Government, in India he pays a considerable levy upon his land, but most often, perhaps, holds it otherwise freehold. In India, Ceylon, and other eastern countries the ancient system of "villages" prevails, these being divisions of country of 500 acres or more, sometimes, but not always, with a central village street or group of houses. Very often some of the land is cultivated, some waste, and most commonly, perhaps, the latter is the joint property of the village, all the villagers being allowed to graze their cattle on it, or to cut wood there. The villages themselves may be "joint" villages, owned in their entirety by the community living in them, who work the land in sections appropriated to each family, sometimes on a more or less cooperative system; but more often, within the tropics, they are not such villages, but each family actually owns (or leases) a piece of land. In the former case the village is assessed as a whole for the payment of the Government tax; in the latter each proprietor is separately assessed. In both cases the village artisans are often paid by a levy on the produce.

In the Federated Malay States, land is regarded as entirely the property of the Government; in fact, "land nationalisation," so much discussed in Europe, is already an accomplished fact in this country. Anyone may buy land from the Government on payment of a premium of one dollar or so an acre, and an annual quit-rent of one or more dollars an acre. Should he cease to pay the rent, or abandon the land for three consecutive years, the Government steps in and resumes possession of it. The original grant of the land from the Government is for 999 years, so that there is no fear of the possessor being disturbed, so long as he continues to work the land properly, but the Government is entitled to revise the rate of quit-rent payable every 30 years. In many ways this is perhaps the best system of alienating land from the Government, for the latter derive an annual income from it, and resume it if abandoned, while the original buyer does not need to expend so much capital on the actual purchase as he does for instance in Ceylon, where he buys the land outright; and thus he has more available for cultivation.

In the West Indies, and in most of the modern British tropical colonies, the land is freehold, and though at one time in the former it was very largely held in big blocks for sugar and other plantations, it is now passing to some extent into the hands of small peasant proprietors.

Except in the thinly peopled countries it is gradually becoming more and more difficult to obtain considerable blocks of land for the larger agricultural enterprises, for the small proprietor usually sticks very closely to his own little patch of land, and refuses to sell it, even if it be almost surrounded by a large estate.

Soils. Speaking generally, the soils of the tropics are very poor as compared with those of the temperate zone. Instead of the comparatively dark colour and damp look of the latter, which is partly due to the larger content of humus, or decaying organic matter, they show a light colour and rather dry appearance in ordinary fine weather, being very poor in humus. Decay takes place so rapidly and so completely that there is but little accumulation of its products.

The soils that occur are of every conceivable kind, depending mainly upon the subjacent rocks. The richest are in general the volcanic soils such as are found in Java, the West Indies, and elsewhere, but there are also very good deposited or alluvial soils in Ceylon, India, the Malay States, and in other countries. And it is worthy of notice, as tending to show that superior richness, provided that the two soils have both all the elements of plant food in fair amount, often makes but little difference, that the growth of most cultivated crops in Java, such as tea, cacao, rubber, etc., is but little superior to that in the poor soils of Ceylon, and sometimes is not so good[1].

Probably as the result of the lack of humus, the tropical soils seem on the whole to be rather less water-retaining than those of more northern countries, and the plants growing in them (in the open) tend to flag rather more quickly for lack of water, though it is true that the sun is so much hotter that this may probably be sufficient to account for the fact.

[1] This, formerly an unexplained fact, becomes clearer in the light of recent physiological work. Cf. Blackman, Optima and Limiting Factors, *Annals of Botany*, xix, 1905, p. 281; Smith, Application of the theory of Limiting Factors to Measurements of Growth, *Annals R. B. G. Peradeniya*, iii, 1906, p. 303.

CHAPTER II

CLIMATE

THE tropics cover so vast an area that it is obvious that there must be a great variety in climates, but in general the types of climate may be set down as two : the moist, near the equator and the sea; and the dry, inland, and usually away from the equator. The former is characterised by a moist air, and a comparatively uniform temperature, with but little daily or annual variation, the latter by a considerable range, often, if it be far from the equator, annual as well as daily, and a dry air; while of course as one ascends the mountains one as a rule comes into a cooler and moister climate.

Every type of climate may be met with in passing from the south of Ceylon to the north of India, so that a comparison of some of the figures for various places lying between these extremes will be useful, while others are also given. The nearer to the equator, other things being equal, the smaller is the annual range of temperature :

	Colombo	Madura	Cochin	Bombay	Surat	Calcutta	Batavia
Mean max.	89	101	91	90	100	96	86
„ min.	72	68	71	68	56	55	72
„ humidity	78	65	80	77	62	78	83

	Manila	Chinchoxo	Lado	Colon	Rio de Janeiro	São Paulo[1]
Mean max.	96	86	88	92	86	94
„ min.	64	67	75	75	62	41
„ humidity	79	85	77	83	78	85

[1] Elevation 2485 feet.

It will be noticed that the range is greater the lower the humidity, in addition to increasing as one passes to the north ; compare for instance Madura and Cochin, which are in approximately the same latitude.

The prevailing character of the climate near the equator and near the sea, as at Colombo, is a very uniform temperature, with rain at all times of the year, but more especially when the sun has just passed overhead. Near the equator, therefore, there are two more specially rainy seasons in the year, at intervals of about six months, while as one goes northward they get nearer and nearer together, till in the far north or south of the tropics they run into one rainy season of a few months duration, as the following tables of rainfall will illustrate.

	Colombo	Trichinopoli	Bangalore	Bombay	Nagpur	Calcutta
Jan.	3·0	1·0	0·2	0·1	0·6	0·4
Feb.	1·7	0·5	0·1	0·0	0·4	1·0
Mar.	5·5	0·7	0·6	0·0	0·6	1·3
Apr.	8·8	1·8	1·3	0·0	0·5	2·3
May	13·2	3·8	5·0	0·5	0·8	5·6
June	8·2	1·3	3·2	20·8	8·8	11·8
July	5·5	2·2	4·0	24·7	13·3	13·0
Aug.	4·5	4·4	5·9	15·1	8·9	13·9
Sept.	4·9	5·3	6·3	10·8	7·8	10·0
Oct.	12·9	7·8	6·4	1·8	2·3	5·4
Nov.	12·7	5·2	1·9	0·5	0·4	0·6
Dec.	6·4	3·1	0·7	0·1	0·5	0·3[1]

Rainy seasons indicated by brackets.

The longer the dry season, the hotter, generally speaking, it becomes, so that in the north of India the heat is often extreme at the end of the dry weather, whereas, near the equator, where there is rain at all times, the highest temperatures recorded are rarely above 90°. The range of temperature is greater in the northern hemisphere than in the southern, where the land masses are smaller, and only in the interior of Australia does the temperature become anything like so high as in north India.

---

[1] Blanford, *Climate and Weather of India and Ceylon.*

Near the equator, and near the sea, the climate is wonderfully uniform, the mean temperatures of the twelve months at Colombo being for example 79, 80, 82, 83, 83, 82, 81, 81, 81, 81, 80, 80, while at Singapore they are almost the same. On the average, in Colombo, the temperature only reaches about 86° during the day, and falls to about 75° at night. In drier places inland the daily range is greater, but the annual range is much the same until one gets far from the equator.

Humidity, other things being equal, increases with elevation. Thus Colombo at sea level, and Hakgala at 5600 feet, have much the same rainfall, similarly distributed, and their average humidities are 78 and 87 respectively.

Another feature which makes some difference to the climate of a place is the exposure upon the mountains. Thus in Ceylon, when the south-west monsoon is blowing, there is heavy rain upon the western side of the mountain chain, while the eastern side is comparatively dry. While the rainfall at Ratnapura, on the south-western side, is 20·78 inches in June, that at Badulla, 50 miles away, upon the eastern side, is only 2·66 inches. In the north-east monsoon, which blows for six months in the year in the opposite direction, the positions are reversed, so that the main wet seasons in the two places differ by about six months, and the periodicity of the phenomena of plant life is also different, Para rubber for instance ripening its seeds at Badulla in February, and at Ratnapura in August.

The actual direction of exposure of a place upon the mountains also makes a difference. In Java and Ceylon, the mornings are comparatively cloudless compared with the afternoons. It therefore follows that, in general, a place with an eastern exposure will get more sunshine than one with an exactly similar exposure to the west. In the extreme north of the tropics, a place with a northern exposure will, other things being equal, be colder than one with a southern exposure, and in the extreme south the reverse will be the case.

The amount of sunshine falling upon a particular place is also a feature of some importance. The temperature in the sun is usually very high, amounting to 140°—170° F., while that in the shade will in general be 60°—80° lower. While in places like Singapore, where the influence of the monsoons is slight, there may be sunshine nearly every day, in places like Ceylon, where they are very pronounced, there may be weeks or even months with hardly a gleam of sunshine during the first onset of the monsoons.

Rain in the tropics usually falls in violent showers, rapidly raising the levels of the streams, making roads and flowerbeds "swim" with water, and doing a good deal of damage by the silting up of stream beds, washing away of soil, etc. The usual shower varies from 0·03 to 3·0 inches, and it falls in a much shorter time than in Europe.

Wind in the tropics is, generally speaking, light compared with that found, for instance, in Great Britain. In the monsoon region of South Asia, near the equator the wind blows fairly steadily for six months in one, and six in the other direction, the year being less evenly divided further north.

In tropical, as in other countries, elevation has a very definite influence upon the climate, the mean temperature— and that for practically all hours of the day and night—falling about 3·5°—4° F. for every 1000 feet of ascent. Thus in Ceylon, to take places with about similar and similarly distributed rainfall, the mean temperature of various months in Colombo, at sea level, runs from 79° to 83°, at Peradeniya, 1560 feet above sea level, from 74° to 79°, and at Hakgala, 5600 feet above sea level, from 58° to 63°. To dwellers in Europe, where the thermometer may easily range from the highest to the lowest of these figures in one day, these may seem trifling differences, but they have a most marked effect upon vegetable life where they go on, as these do, all the year round. Hardly a plant grown in the botanic gardens at Hakgala is the same as in the gardens at Peradeniya, and this is not from any wish to keep the collections dissimilar, but because plants which will grow at the latter place will often not grow at the former except under glass. With the exception of camphor and tea, which come from much further north, and are most accommodating to temperature, but few cultivations can be successfully carried on in both places.

The range of temperature varies according to the slope, to some extent, and on open plains at high elevations there is often a very considerable range of temperature, making the climate very unlike that of places lying upon the slopes quite near by. Thus at Nuwara Eliya in Ceylon, which lies upon an open plain at an elevation of 6200 feet, the thermometer ranges between 28° and 81° during the drier season of the year, while at Hakgala, only six miles off, and 600 feet lower, the extremes are about 37° and 79° during the same period, Hakgala lying upon the ordinary mountain slopes. Consequently, perhaps, many European plants of the north succeed at Nuwara Eliya, while they merely struggle for life at Hakgala. The greater range of temperature on the plain is probably largely due to the greater radiation that goes on; and it will be noticed that there is more difference between the minima than between the maxima.

The character of the soil also has to some extent an effect upon the climate, a sandy soil being liable to get much more heated during the day and cooled at night than a clayey one, so that there is a greater range of temperature upon the former. Drainage of the soil, more particularly in swampy land, thus has a tendency to make the range of temperature greater.

The effect upon the climate of the clearing of the forests in a country has been a fruitful source of dispute, many of the disputants ignoring the fact that it need not necessarily be the same in all countries. So far as the tropics are concerned, its general effect seems to be to make the climate warmer and drier. In Ceylon, for example, at Peradeniya and Kandy, 1600 feet above sea level, most of the houses built prior to 1850 had fireplaces, which are now quite unnecessary, all the forest having been cleared from the neighbourhood, and the mean temperature having apparently risen. In the Federated Malay States, the climate at corresponding elevations appears to be slightly cooler or at least more uniform and damper than in Ceylon, the whole country being much covered with forest.

The clearing of the forest acts in a disastrous way upon the streams, these being now much exposed, and consequently liable to dry up during dry weather. Most of the streams which rise in the lower parts of the western mountains of Ceylon now dry up during February and March, but those which rise above 5000 feet—land above that elevation being kept in its natural condition of forest—remain running during that period.

Not only does clearing expose the soil to the sun, but also to the wind, which does not blow in the forest, and which has a drying effect. Shelter belts of trees have had to be planted through the tea and other crops throughout many planting districts, to check the sweeping of the wind over the fields.

[The climate of southern tropical Brazil is so different from that of corresponding latitudes in the north, e.g. Calcutta, that its agriculture partakes to some extent of the character of that of the temperate zone. At Rio de Janeiro, for example (22° 50′ S.), the mean temperatures of the various months range from 66° to 78°. The mean maximum is about 86°, minimum 62° (cf. Calcutta). There is well-distributed rain throughout the year, so that the place on the whole perhaps looks, though it does not feel, just as "tropical" as even Singapore or Java. The temperature in the sun is comparatively low, reaching about 133° at the maximum. The country inland is a plateau, with an elevation of 2000—2500 feet. Here the climate is 6—10° cooler; the rain is chiefly in the summer, and many temperate-zone cultivations, even such as apples or strawberries, can be successfully carried on, whilst cattle-raising is a very large industry.]

CHAPTER III

POPULATION AND LABOUR

THE total population of the tropics is large, yet not so great as that of the temperate zones, which have about the same area. India, Ceylon, Java, and some of the small West Indian islands are thickly populated, but in the rest of the tropics the peopling is extremely sparse. Of late years the natives of India and Java have begun to emigrate to other countries, and this may be expected to go on more and more; but as yet they in general ultimately return with their savings to their native land.

The following rough figures of populations and densities are instructive, especially when we remember that South America, at any rate, is probably as productive as India:

Country	Area in sq. m.	Population	Density per sq. m.
India	1,093,074	243,750,000	223
Ceylon (W., S., and Centr. Provs.)	5,865	2,074,000	355
Java	50,557	34,157,383	675
Mexico	768,883	15,063,207	19
Brazil	3,298,870	24,309,000	7
Jamaica	4,450	832,000	187
Barbados	166	200,000	1204

Now nature is fairly prodigal in the tropics, and owing to the smaller wants of the people a larger population per square mile can probably be supported by agriculture than in the temperate zone, though the agriculture in general is inefficient. While in the United States two men are enough for 50 acres of rice, in the tropics 25 to 50 will be needed in many districts.

The races that inhabit the tropics are very numerous and varied. The majority are natives of British India—Bengalis,

Mahrattas, Tamils, Telugus, Burmese, and many others of less
note. In the south-eastern parts of Asia the Malayan races are
of importance, more especially the natives of Java. Africa is
mainly inhabited by negro races, and the same is the case in
the West Indies, while Mexico and South America are chiefly
the home of the mixed race, derived from the Spaniard or
Portuguese, negro, and Indian.

Speaking in a broad general way, all these races have
similar faults regarded from the agricultural point of view. In
particular, they may all be justly accused of what we may
perhaps term in a general way indolence. However hard they
may have to work upon their own properties to make a liveli-
hood, the general principles upon which they act would seem to
be—to do no work that can possibly be avoided, never to do
to-day what can possibly be put off until to-morrow, and to do
as their great grandfather did and because he did it. It can
be readily seen, therefore, that to induce them to progress in
agriculture, or in anything else, is a work of extraordinary
difficulty. Such people show no desire for progress, and have
no enterprise in taking up new industries or undertakings.

In fact, it would appear that, as with other people, the chief
stimulus to progress is increasing pressure of population. So
long as the natural capital of forests exists, and the inhabitants
are but few, so long do the people subsist as much as possible
upon chena, a very large area being required for each individual.
As the population increases under settled government, chena is
perforce given up on the introduction of more regular methods
of cultivation, which in turn are improved as the number of
people increases. The two things of course go together and
react upon one another, every improvement in agriculture
being followed by an increase in population up to the limit of
subsistence, unless checked by other factors. This limit has
not yet been reached in much of tropical America and elsewhere.

Not only is the tropical native characterised by indolence,
but also by want of foresight. The man who looks forward
more than a few months is a very provident individual indeed.
A not untypical case was lately furnished in a certain district of

the north of Ceylon. Getting a very large crop of rice in 1903, the villagers sat down to eat it, and grew not a blade until 1905, when their seed rice was almost all that they had left; this was sown, and was attacked by a bad outbreak of the "arakkodiyan" caterpillar, with the result of famine in these villages, whose inhabitants had practically done not a stroke of work for two years. Famine having come, of course the Government was called upon to help them out of their difficulties.

Ignorance, often of the most pronounced kind, is another prominent quality among the poorer tropical natives, as among the poorer folk in other countries. Poverty, in the sense of lack of any money with which to buy things, is also a very strongly marked feature in ordinary village society, though poverty in the sense of actual dearth of things to eat and to wear is fortunately much less common, and in the more equatorial countries like Ceylon and Java is almost non-existent.

Other obstacles to any agricultural progress are the remarkable conservatism of the people, and their slavish adherence to ancient custom, their fondness for home, and consequent unwillingness to move into new districts where they might have a better chance in agricultural matters, and their prejudice against anything that smacks of novelty. All these matters will be considered again below.

On the other hand, it must not be assumed that all the agricultural characters of the tropical races are necessarily bad, though they may be far inferior to the white races or to the Chinese. The manner in which they are willing to continue the cultivation of rice and many other products, though "there is no money in them," is on the whole distinctly commendable —within reasonable limits—and the leanings towards cooperation that many eastern races at any rate exhibit are in the highest degree praiseworthy, and to be fostered to the utmost. Cooperation in agriculture is becoming one of the most important factors in its progress in Europe and America. In Ceylon, to take an example, the villagers often cooperate in the care of their rice fields, sowing each man's field in turn, or reaping it in turn, instead of each man having to do all his own work.

By a judicious handling of this principle of cooperation, there is little doubt that the agricultural prosperity of many eastern villages might be increased, while at the same time those villages could produce products for export—a thing they at present do not. Were they for example to devote a certain portion of the "common land"—a thing that exists in very many eastern villages—to the growing of "export" crops, a considerable industry might gradually come into being. But it is highly improbable that this could be effected at present without compulsion.

In sharp contrast to the tropical races are the settlers among them from the north—the Europeans, the Americans, the Chinese. Of these, the last named seem to be the only race capable of settling and breeding in the tropics without any serious loss of stamina, for the "country bred" Europeans or Americans of the West or East Indies have to an appreciable extent the characters of the native races among whom they were brought up.

In such densely peopled countries as India and Java the people have necessarily to work comparatively hard to acquire a living at all, and when the density, as in parts of Madras, is so great that the people live upon the borders of famine, they are more or less willing to emigrate to other countries where they can get greater wages, though they are rarely prepared even then to settle down in such countries. The hundreds of thousands of Tamil coolies who go from South India to Ceylon to work upon the tea estates and at other occupations practically all go back again at one time or another. Their great object is to save enough money in their temporary home to be able to return to India after a few years, there buy land and settle down in their old home. Even the bulk of the Indian coolies who go so far afield as Africa and the West Indies ultimately return to their old country. Only in Mauritius and in Guiana is there any important native population of British Indians, and even in those countries a few hundred thousand is the total after many years.

Coolies—to use the common Indian word for men upon daily pay—who go from the densely peopled countries, having learnt at home to work comparatively hard, are as a rule ready to do a fair amount of hard work, whereas the actual inhabitants of thinly or insufficiently peopled countries are as a rule very "lazy," nature being so bountiful to them that they do not need to work hard to make a living. It is but comparatively rarely that one finds an individual that has ambition to "better himself," *and* willingness to work hard for that end. It therefore follows that in thinly inhabited countries it is necessary to import labour if any serious work is to be done, especially by white men, or if any agricultural progress is to be made. Thus Ceylon[1] and the Federated Malay States import labour, the former from India, the latter from India, China and Java; the more thinly populated West Indian islands import labour from the more thickly populated islands and from India; Hawaii from Japan; southern Brazil from Italy; whereas India and Java do all their own work with their own inhabitants.

Southern tropical Brazil, as explained under Climate, has really a climate more comparable to that of the temperate zone. White men can live with less strain on the health than in tropical Asia, and even breed there. The great industry of coffee, the largest exporting industry of the tropics, is mainly in the hands of white or nearly white Brazilians. The labour is also chiefly white, especially Italian, Spanish, and Portuguese.

---

[1] Ceylon (or at least S.W. Ceylon) is not thinly populated, but the Sinhalese are averse to hard or regular work, which has therefore to be done by the Tamils imported from South India, especially in the colder "up country" districts where tea is chiefly cultivated, and in which the Sinhalese do not willingly live.

CHAPTER IV

TRANSPORT AND CAPITAL

Transport. Without some means of transporting goods to a more or less distant market, agriculture cannot be conducted upon the large scale, and the cultivator must consume his own products. If transport is difficult and costly, he is necessarily limited in his markets, whereas good and cheap transport multiplies the value of his produce by extending his market. Until this is provided, it is quite idle to expect any extensive agriculture to be carried on, unless—as occasionally but very rarely happens—the produce is so valuable that there is still a profit left after meeting the expenses of costly carriage. This was the case, for example, with india-rubber or with gutta-percha some ten years ago, and is the case with some few minor products at the present time. Such collection cannot, however, be termed agriculture.

The most primitive mode of transport at present existing, and one very common in Africa at least, is the carriage of goods upon the heads of coolies along narrow paths winding through the jungle or over the plain from one village to another and to the nearest town. As one man can only carry a moderate load, and for a moderate distance in one day, it is obvious that this method, apart from other disadvantages, must be very costly and consequently that it can only open up distant markets to a very limited extent, the profits in most forms of agriculture being insufficient to stand heavy expenditure upon carriage.

A step in advance of this is to have carriage along the paths by means of pack animals, usually bulls or ponies. By this means larger loads can be carried, and at a cheaper rate, and this method is as yet not uncommon in many parts of the tropics, especially where the cost of making proper roads is very great.

The first real step towards modern transport facilities is, however, the provision of roads along which wheeled vehicles can be driven. By this means transport is rendered much cheaper and less precarious, and most of the more advanced countries in the tropics have now reached this stage to a greater or less extent. Some, such as Ceylon, the West Indies, India, have now got a very widespread and perfect system of roads, forming quite a network over the country.

But with the interest in tropical agriculture that is now being felt in many quarters, and the extension of agricultural departments, and other organisations for the encouragement of agriculture, it will probably gradually be found that the present systems of roads, perfect though they may be, are altogether insufficient for the purpose. If the villager is to grow "commercial" crops, he too, even more than the more wealthy proprietor, must be provided with cheap transport to the markets, instead of the present system of footpaths and coolie carriage. In a report upon the agriculture of the Federated Malay States we have pointed this out, and suggested that the whole country should be marked out by road reservations at distances of about a mile apart in each direction, somewhat as has already been done in the Western United States of America. There is no need actually to make the roads in these reservations, but the latter should be there before the country fills up, when it would be very much more difficult and costly to make them. By this means the country would become broken up into blocks of about a square mile each, so that every portion of land would have access to a public road, for of course where the blocks were to be sold in small lots, roads should also be reserved into the middle portions of them. In this way the purchaser of any kind of agricultural produce would have easy access to the places from which he has to buy it, or the producer easy access to the markets where he has to sell it, and so a considerable step would have been taken in agricultural progress, for the small producer cannot afford to carry his produce long and toilsome journeys to market. This is a matter requiring early and careful consideration in all tropical countries, especially those with "spare" land.

With the advent of the motor car and of the motor lorry, a new era seems to be about to dawn with regard to agricultural progress in the more rural districts, for these vehicles will be able to collect produce more rapidly, and from greater distances from the towns, than the horse or bullock vehicles as yet in use upon the roads.

Railroads form a yet further stage in progress, and go, generally speaking, with an export trade. They are now very largely developed in India, and to a considerable extent in Ceylon, the Federated Malay States, Brazil, the West Indian Islands, and Java, but in the remainder of the tropical zone they are in general conspicuous by their absence. To work a railroad with financial success of course means that there must be a considerable amount of cultivation in the country which requires to send its produce to distant markets—unless there is, as in the Federated Malay States, a considerable mining industry—and as yet this only exists in comparatively few countries. In Brazil, the opening up of the country is done by railroads as much as, or more than, by roads.

Lastly, when by means of roads and railways the agricultural produce has reached the port, it must be carried away by some cheap and efficient means of transport. This is already provided for the great majority of tropical countries in the numerous lines of well appointed cargo steamships which ply almost throughout the world.

We have not yet mentioned, except in connection with steamships, water carriage, which almost forms a genus of transport to itself. In a very large number of tropical countries, the streams are sufficiently large, and free from rapids, to be available for the passage of at any rate small boats. Lower down larger boats or even steamers can ply upon them, and on the whole, though slow, this is perhaps the cheapest mode of transport, whilst also available at a very early stage in the development of a country. Thus it is that the great valley of the Amazon has been able to export many articles of produce in considerable quantities, though it is quite unprovided with a proper system of roads.

Apart from this "natural" water carriage, there is also a very important form of water transport, in artificially made ditches or canals. This is very well seen in the coastal lands of the Federated Malay States, where the great sugar estates have cut extensive systems of canals, upon which the sugar cane is dragged to the factory in low open boats, and manure and other products are also transported. This method of transport is very valuable, and gives these estates a measurable advantage over those of the West Indies and Java, where the cane has to be carried by rail or by cart. Canals are largely developed in India, Ceylon (where they were made in Dutch times), Guiana, and elsewhere, and form a valuable means of transport for any but very perishable goods.

Capital. This subject only requires a very brief mention, but must not be omitted, as agriculture largely depends upon the proper supply of capital; so long as no capital is forthcoming, so long can there be nothing but the smallest peasant industries, so long can there be no export trade worth mentioning, and so long might the country, so far as the remainder of the world is concerned, just as well be non-existent.

The great bulk of the capital sunk in large agricultural enterprises in the tropics is of course from Europe or America. The planting enterprises of Ceylon, India, Java, Hawaii, and other places are mainly financed from "home." At the same time, there is a small and steadily increasing amount of local capital available in the more wealthy tropical countries, like India, Brazil, and Java, and this capital is showing an increasing tendency to invest in agricultural industries.

Capital will not be invested in any country until there are satisfactory conditions as regards land, labour, and transport. As will be pointed out elsewhere, these conditions were first fully satisfied in the old slavery days in the West Indies, and the great sugar industry sprang up there. With the abolition of slavery, labour ceased to be in a satisfactory state, and Ceylon, with plentiful cheap labour at her very doors, took the place of the West Indies as a field for the investment of British capital, and has held it ever since, though many rivals have sprung up, especially, in recent years, the Federated Malay States, in which the great rubber-planting industry has grown to such dimensions.   British capital is also being invested, in greater or less amount, in the African colonies, and in Java, Sumatra, Brazil, and other foreign countries or settlements. Foreign capital mainly goes to the various foreign tropical colonies, especially the Dutch Indies.   Brazil and other South American countries, and India, on the other hand, work mainly with local money, though it must be pointed out that the common people of India at least are very heavily indebted.

Not only is capital required for the large enterprises, it is also required, in small quantity it is true, for the small, and the practically absolute lack of capital, even a few shillings, is the great bar to progress in village or peasant agriculture.   Even as it is, in perhaps the majority of cases, the small crops growing upon the land are mortgaged to money-lenders, who have advanced small sums at a rate of interest from 40 $^{\circ}/_{\circ}$ upwards. Serious attempts to get over this difficulty are now being made in many parts of the tropics, usually by the establishment of Cooperative Credit Societies, upon the lines so successful in Europe.

CHAPTER V

DRAINAGE AND IRRIGATION

As a rule, owing to the heavy nature of the rainfall, drainage is a matter of necessity in the tropics, more especially nearer to the equator, where more rain falls, and on irrigated land, where water is artificially supplied. While in North India drains of the kind seen in Europe are at times employed, as a rule, if there be any drains at all, they are simply open watercourses cut at intervals. On hilly ground they follow comparatively gentle slopes around the declivities, and do not run straight down the slopes.

Occasionally, as for instance in the coastal region of the Malay Peninsula, such drains are not enough, on account of the very heavy rainfall, the very flat nature of the country, and its very slight elevation above sea level. In such cases large drains, often in fact small canals, have to be cut at fairly frequent intervals, and it becomes a matter of great importance, before opening land, to make sure that it will be possible to drain it. The first comers of course will be all right, but later comers may have to buy up land from their predecessors to get their own drains through to the sea or to a river. In such cases we have suggested that the Government should at an early date mark out the country into approximate squares of a mile or so by lines of reservation for drains (which would of course also ultimately supply canal transport), just as we have suggested for roads, so that a purchaser of land may find that it abuts somewhere upon a drainage reservation, along which the Government will then make a drain to convey away his surplus water. Of course in such cases land would only be sold near to existing drains, not far away back in the forest.

Irrigation is a matter of great importance in the tropics, because near the equator, where the rainfall is plentiful enough, the standard crop is rice, which requires definite irrigation, and because further away from the equator the rains only fall for part of the year, and are often uncertain, so that without a guaranteed water supply the raising of crops would be a very precarious matter.

In some places, where there are no streams, the rain water is simply held in the fields by damming them up, but as a rule the water is obtained from the streams, little or big, in the neighbourhood, by damming them up by what are often called anicuts (weirs), and thus diverting the water into the fields. These anicuts may be of all sizes, from the tiny dams in use in southern Ceylon, of a few yards in length across a little brook, to the stupendous anicuts across some of the large rivers in India, and which irrigate hundreds of square miles, often at a great distance.

By means of the anicut, the water of the stream, which would otherwise simply run to waste, is prevented from doing so before it has done all the irrigation required of it. It is diverted into a channel which only falls at the minimum slope, and is consequently made to water as much land as possible, to which it is conveyed by a system of canals and sluices. The canals continually subdivide, and form a system not unlike the branches of a tree. In the simple irrigation of a small valley, as in the low country of south Ceylon, no irrigation sluices or gates are definitely made, but the water is simply dammed up or diverted as required by hand labour with piles of mud. In the great irrigation works of India, on the other hand, most elaborate systems of gates, sluices, and canals are made, and the water is distributed through these under skilled superintendence.

At first the Indian Government only made the main channels, and left the cultivators to construct the minor channels for the actual distribution, but this led to great abuses and serious waste, and now the whole system of canals is made by the Government in the first instance.

Where the water has thus been provided by the Government

at a great cost, an irrigation rate is charged upon all the
land watered by it, and in many parts of India the irrigation
works pay a good dividend through these rates. Thus in
parts of Madras, the rate is Rs. 7½ (15s.) an acre a year, and
for this a certain fixed amount of water is allowed. In the
south of Ceylon, on the other hand, where the work of making
the irrigation dams, etc., is simple and cheap, and is done by
the people themselves, there is a terrible waste of water, though
luckily there is so much rain that this very rarely matters.

One of the most wonderful systems of irrigation that ever
existed is that which was put into practice in the north of
Ceylon in the early days of the Sinhalese monarchy, 2000 years
ago, which fell into entire ruin during the Tamil invasions from
700 to 1300 A.D., and which is now, at great cost, being slowly
restored by the Ceylon Government. The north of Ceylon is a
"dry" country, i.e. it only gets rain for about four months in
the year, and must have irrigation. Almost every valley was
dammed up, the country being gently rolling, by an earthwork
or "bund" within 20 or 30 miles of its head, and other bunds,
gradually getting longer and longer, and less and less high as
the sea was approached, were made across the valley at intervals
of a few miles, lower down. During the rainy season these
reservoirs became filled. The overflow from the first "tank"
(to give the reservoirs the name by which they are known in
Ceylon), together with the waste water from the rice fields
below it, was of course caught in the second tank, and so on.
Not only so, but from the uppermost tank a canal was taken at
the highest possible level, winding round the side valleys at as
gentle a slope as possible, and feeding the tanks that were also
made in these valleys. In this way almost the whole of every
valley was made irrigable, and there was practically no water
allowed to reach the sea until it had done the maximum of
work. Some of the tanks were of enormous size; Kalawewa,
for example, now restored, has a bund about 6 miles long, and
60 feet high at the centre of the valley, while the tank is about
5 miles by 2, and in the old days, when the water was retained
at a higher level, was about three times that size, while other
tanks are even larger. The canal on the north side of Kalawewa

runs for 55 miles along the side valleys, feeding all their tanks, and is about 60 feet wide.

In many districts irrigation has to be from wells, and every form of appliance is in use, from simple hand carriage of the water—the well being made with a sloping side to enable one to walk down to the water—through more and more perfect raising implements worked by bullocks or by well sweeps, to modern continuous chain pumps, etc. This form of irrigation is particularly suited to gardening work, tobacco or vegetable cultivation, and so on, and the arrangements for distributing the water are often very perfect, the "flower beds"—if such a term may be used,—being made with little banks round them, and the water led to them in little canals.

Irrigation by windmill-pumps, such as is so common in the United States, is almost unknown in the tropics, for the wind in the driest weather is often absent, and blows hardest in the rains. Partly in consequence of this, pumps worked by oil or gas engines are coming in in some places.

The necessary concomitant of irrigation is drainage, and care must be taken to give the soil no more water than will drain away before the next application of water. Heavy clayey soils are thus in general unsuited to irrigation, which succeeds better on friable soils. A good deal of trouble sometimes arises from the top layers of the soil becoming alkaline, often for want of proper drainage. Irrigation results in good and reliable cropping, but is of course exhaustive to the soil, which will probably want manure much sooner[1].

[1] As many who have read the manuscript have complained of the absence of description of the irrigation works of Egypt, the north of India, South Africa, etc., the opportunity may be taken to point out that none of these are tropical.

CHAPTER VI

TOOLS, TILLAGE, MANURING, CROPPING, ETC.

Tools. The more complex and efficient tools, such as are so largely superseding hand labour in Europe and America, are but little employed in the tropics. The reasons for this are several, the chief being that hand labour has hitherto been so cheap that there has been but little demand for labour saving, that the complex tools require good workmen to use them, and good mechanics to mend them, neither being readily forthcoming in the tropics, and that the better tools are in general too expensive for the ordinary cultivator to buy, while cooperative purchase, such as is so common in France, Belgium, and other countries, has not yet come in.

For simple tillage of the ground, the most common tool in the more equatorial countries is probably the large hoe, or mămŏtĭ, as it is called by the Tamil coolies of Ceylon, while further north the plough is far more common. The mamoti is a very strong and heavy hoe, with a handle about 3 feet long, and a blade at right angles to it, 9 inches wide, and 7 inches deep, but varying according to the work it is designed for, those used in wet rice fields, for instance, being much larger and with longer handles. With it the coolie digs, by swinging it like a pickaxe, and he also uses it for gentle digging, scraping. and for other purposes. The spade is hardly ever used.

The plough, used in India and tropical America, and in rice cultivation in the equatorial countries, is usually a primitive instrument, as a glance at Plate XXII will show. It consists essentially of two pieces of wood fastened together at right angles, with a metal point to the horizontal one, and drawn by bullocks in dry fields, buffaloes in wet ones. It performs its work, however, with some degree of efficiency, and is both very cheap and very easy to mend if anything should go wrong, two points which appeal with very great force to the ordinary tropical villager, with little or no money, and far from any skilled help. It does not however cultivate deeply, but only to a depth of 3—8 inches, and does not turn the soil over.

Cultivators, in the American sense of the word, i.e. machines with a number of teeth to tear up the soil, and drawn along by hand or by horses or bullocks, are as yet but little employed, being too complex, too expensive, and too difficult to mend for the ordinary villager to use them, and but little wanted yet on the ordinary European estate, on account of the cheapness of hand labour. Locally made cultivators, with the parts of wood tied together with string, are, however, in use in parts of Madras and elsewhere in India, as also are locally made seed-drills and other tools. The harrow is commonly replaced by a log of wood with or without a horizontal metal blade in front of it, drawn across the field, and increased in weight by the driver standing upon it.

The pickaxe is commonly used for digging holes, removing stone, and for similar purposes. The rake is also not uncommonly used, in the same way as in Europe. A very useful tool, especially in the West Indies, is the cutlass, with which weeds are cut down, trees pruned or lopped, and even holes dug. Grain is usually cut with the sickle, and in fact all tools are both simple and primitive in most places.

Manuring is in general just as necessary in the tropics as in the temperate zones, if good results are to be obtained for any length of time on the same ground, and it is the saving of the cost and trouble of manuring which is one of the most attractive features to the ordinary unthinking villager in the practice of chena, described in Chapter I. Both European planters and natives alike prefer to get new forest land to plant upon, for it is so much richer in plant food, but of course such land becomes every year more and more scarce, and in general it may be said that every tropical cultivation requires manure.

Whether it gets the manure, however much it may require it, is a question of another kind. Perhaps the majority of tropical natives are unable to afford any manure worth mention. For instance those of the greater part of India use cow dung, which is almost the only available manure, as fuel, and have little else that could be used for this purpose. The slow but certain result is the gradual impoverishment of the soil to the lowest stage of productive capacity that its natural constitution will permit.

Even in a country like Ceylon, where vegetable matter is cheap and easily obtained, manuring is by no means common among the natives, though in the far north of the island large quantities of green stuff of various kinds are collected for manuring purposes. But on European planting estates a different state of things is evident, especially in the East, where for years the planters have had the advantage of skilled scientific advice in manuring. Nearly all Ceylon tea estates are now manured with great care and economy, with the result that the export of tea, which seemed to be reaching its maximum at about 135 millions of pounds, has gone up to a new maximum of about 190 millions. In India too, tea manuring has reached a high pitch of perfection, and in the West Indies manuring is carefully applied to sugar, cacao and other plantations, in South America to coffee, etc.

While in general farm-yard manure is the best, in practice there is not enough of it, and artificial manures, such as bone-dust, basic slag, cotton-seed cake, etc., are used. The constituents usually lacking in soils are lime, potash, and nitrogen.

A method of manuring, which is very popular in Ceylon, Java, and India, is what is called "green manuring." This consists in growing, between the rows of the permanent crop, rows or broadcasts of some plant belonging to the family of the Leguminosae (peas, beans, clovers, vetches, etc.), which have the property of taking up nitrogen (a constituent in which the soils of the tropics, owing to their lack of humus, are generally deficient) from the air. After they have grown to full size, the plants are cut down, and oftenest ploughed or dug into the ground. In this way they increase the contents of the soil in organic matter and nitrogen at a very small cost.

Another very common method of manuring in the East is folding cattle, goats, or sheep upon the land, during the drier weather. A flock of 100 sheep will sufficiently manure an acre in about 20 nights.

Rotation of Crops, with which so much is done to get better returns in agriculture in colder climates, is systematically practised in Java, Ceylon, India, the West Indies, etc. The great difficulty in the way of its general practice is the fact that so many of the tropical crops, e.g. tea, coffee, rubber, cacao, coconuts, are perennials, and consequently rotation is impossible with them, or that they are crops like rice, with which rotation is difficult. In Java the rice crop is regularly rotated with various vegetable and other crops grown on the fields when dry.

Mixture of Crops, which seems to bring in its train some of the advantages of rotation, is very common, especially in the more equatorial parts of the tropics, such as southern Ceylon, Malaya, the West Indies, etc. In Ceylon, for example, the great bulk of the country inhabited by the Sinhalese may be roughly divided into "high lands" and "paddy (rice) fields," the former being the higher lying lands, the ridges between the valleys in fact (Pl. III, p. 46), which cannot be reached by the irrigation water. Upon them the villagers grow a great mixture of crops, from trees such as coconuts, mangoes, jaks, silk-cottons, kituls, etc., down to herbaceous plants such as yams, etc. Usually they leave the ground covered with a miscellaneous turf of weeds and grass, and the cattle graze upon it. The plants are not arranged in any definite way, nor are two of the same kind necessarily put together, but they are simply left anyhow upon the land, much as they might grow in a jungle containing only those species. Now the various plants of course take different quantities of food stuffs from the soil—some take much lime, some little, some much potash, some little, and so on, so that it is quite probable that the total result is to drain the soil of its food materials at a rate proportionate to what it can supply, and thus to exhaust it at a far slower rate than would one single crop, which would use up some single constituent of the soil at a rapid rate.   In fact, the group of plants growing on the soil forms a "plant society" like the natural plant societies that grow on any piece of soil left to nature.   On a moor in Scotland, for instance, there may be a very large amount of heather, a small amount of bell-heather, and smaller amounts of rockrose and many other plants, and on any two similar pieces of ground the same plants will always be found in about the same proportions.   Now rough observation shows that something not unlike this is the case in these mixed gardens of the villagers, they nearly always containing the same plants, and in not dissimilar amounts.   It must not for a moment be supposed, however, that the villager has adopted this method of "cultivation" with any advantages of this kind in view, but rather it is that by using this method, the troublesome labour of cultivation is practically entirely done away with, for he never tills the soil among his mixed crops.   Though his return is very small from this method of cultivation, it is probable, therefore, that he gets one of the two great advantages of rotation, though of course he loses the other, of the proper tillage of the ground for which opportunity is given by the change of crop, for example from wheat to roots.

Not only is there this mixture of perennial crops, but mixture of annuals is very common in the East: pulses are sown among the grain, different kinds of grain with one another, and so on.   Here again the gain is somewhat like that obtained with rotation, or the season may suit one and not the other, so that there is not a total failure.

CHAPTER VII

PLANT LIFE IN THE TROPICS. ACCLIMATISATION

THE agriculturist coming from Europe to the tropics must entirely alter his point of view in regarding the vegetable world. No longer is there any interruption of the growth and activity of the plants by a winter. On the other hand, such interruption as there is comes rather in the hottest part of the year, the dry season. Near to the equator the dry seasons are so short that vegetation goes on almost uninterruptedly, but further to the north or the south, there is a dry season, of length increasing as we get further from the equator, and in this season the growth of the plants is little or none. Where there is a really long dry season, as in northern India, irrigation, as already explained, is a necessity if crops are to be grown for more than a comparatively small portion of the year.

The agriculturist must learn, not only what are the most suitable times of the year for sowing and for planting out— usually the wet seasons—but he must learn to perform all the other operations of husbandry—pruning, manuring, cropping, etc.—with reference to the seasons. In most of Ceylon, for instance, the great planting season is October–November, and annual crops are reaped in February–March.

The tropics possess, generally speaking, a great many species of plants. Even Ceylon, only five-sixths the size of Ireland, possesses more than twice as many as the whole of Great Britain and Ireland. And on the whole, perhaps, they similarly outnumber the temperate zones in the number of useful cultivable plants; but in any one country there are usually but few, and there are many others which may be brought in and made to grow satisfactorily there, or "acclimatised," as it is called.

Acclimatisation of plants in the tropics is very old. It has been very vigorously prosecuted, and with great success, from the first settlements there of Europeans, the Portuguese having been especially active in this respect. Plants were very early carried from the New World—especially the West Indies —to the Old, and *vice versa*. Coffee was introduced to America, it is said, by Louis XIV of France, who sent a ship out to Hayti with a single plant on board. On the way the water supply ran short, and the captain heroically shared his own water with the plant, and brought it successfully to the West Indies. It is said that the mangoes in some of the West Indian islands owe their introduction to the capture of a French warship, which was taking them to one of the French islands. A vast amount of acclimatisation has gone on, and in many cases the acclimatised plants have formed the basis of successful industries in their adopted homes, e.g. coffee (Asia, Africa) in Brazil, tea (Chinese and N. Indian), cinchona and cacao (South American) in Ceylon, rubber (South American) in Ceylon and Malaya. Not only have useful plants been acclimatised, but also innumerable weeds, usually carried unintentionally in packages of seeds, etc. Ceylon has quite a large flora of such weeds, which are almost all Mexican or West Indian, the reason apparently being that Ceylon being a forest-clad country had no weeds of its own which could take their place in the cleared ground, so that those introduced from open countries had a clear field.

With the advent to the tropics of the Dutch, and later of the English, the acclimatisation of plants was put upon a scientific and systematic footing, Botanic Gardens being opened in most of the tropical possessions for the express purpose, among others, of introducing, and trying experiments with, the plants of other countries. The history of the Ceylon gardens, perhaps the most successful of all in the British colonies, will illustrate the general history of all. The famous gardens of Peradeniya, near Kandy, in the central province of Ceylon, were opened in their present site in 1821. Concerned until about 1850 mainly with the investigation of the wild flora of the colony, they began about that time to introduce in considerable number the useful plants of other countries. Among the many valuable things introduced, mention need only be made of cinchona—introduced in 1861, and forming the staple industry of Ceylon for many years—of cacao—also an important industry in the island—of tea, now the staple export industry of the colony, originally introduced by the gardens in 1832 or earlier, but subsequently mainly brought in by private agency, and of rubber, introduced from South America by the Indian Government, aided by the Botanic Gardens of Kew, and now rapidly becoming the second or third most important industry in Ceylon. Without the aid of the Botanic Gardens, Ceylon would have remained a small and unimportant "native" possession. In the same way the West Indies owe many of their most valuable crops to the Botanic Gardens there, and the Malay Peninsula is becoming a rubber-country as the result of the work done in the gardens of Singapore. But, for the future, this acclimatisation work will be done mainly in the new countries, e.g. in tropical Africa, where cacao, introduced only a few years ago, is already a very important industry.

It is obvious that as time goes on, this introduction and acclimatisation of foreign products in any one colony or possession must decrease in importance, for the simple reason that most of the new products that can possibly be brought in are now introduced, and the chance of finding anything of great value becomes less with every year. Thus during the last twenty years the Ceylon gardens have not been able to introduce anything of much value, though they have been able to bring in a few minor fruits, shade trees, and other things, and during the present century great changes have come over the organisation of the establishment, which has expanded into a department of agriculture, to suit the changed needs of the colony.

The work of the colonial botanic gardens has of course been mainly cooperative, the gardens exchanging plants with one another, aided in the exchange by the central garden of Kew. But, just as the acclimatisation work of the larger colonies, at any rate, has sunk into comparative unimportance, and as the facilities for direct shipment of plants from one part of the globe to another have increased, so the exchange work of Kew has decreased in importance to the larger colonies.

The old cry for new products—that is, products not as yet cultivated in the country—must now be modified.   Ceylon is an interesting case in point.   At one time coffee formed $95°/_o$ of the value of her exports.   Tea, which has taken the place of coffee in the mountains, though it covers a larger area than coffee ever did, now only forms about $32°/_o$ of the value of the exports.   In addition to this, Ceylon cultivates on a commercial scale, rice (not for export), coconut palms, palmyra palms, cacao, rubber, citronella oil, cinnamon, cardamoms, coffee, tobacco, besides smaller (but usually growing) areas of camphor, vanilla, coca, lemongrass, cotton, nutmegs, cinchona, annatto, cassava, fruits[1] and vegetables[1], a very varied and imposing list of products.   There are now practically no new products of the old kind which can be introduced into the country, and in which, as was the case in tea, the competition is only with the products of the tropical or sub-tropical races of mankind, or, as is the case in rubber, with the product of wild jungle trees, collected by very rough methods.   Almost everything of value in tropical agriculture is now in the hands, somewhere or another, of Europeans, Americans, Chinese or Japanese, and in starting any new product in any country a fierce competition will have to be met from countries already growing that product.

[1] I.e. for export; there are large areas devoted to growing these products for home consumption.

CHAPTER VIII

AGRICULTURE IN THE TROPICS IN PRIMITIVE TIMES, AND ITS GRADUAL CHANGE

BEFORE the advent of the European races to the tropics, agriculture may almost fairly be called non-existent there, except in the more civilised countries such as India, by reason of the comparatively savage habits of most of their inhabitants. It is not intended to imply that nothing was cultivated, for that would be entirely incorrect, but that no systematic and regular cultivations were engaged in. As in early days there was practically no export trade, the products cultivated were of course in general those that could be used in the countries themselves, such as rice, yams, fibres, drugs, oils, etc. It must also be remembered, that, as pointed out in Chapter VII, as there was then little or no intercourse between the different countries in the tropics, the supply of useful plants was far less varied than it now is. Rice, for instance, was probably unknown outside of Indo-Malaya.

In general, then, the principle upon which early agriculture was conducted was of the simplest—grow all you need, and consume all you grow. And in very many countries in the tropics agriculture as yet has practically not got beyond this stage. In the older and more civilised countries however, such as India or Ceylon, matters have always been more complex than this, owing to the presence of land owners and other capitalists. Upon the land belonging to such people, the poorer villager has in some countries had to work as a slave, in others has had to rent the land for his own use, usually on a system of shares, the owner taking say 50°/₀ of the crop as rent. In yet other cases, the villager has perhaps owned his own land, but has had to pay a heavy tax to the chief of the district. A relic of such taxation was kept up in Ceylon until about thirty years ago, the villager having to pay to the government $10\,^{\circ}/_{\circ}$ of the rice that he grew.

Almost the only countries where agriculture was carried on in any systematic way in early times were those inhabited by the Indian races (India, Ceylon, etc.), where agriculture has always been counted an honourable profession, and where the cultivators were usually among the highest castes of all. It appears also to have been of some importance in tropical America (Mexico, Peru, etc.) prior to the advent of the Spaniards.

Partly perhaps in consequence of the unsettled nature of the country, and the risk attaching to the cultivator who should settle down in one place to cultivate any crops for a long period of time, the system of chena or ladang cultivation briefly described in the first chapter sprang up and became of much importance, though of course it is obvious that the first clearings in any forest-covered country must be of the nature of chena. To this day, it is one of the standing minor grievances of the eastern native against the British government that he is not allowed free and unrestricted chena in the crown lands. The fact that such practices are utterly destructive of the natural capital of the country does not in any way appeal to him—so long as there is land left to chena he considers that he should be allowed to chena it. In the more densely peopled districts and countries the practice has gone out perforce, but in more thinly peopled places it is extremely popular.

The most common argument in favour of chena used by natives of countries in which it goes on is that the land is so poor that it will not allow of any other method of cultivation. This is disproved by the fact that in places where chena used formerly to be common, as for instance in the western province of Ceylon, it has now gone out, and the land is continuously cultivated, by the success of European planting enterprises in chena countries, and by actual experiment, as at Maha-iluppalama in Ceylon, where land in the midst of a chena district has proved to be capable of continuous cultivation.

In very early times there was a small trade, at first chiefly overland, later in Moorish or Persian ships across the Indian ocean, in the products of eastern countries, chiefly spices, for which high prices used to be given, but this trade was extremely small, and most of the spices were not cultivated, but obtained from wild plants.

Though the early practices of agriculture yet survive in many eastern and other countries, the whole conditions have been altered by the appearance in the tropics of the white races of the north. Apart from their direct influence upon agriculture, their presence, and the settled government which they have brought with them, and which would seem to be a thing outside the capacity of the tropical races, has enabled the simple village agriculture of former times to extend and spread in all directions with the growth of population, until now, in Java, India, and Ceylon, for instance, there is far more of it than there ever was in primitive times.

From very early times, the existence of the nations of Europe, as above explained, has caused a slight trade mainly in spices, but the want of proper transport facilities, among other things, checked the development of any large or important trade. Transport by water was of course the first to become important, and hence the first places in the tropics to be opened up were the islands, such as Ceylon and the West Indies, coast places, such as Madras, and the valleys of the great rivers, such as the Amazon.

When the sailors of Portugal and other European nations had found the way to India and the East, and to the West Indies, they brought the markets of the north for the first time really within the reach of the people of the tropics. Very much the same process went on in all places, and is going on to-day, as the recent history of the West African coast illustrates. The first stage is the establishment of factories and trading settlements at the river mouths, which buy the produce grown in the interior by the natives, and export it. The general inefficiency of the natives and their methods, and the insecurity and dangers to which the traders are exposed next leads to the conquest and opening up of the country. Nowadays such work is generally done by the Government, and the conquered country is treated as a colony, but formerly, as in the case of the East India Company, the exploitation or development of the country was often placed in the hands of a great trading company. Such in general have been the methods in which English and Dutch colonies in the tropics have been formed, whereas in the case of the Spanish or Portuguese colonies of an earlier date, the usual method was simple conquest at the very first. The trading companies, and after them the Governments, of the eastern colonies, for a long time worked upon very crude principles, usually endeavouring to establish monopolies and keep out competitors, as was for instance the case for many years with the cinnamon culture in Ceylon (see pp. 82, 86, 87).

Once Europeans had entered the countries of the tropics in the capacity of masters, the introduction of the more modern systems of agriculture was assured. The first great development in agriculture in the tropics was of course the sugar trade of the West Indies, which was worked by European planters with the aid of slave labour. The next was the coffee industry of Ceylon. In general, the alteration brought about by Europeans in native agriculture may be almost said to be due to their development of improved methods of transport. The old native countries had practically no methods of transport but by coolie or bullock carriage and by water. The Europeans introduced good roads, then railways, and often canals, which have opened up the countries, and made agriculture for the purposes of export at last reasonably possible.

The invasion of the European races also altered finance in the tropical countries. At first the white races were merely in trading settlements at the mouths of the rivers, but they were not long content simply to trade with the natives. Very soon an exploitation of the countries began, with the aid of European capital. Later the whites conquered the countries, and wanted to settle in and cultivate them themselves, as the only means to ensure large and regular supplies for export. The first example of this kind of thing, as already indicated, was the great sugar industry of the West Indies, where the white planters set themselves to cultivate sugar with the aid of slave labour imported from Africa. This was for a long time a very prosperous under-taking, but was terribly thrown back by the liberation of the slaves, and so far as the British West Indies are concerned, has hardly yet recovered its lost ground.

The abolition of slavery practically threw the West Indies out of the competition, which was now beginning, in tropical agriculture under European management, and the countries with cheap labour came to the fore, more especially Ceylon, which now began to develope its great coffee industry. India and Java also have taken a great part in this development.

The history of agriculture in the British colonies has practi-cally been the history of the planting enterprises, whereas in Java the Dutch put into operation the famous "culture system" of van den Bosch, compelling the natives to give a part of their land and a part of their labour to the cultivation of "export" products, such as indigo, sugar, and coffee. This system[1], which is now all but extinct, had a great vogue for many years, and appears to have had no small share in making Java such a nation of comparatively energetic and skilful cultivators as it now is.

Ceylon, generally speaking, has led the way in the various European planting enterprises—first with coffee, then with cinchona, cacao, tea, cardamoms, rubber, and other things. The West Indies have cultivated sugar, fruits, tobacco, and of late cotton. India has had successful planting enterprises in indigo, tea and coffee, Java in sugar, cinchona, spices, tobacco, tea and coffee, the Sandwich Islands in sugar, West Africa in cacao, South America in coffee, cacao, etc., and so on.

The great development of European planting enterprise in the more civilised and opened up countries has of course quite revolutionised the primitive agriculture or rather has built up a modern agriculture beside it. Though there is still much of it, probably more than in primitive times, it is now quite overshadowed in importance to the world at large by the European enterprises, which provide the material for a large export trade. Whether planting in the tropics will always continue to be under European management is another question, but the northern powers will not permit that the rich and as

[1] For details, see Part III, Chapter II.

yet comparatively undeveloped countries of the tropics should be wasted for them by being devoted merely to the supply of the food and clothing wants of their own people, when they can also supply the wants of the colder zones in so many indispensable products.

The success of the European planters has had the effect of stimulating the natives in many places to imitation or rivalry, and in Ceylon, for instance, there are now a large number of native planters, cultivating mainly coconuts, but also engaging in the tea, rubber, and other industries. And the number of such men continues to increase. In Southern Brazil the great coffee industry is mainly in the hands of Brazilian natives, but these are so largely pure white men that for the purpose of this chapter they may be regarded as Europeans, from whom they are of course descended. In India and West Africa various "commercial" industries are entirely in native hands.

PART II

THE PRINCIPAL CULTIVATIONS OF THE TROPICS

CHAPTER I

RICE AND OTHER CEREALS AND FOOD PLANTS

Rice. This is one of the oldest and most important cultivations in the world, this grain forming the staple of the food of the Chinese and Japanese, the southern races of India, the Malay and Javanese, and other races, besides being very largely consumed in temperate climates. In recent years its cultivation has also been undertaken by white men, in the southern United States, with very good results, the yield obtained by the use of machinery being greater in proportion to the cost of the labour than that obtained in the tropics.

The varieties in which rice (*Oryza sativa*) is found to occur are legion, especially in India, where almost every district has its own. This is probably due to the fact that there has been but little intercourse, or exchange of seed, between the different districts. The two main kinds of rice are "hill" and "swamp," the former growing without special irrigation and up to a greater height in the mountains, the latter more a lowland and irrigated form. The former is now mostly grown by the semi-wild races, such as the Indian hill-tribes, the Sakeis of the Malay Peninsula, and others.

Among the swamp rices one of the most important varietal distinctions, from a practical point of view, is the time required from sowing to reaping; thus there are "three-month,"

I. Terraced Rice Fields near Kandy, Ceylon

"four-month," etc. rices, up to six and nine month. It is almost needless to point out that the yield is in general greater the longer the ripening period, but of course the kind grown in any one district must depend on the length of time during which water is available. Six-month rice will be useless if there is only water for four months.

Swamp rice requires to grow in a few inches of water until its seeds are all but ripe, consequently it needs to be cultivated in fields which are enclosed in little banks of earth to prevent the water from getting away, and to have regular irrigation provided for it, even in wet countries. The most economical districts for rice cultivation, therefore, other things being equal, are the great flat alluvial lands about the lower courses of the large rivers, as in Bengal, Madras, and Lower Burma, but rice can be cultivated anywhere that there is water available, and the soil suitable. On the large flats the fields can be correspondingly large, while as we get into more rolling country they become smaller, and require more terracing, until at last, in really hilly country, the fields become very small, often not more than a few square yards, and irregular in shape, and exhibit marvels of terracing, as may be seen in the picture of the terracing in the Kandyan country of Ceylon (Plate I). In these terraced fields, of course, the water is passed down from one field to another, but to bring it to the topmost field often requires considerable engineering feats, the water being brought for long distances in channels winding round the faces of the hills. These channels often run for miles over very difficult pieces of mountain country.

In some places there are no streams that can be impounded for purposes of irrigation, and the rice has to be grown with the ordinary rainfall, the rain being simply retained in the fields by the banking up of their edges.

Being the cultivation of the national food, and a cultivation of almost immemorial antiquity, the growth of rice in Indo-Malaya is hedged round with many superstitious observances, which differ from country to country. A brief description of some of the ceremonies observed by the Kandyans or mountaineers of Ceylon may perhaps suffice as an indication of these. "The goiya (cultivator) presents himself before the Neket-rala (village astrologer) on a Monday or a Wednesday with the customary offering of forty betel leaves and areca nuts, and expresses his wishes in a humble attitude. The Neket-rala then informs his petitioner, after certain astrological calculations, of the circumstances upon which the success or failure of his undertaking depends. On an auspicious day (according to the Neket-rala) the goiya, after partaking of the morning meal, wends his way to his land with a mamoti (see above, a kind of hoe), his face turned towards the favourable direction of the horizon as indicated by the astrologer. Should the goiya on this journey encounter sights or sounds which portend failure, e.g. the hooting of an owl, the cry of a house lizard, the growling of a dog, the sight of persons carrying weapons capable of inflicting injury, etc., he immediately turns back and retraces his steps homewards. Again the Neket-rala has to be approached in the manner before described, and consulted as to a lucky hour. Were the goiya to meet with a milk cow, vessels filled with water, men dressed in white, etc., when he sets out towards his land, it is considered very propitious.......On the following day the goiya entertains such of his fellow-villagers with rice-cakes, milk-rice, etc. as are willing to cooperate with him in the cultivation of his field. At the lucky hour, these villagers armed with mamoties proceed to the land, headed by the owner, and turning their faces in the direction of Adam's Peak give out the cry of Ha pura hodai (Ha, a good beginning).......

"When the field is ready for sowing,......on the advent of a lucky hour, the goiya leaves his dwelling after having recited a number of religious stanzas, bearing an areca-nut flower and a pata (handful with the fingers stretched out) of paddy (rice in the husk). Having arrived at his field, with his eyes turned towards the favourable region of the sky, he buries the paddy in a corner of a ridge, having first moulded the earth at the spot so as to resemble a peculiarly shaped symbolic figure, and lays the areca-nut flower on the top of the mound.......The High Priest of Kotmale Pansala informed me that the areca-nut flowers were intended as an offering to the gods, who are held to have a great love for them, while the paddy is believed to be taken away to provide for a meal.

"The time of ploughing is one of great solemnity to the Kandyan paddy cultivator. The Neket-rala is again consulted for the purpose of finding a lucky hour.......

"Thinning is done by the women when the paddy is about three months old.......No one dare cross the ridges with an open umbrella while the women are at work, unless there be urgent need for so doing, and permission be first obtained, otherwise mud, etc. are thrown on the intruder, whoever he be.

"Paddy is liable to be attacked by a grub...which sucks the juices of the plant.......In the Anuradhapura district, sand, after being 'charmed,' is scattered over the field, and offerings are made to *Jyan* and *Abimana* Dewiyos with a view to inducing their intercession to stay the ravages of the pest.......

"When the paddy is approaching maturity, other ceremonies are gone through; the goiya after purification places three ears of grain on a leaf of the Bo tree, which is held in great veneration for reasons too well known to need mention[1], and buries them in the kalavita or threshing floor, at the same time chanting some mystic words, invoking the gods to protect the crop from flood, fire, birds, and wild beasts.......The Neket-rala, attired in fantastic dress, describes a peculiarly shaped figure with ashes on the kalavita with a view to preventing sorcery and other evil influences.......Another rite of a peculiar nature follows this.......It consists of digging a circular hole in the field and placing inside a model of the sacred footprint of Buddha, a husked coconut, a creeping plant, clusters of areca nuts, leaves from the hiraspalu and tolabo, and covering these with about three bundles of straw[2]."

When such complicated ceremonies are gone through for such simple operations as are involved in the cultivation of rice, it is not surprising to find that the methods of cultivation are

---

[1] This tree (*Ficus religiosa*) was that under whose shade Gautama attained his Buddhahood. Almost the oldest tree in the world of which there is any historical record is the sacred Bo at Anuradhapura in Ceylon, planted there in 288 B.C.

[2] Ceremonies observed by the Kandyans in Paddy Cultivation, T. B. Pohath-Kehelpannala, *Journ. Anthrop. Inst.* November, 1895.

themselves very old and leave much to be desired in economy and efficiency. Not only so, but each country adheres rigidly to its own methods, and refuses even to try those of another country. Ceylon is very backward in that the method of sowing is by broadcasting, while Java, which is very advanced in the careful transplanting of the rice, and the rotation of crops upon the rice fields, adheres to the system of cutting each ear separately with a penknife, at enormous labour cost. A brief description of some of the methods of cultivation may be useful, but it must be remembered that each country has its own.

Two crops of rice are obtained every year in the wet districts of Ceylon, but as a rule only one from any one field. The fields are allowed to be thoroughly saturated by the heavy rains of the commencement of the monsoon, and are then turned over with the mamoti, and ploughed with a primitive plough. They are then puddled, usually with the feet, or with a mamoti, and levelled over into a thin creamy paste, on which the seed is sown by broadcasting—a most wasteful method, but one, which being the "custom," and comparatively cheap as regards labour, is rigidly adhered to. When the seed has germinated, the water is admitted again, and the rice left to grow, with perhaps an occasional weeding, until harvest time, when as the grain ripens, the water is once more turned off, so that the final ripening is done upon dry ground. The crops are so timed that this ripening shall take place in the drier weather of the monsoon, i.e. from January to March, or from July to September.

The grain is harvested with sickles, and heaped into small stacks. It is threshed in the same old way that is described for corn in the Bible, by being laid upon the ground, and bullocks driven round over it. It is then winnowed in an equally primitive fashion, by being thrown up into the air from flat basketwork trays, and caught again, the chaff being blown away meanwhile.

In Madras the general systems of cultivation are not unlike those in Ceylon, but more efficient, and the yield is greater. About 11,500,000 acres are devoted to rice, or fifteen times

II. Rotation of crops on Rice Fields in Java

as much as in Ceylon. Manuring, especially in the form of cattle-penning on the land, is employed, but generally only when two crops are to be taken off the land in one year. In Burmah there is a very large area given to rice, the yield is good, and the annual production is perhaps 5,500,000 tons, a large quantity being exported (1,750,000 tons).

In Bombay the yield is on the whole larger than in Madras, and manuring, both heavy and *ráb*, is carefully practised. The latter consists in growing the young plants upon seed-beds on which a mixture of dung, leaves, rubbish, etc., has been slowly burnt.

Bengal, though most of it is not, strictly speaking, within the tropics, is one of the greatest rice-growing countries of the world, and as the bulk of the rice is grown in the summer, we may for the nonce regard it as tropical. Three main varieties of rice are grown, *aus*, the early crop, sown in spring and reaped in August and September, *aman*, the main crop, sown in April–June, and reaped November–January, and *boro*, reaped in the spring. *Aman* is by far the most important. It is sometimes sown broadcast, sometimes transplanted, and is not infrequently, especially in jute districts, rotated with jute, etc., the order often being rice, pulse or oilseed, jute, pulse or oilseed, rice. What manure is available is carefully applied. About a third of the 75 million acres of rice in India are in Bengal, which exports about 200,000 tons to other countries.

Java is also a great rice-growing country, and exports about 40,000 tons of rice a year. Owing to the hilly configuration of the island, the rice is mainly grown on small terraced fields, as in Ceylon. As soon as the crop has been gathered, the water is allowed into the fields sufficiently to soften them, and they are then cultivated with every kind of vegetable, prominent among these being sweet potatoes, which by the way are the only rotation crop employed in Ceylon.

Siam and French Indo-China are also great rice-growing countries; the latter exports about 1,360,000 tons a year.

In recent years, with the influx of Indian coolies, and their partial settlement, rice has become an important article of cultivation in Mauritius, Guiana, Trinidad and elsewhere.

British Guiana is already exporting this grain. Brazil also grows a large area of rice, exporting 135,000 tons in 1920.

The yields of rice obtained differ very much from country to country. In Ceylon about 700 lbs. per acre is probably the average in the more thickly populated districts, in India probably 990 lbs., while in the Malay Peninsula about 2000 lbs. is often obtained, and in the Tinnevelli district of southern India even more, so that in 1903 the best rice land there was selling for Rs. 2000 per acre (£133). The natives of these countries, however, do not regard rice cultivation from a commercial point of view, and there is not the least likelihood of their giving it up in favour of anything more profitable.

Rice is a somewhat difficult grain to husk. The common method in Ceylon and elsewhere is by means of a heavy pestle and wooden mortar, while in much of India it is first parboiled and dried, and then husked in the same way.

Nothing is more striking to the outside observer than the obstinate way in which the natives of each country cling to their own particular methods. In Ceylon they object to transplanting on the ground of its greater expense, the fact being that though it uses less seed, it costs more in labour. In Java, on the other hand, they transplant the rice most carefully, and treat it with great care and efficiency, but when it comes to the harvesting, they cut each ear separately with what is practically a penknife. Yet, in spite of all effort, this custom is rigidly adhered to, as the harvest time is the great festive season, when all the villagers turn out into each field in turn, well dressed, and engagements are then mostly contracted between the young people.

One great difficulty in the way of any improvement being introduced by Europeans into this cultivation is the fact that there are hundreds of very small varieties, many of which look to the botanist exactly the same, but which the native almost at sight distinguishes, saying that the one will suit one kind, the other another kind, of soil, or that he can eat the one, but does not like the other. The native understands his own varieties, his own ways of cultivation, his own taste, to a nicety, and resents any interference, in so far as he is not contemptuous

III (a). High Lands and Paddy Fields

III (b). Winnowing Paddy

about it; while one not knowing the niceties of flavour, etc., is liable to great mistakes. The Tamil coolies of Ceylon, who come from the southern parts of Madras, live on the imported parboiled Indian rice, refusing to touch the Sinhalese rice, which they say gives them indigestion; while the Sinhalese say that there is no nourishment in the Indian rice. Analysis shows, we may mention, that rice contains about 7.3% of albuminoids and 78.3% of starch, and is thus hardly so good a food as wheat.

It is at present idle to imagine the natives of eastern countries going in for machinery and modern methods, such as are so successful in the United States, and for the improvement of rice cultivation we must look to other and minor things. But, as has been elsewhere indicated, we must be very sure of our ground before we recommend any measure to the native for adoption. To take an illustrative case from Ceylon—a planter living near Peradeniya suggested to the villagers that they should manure their fields, and offered, as they could not afford to buy the manure, to give it to them. This was accepted, the manure was applied, the plants grew splendidly, about half as tall again as usual, the planter was delighted. But when harvest time came, the village headmen came and offered to give him all the crop, if the villagers might be allowed to keep the straw. On examination, it turned out that the "paddy-fly" had eaten out the contents of all the grains. Whether this was merely a coincidence, or whether it was that the extra vigorous growth of the shoots had made the grains more tender, is uncertain, but the result of the experiment was a disastrous failure, and the villagers there have acquired a prejudice against manuring which may last a century or more. And yet there is no doubt that a carefully thought out scientific system of manuring, combined if necessary with improved precautions against the paddy-fly, would improve the crop. But the important point is that all such proposals should receive the most careful and exhaustive trials *before* being recommended to the villagers.

To indicate briefly some of the directions in which it would seem possible that improvement may be effected: paddies of different durations of ripening from those already employed might be tried in the villages, for instance "three-month" paddies in districts at present only using "four-month": paddies of similar duration, but of better quality, should be tried: experiments should be carefully tried with improved tools, especially ploughs: transplanting should be introduced in place of broadcasting, in districts where it is not now practised: harvesting might be improved by the use of the scythe in place of the sickle: threshing by the use of the flail: the use of water might be more economical.

Another way, again, in which it is likely that great improvement might be introduced in most countries, is in the practice of rotation of crops. During the period in which the fields lie idle, they should be planted with other crops. This is at present only done systematically in Java and India, where the fields are planted with sweet potatoes, jute, pulses, etc. It would seem likely that if the same crop were not always used, and if a leguminous crop were occasionally introduced into the series, a better effect might be produced. For example, let the course of the crops be rice, sweet potato, rice, peas or beans or other leguminous crop.

There are many other ways in which small improvements might be introduced into rice growing, without giving too great a shock to the prejudices of the villagers, but improvement must be very gradual and cautious, and every step must first be carefully tested.

Dry Grains. This term, used in Ceylon to describe those cereals which are not grown with the aid of irrigation, is a convenient generic term to use for these plants, of which there are many, grown over very large areas in India and elsewhere. The term Millets might almost as well be used, the bulk of these grains being millets, but would not cover quite all of them. Next only to wheat, maize, and rice, these are the most important food grains, and it is probable that about a quarter of the population of the world lives upon them, though they are more unfamiliar in Europe than rice.

India is more especially the land of dry grain cultivation. In the drier districts, which make up a large part of India, it replaces rice. The fields are usually tilled with the plough and harrow, the latter having frequently such large teeth and being so heavily loaded that it is practically a cultivator, and the seed is sown with a drill, or broadcasted. Most of these grains ripen in a few months, and are then usually harvested with the sickle, and threshed with bullocks, as described under rice. The straw is often valuable as fodder, and many varieties are grown expressly for fodder purposes.

Among the more .important of these grains are (1) the Great Millet or Guinea Corn (*Sorghum vulgare*), variously known in different parts of India as juar, jowar, jowari, cholam: it occurs in a vast number of varieties; (2) the Bulrush Millet (*Pennisetum typhoideum*), or bajri, or kumbu; (3) the Maize or Indian Corn (*Zea Mays*); (4) *Eleusine coracana*, the Ragi or Kurakkan; (5) the Italian Millet (*Setaria italica*) or kangni; (6) the Kodo Millet (*Paspalum scrobiculatum*) whose grain is at times liable to be poisonous (it is supposed from the development of a fungus in it); (7) the other millets (*Panicum* species).

Guinea corn is grown on 8,000,000 acres in Bombay, and 4,000,000 in Madras, as well as elsewhere in India. The soil is generally manured by cattle-penning and in other ways, and the seed most commonly broadcasted. The grain contains more albuminoids and less starch than rice, and is a good food, while the plant makes a good fodder and is much used for this purpose. Guinea corn is largely exported, especially from Bombay to Aden, Arabia, Abyssinia, etc.

Bulrush millet is especially grown in Bombay, and covers 8,000,000 acres in tropical India. It is a summer crop and reaped about September. The analysis is like that of Guinea corn.

Maize, or Indian corn, a native of America, introduced to the East by the Portuguese, is cultivated all over India and Ceylon, but only on the large scale in the northern non-tropical parts. It shows a great range of varieties, apparently depending to a large extent upon climate. New varieties introduced anywhere tend to go to the local form by crossing, and disappointment has consequently attended efforts to improve the Indian forms by acclimatisation of good American kinds. In tropical America this grain is very largely cultivated in different varieties from sea-level to 7000 feet and even higher, yields two crops a year, and a large return per acre. Cakes and bread are made of the bruised or ground corn, the green cobs are eaten, spirit is prepared from the corn, the young plants are used for fodder, etc. It makes in fact one of the great staples of the food of the population.

A careful study of the capabilities of the different varieties, and of their suitability to different districts, would well repay itself, for there are very large areas suited to this crop, and there should be a large export, as well as production for local use.

Ragi is grown in Madras on 1,500,000 acres, in Bombay on 800,000. Though a poor food, the straw is good fodder.

In the East these grains are very popular as chena crops; in the West Indies they are grown as a minor food crop, but rarely in large areas. In Africa they are also common and might perhaps with advantage be more largely grown in South America, etc.

The dry grains being so important a part of the food supply of the world, it is obvious that attention should be especially devoted to them, with a view to making the cultivation more efficient and remunerative. It is, however, difficult to do much in this way, in dealing with the very poor people who mainly cultivate these grains

The different varieties should be carefully tested against one another in different districts, and a careful study should also be made of the possible rotations or mixtures of crops. In most of India these grains are as a matter of fact even now sown mixed with pulses, etc.

Other Food Crops. There are many other plants grown in the tropics for food, and it would lead too far to go into details with regard to them, but a brief account of the more important of them will be given.

Yams. Strictly speaking the name applies only to the tubers of species of Dioscorea, but it is often applied to all tubers, even potatoes being known as yams in Ceylon. The four best of the many Dioscoreas used are usually supposed to be the white yam (*D. alata*), the negro yam (*D. sativa*), the Guinea yam (*D. aculeata*), and the cush-cush yam (*D. triphylla*), but there are very many others eatable out of the 150 species of which the genus is composed. Most of them, and all the best, have underground tubers like potatoes, but of very variable size, from a few ounces in some kinds up to 40 lbs. weight in others.

Yams are propagated like potatoes from pieces of the tubers, and are planted in rows, with sticks to climb upon. The tubers are ripe in eight to twelve months, and are usually dug up and put by to keep. The yam is used as a vegetable like the potato, and cooked in various ways. Properly cooked, a good yam is an excellent vegetable, though English people seldom enjoy it.

Cassava, Manioca, or Tapioca (*Manihot utilissima*) is one of the great food plants of the tropics, besides being consumed in colder climates. It is a native of South America, and was very early introduced into Asia, where it is extensively grown in the Malayan countries, Ceylon, etc. It is also very largely cultivated in the West Indies and throughout the warmer parts of South America. It is a shrubby plant, usually about eight feet high, and produces enormous tubers upon the roots. These are full of starch, and it is for them that the plant is cultivated.

There are two varieties in cultivation, the sweet and the bitter. The latter gives the best return, and is the more popular, but its tubers contain prussic acid, and are dangerously poisonous until the acid has been dissipated by boiling or heating.

The plants are set out as cuttings, and the roots may be gathered at about eight to twelve months old. The tubers are carefully dug up, and are usually washed, peeled, and grated small, while the resulting pulp is hung in a compressible bag, with weights upon it, so as to squeeze out the poisonous juice. The meal is then baked or otherwise cooked. In some countries the tubers are eaten like yams.

The poisonous juice is often boiled down in the West Indies, until it forms a treacley compound, which is highly antiseptic and is known as cassareep. It may be used for preserving meat, and is an ingredient in many sauces.

The tapioca of commerce (mostly exported from Singapore) is the starch of the tubers, heated so as to burst the grains.

Sweet Potato (*Ipomoea Batatas*). This is another very common vegetable in the tropics, as in the United States, and is one of the best of culinary vegetables. It occurs in very numerous varieties, and is specially popular as a rotation crop in rice fields. It is a small climber, not unlike a true yam in habit, and is cultivated in the same way, and the tuberous roots eaten.

Arrowroot (*Maranta arundinacea*). Though the best arrowroot of European commerce comes from Bermuda, the plant is usually a tropical cultivation. The tuberous root-stocks are full of starch, and the plant is cultivated like Cassava.

Sago. The sago palm (*Metroxylon Rumphii* and other species) is an important cultivation in the Malayan region. It is a short palm, which only flowers once, as do so many palms, after a long period during which it is saving up food material with which to do so. Just before the flowering stalk arises, the stems are cut, and their pith, which is very rich in starch, scraped out and washed.

Aroids. A good many members of the family Araceae or Aroideae are also used as food, especially in the strictly equatorial regions. Perhaps the most important are the taro (*Colocasia esculenta*) of the East Indies, and the tanier (*Xanthosoma spp.*) of the West Indies.

Food for Animals. The cultivation of fodder plants is hardly yet a definite industry in the tropics except in India, where considerable areas are cultivated in Guinea corn, millets, and other plants for fodders. But many of the cereals cultivated, and especially the dry grains, furnish good fodder. Large areas of Cuba and of other countries are now under Guinea grass and other fodder grasses. An important minor industry in Ceylon and other places is the cultivation of

Guinea and Mauritius grasses for sale to the proprietors of horses and cattle in the towns.

In southern Brazil there is quite a large cattle industry (including dairying) upon the drier country of the plateau (p. 10), where the beasts feed chiefly upon the natural grass. Pigs are also raised in large numbers.

In the more equatorial countries, one of the great wants is that of proper grazing land; the cattle get a little grazing on the dry paddy fields after the crop is cut, and are usually turned out more or less untended to graze where they can, but real pasture land is almost unknown. In India they are usually grazed in the fields, or among the trees upon crown forest lands, under charge of small boys. But a very real want in all the more equatorial countries is pasture land, and much improvement of cattle cannot be taken in hand unless the question of proper feeding is at the same time solved.

CHAPTER II

SUGAR

Cane Sugar. This is the classic tropical cultivation, so extensively engaged in in the West Indies in the days of slavery, and is still one of the largest industries in the tropics, in spite of the competition of European and American beet sugar. It is most extensively pursued in Java, the Sandwich Islands, Brazil, Guiana, the Malay Peninsula, Cuba, and in the British West Indies, while in India there are about 2,850,000 acres devoted to cane, though all but about 200,000 acres are in the northern non-tropical parts.

In the early days of the European occupation of the West Indies, this cultivation was practically the only one engaged in, and owing to the great profits made in it, thanks to absence of competition, slave labour, and other things, it gradually took up a great part of the country, including large areas of soils which were in reality unsuited to it. The first blow to this prosperity was of course the abolition of slavery. The second was the competition of beet sugar grown in Europe, the yield of sugar from the beet being continually improved by scientific selection. The third was the continuance of the West Indian planters in the old ways, suitable enough for the past generation, but out of keeping with modern progress. They continued to grow sugar in small areas and to have a factory for each small estate. With all these factors against it, cane cultivation in the British West Indies has in recent years sunk to a very low level of prosperity. From a modern point of view, the third disadvantage named above is probably the most important. In Cuba, Java, Hawaii, and elsewhere, sugar is cultivated on a very large scale, and enormous factories are

IV. Sugar Cane in Java

erected, which of course can contain the very latest and best machinery. Such estates continue to show a good profit, though the small West Indian concerns do not. There is probably no industry in the tropics in which specialisation has gone so far, and in which consequently large estates, and giant factories, are so much required. The small *maker* of sugar can only survive by being specially bolstered up, but the small *cultivator* is of course all right, for he can devote his attention to growing the cane in the best way, and sell it to the large factory near by, as in fact is done on a fairly large scale in Java, the Malay Peninsula, and elsewhere.

What the writer saw in Cuba may very well illustrate the general tendency in sugar cultivation. An American merchant many years ago had a small sugar estate left to him in payment of a debt. At first intending to sell it and be done with it, he, on second thoughts, went down to look at it, and soon decided that the expenditure of a little capital would perhaps give it a chance. This was done, the estate paid its way ; presently one of the owner's Cuban neighbours was so hardly pinched by bad trade that he sold his estate to the American, who closed the factory upon it, dealt with the cane at his own now enlarged factory, and put the former owner, a careful man, upon the place as cane-growing superintendent. This process went on, and one by one the surrounding estates were sold to the growing American business, till now, after thirty years, its rich proprietor owns about 15,000 acres of sugar-cane, and runs a colossal factory dealing with the whole produce of this area. I was informed that the same process was going on in four or five districts of Cuba, and that the whole sugar industry of the island was falling into the hands of a few wealthy Americans or American companies. In some of the British West Indies, e.g. in Montserrat, sugar has come to be a peasant cultivation, the landowner providing the land and the sugar works, the peasant cultivating and manufacturing the sugar, each party then taking one-half of the net proceeds. Sugar is thus very cheaply produced, for the peasant does not set much value on his time, and the landowner spends little, but the land tends to become steadily impoverished.

In India, on the other hand, the problem is quite different. The cheapening of sugar by the competition of beet-sugar, and other causes, have enormously increased the local consumption, though they have thrown India out of the export trade; in fact, it now imports enormous quantities (about 260,000 tons a year) from Java, and the amount is increasing year by year—though India ought to be able to supply herself. The local demand is mainly for the coarse unrefined *gur* or *jaggery*, which can be produced more cheaply than any imported sugar. The cane, which is grown in small areas, and often in rotation with wheat, rice, pulses, and other crops, is crushed between wooden rollers and the juice boiled down till it will condense on standing.

Sugar (*Saccharum officinarum*) grows best on rich porous clays and on alluvial soils at sea level, and does not mind the near neighbourhood of the sea. It will not succeed in the hills. It sets no seeds as a rule, and is propagated by cuttings, which are nowadays usually planted about five or six feet apart. In from 12 to 14 months (in the West Indies) the shoots from these cuttings are ripe for harvesting, when they form bunches of waving stems, about 6—12 feet in height, and looking not unlike gigantic grasses, as indeed they are.

They are cut close to the ground with cutlasses, and brought into the factory. Owing to their enormous weight the problem of carriage assumes great importance in sugar cultivation. On large estates in the West Indies and elsewhere, they are generally brought in by light railroads or tramways laid down in the fields, sometimes worked by horses, sometimes by locomotives. In the Malay Peninsula, on the other hand, the land lies very low, and small canals have been made throughout it, upon which the cane can be hauled in barges, at a great saving in cost. This, I was informed by the manager of the largest company engaged in sugar cultivation there, gives the estates a very measurable advantage over those of the West Indies, in which he was for several years engaged in the cultivation of sugar.

In British Guiana, it is stated that 30 tons of cane per acre are regarded as a good crop, and yield 25 tons of juice, but this evaporates to about 36 cwt. of sugar. Even so, it is evident that the crop must be a very exhausting one, and indeed rotation of crops is commonly practised with sugar.

In many countries the canes are not replanted after every crop, but the stumps, or rattoons, as they are called, are allowed to grow up again for two or more years.

Once in the factory the sugar cane goes through a variety of processes. It is first passed through large and heavy rollers, which crush out the juice. As a rule it goes successively through two or three sets of such rollers. The refuse cane, known as megass, is commonly used as fuel for the engines in the factory, and is carried to them by elevators. The juice is next clarified by being mixed with unslaked lime, and heating, when the acids are neutralised, and the twigs and other debris contained in the juice rise to the top and are skimmed off. It is then concentrated by heating in several successive boilers, usually under lower and lower pressure, and finally the thick pasty mass is poured out to stiffen into sugar and then arranged in such a way as to allow the uncrystallisable "molasses" to drain off. It would lead beyond the scope of this work to describe the processes in detail. The work requires, and in every modern factory receives, the attention of a skilled chemist—one reason among many why the small factory cannot hope to succeed against the big one.

Some of the sugar factories in Cuba, Hawaii, and the Malayan region are upon a colossal scale, the machinery in them representing large capital expenditure. Big machinery crushes, boils, crystallises, and does the other work of the factory much more economically than small, and obtains a greater percentage of sugar from a given kind of cane.

Until comparatively recently, even in the most advanced countries, the cultivation of the cane was more or less casual, attention being rather devoted to the improvement of the machinery to deal with it; and it remains in this condition in India and elsewhere. Now, however, stimulated by the example of beet-sugar, in which wonderful improvements have been introduced by careful selection of the tubers, and in other ways, careful and well-organised attempts are being made in Java, the West Indies, and elsewhere, to improve the yield of the cane. Already several new varieties have been created, which bid fair to give much better returns. It has also been found that the cane occasionally bears fertile flowers, and attempts have been made to gain the benefits due to cross-fertilisation. Some of these crosses also promise well.

The general indications point to sugar remaining a very important industry in Java, Cuba, and other of the more advanced countries, but to its more or less dying out, or becoming a peasant cultivation, in the smaller West Indian Islands. One of the most obvious improvements, in such countries as India, is separation of the manufacture from the growth, and specialisation of the former into very large factories, with trained chemical assistance. Trial of new and improved canes may be recommended, and the production of improved forms. Careful study of rotation of crops upon sugar land is also required, for sugar is a very exhausting crop, and requires to be alternated with other things. Green manuring between the rows of sugar might also be of advantage. In India a special problem is presented, to grow sugar adapted to local needs, and this the more as foreign and cleaner sugar seems to be becoming annually more popular there.

Other Sources of Sugar. Many of the palms have the habit of flowering only at the end of their life, either in one large mass of flowers, or in several consecutive ones. From such palms, and from the Coconut and Palmyra and other palms which do not do this, sugar is obtained in many tropical countries, by tapping the flower stalk, collecting, and evaporating, the juice. A coarse brown sugar named jaggery is thus obtained, and it is in general a sweet and good sugar, extensively used in tropical lands. Careful comparative investigations, and perhaps selection of seed, are badly wanted in reference to this industry, which is very important locally in the tropics, no less than 480,000 tons of sugar being made annually in India from palms.

CHAPTER III

TEAS

Tea. The tea plant (*Thea sinensis*) is originally a native of south-west China, Assam, and Manipur, occurring in several varieties, of which the true "China" with rather small, and the "Assam" with rather large, leaves are the best marked. It has been largely cultivated in China and Japan for a very long time, and has always formed a staple of the consumption of those countries. From about the middle of the eighteenth century it came largely into use in Europe, but the supply was for a very long period entirely or almost entirely from China, and the great tea merchants were mostly in Foochow and Canton. About 1835, through the efforts of the Botanic Gardens in Calcutta, the cultivation was introduced into Assam, and from almost the very start it has proved successful there, until now Assam is a very large producing country. It was not tried commercially in Ceylon until considerably later, when the collapse of coffee rendered it obligatory to find something else to grow instead of it, but about 1875 the first tea was exported from Ceylon, and proved to be profitable. During the early eighties there was a tremendous rush into tea in the island, and by 1896, when the rush began to fall off rapidly, the area planted in tea was no less than 380,000 acres, and it has remained at that figure since, with trifling change. At a later period it was introduced into Java, and that country now has some 210,000 acres in tea cultivation. It has also been introduced into the West Indian islands, and into other countries, but in none of them is labour sufficiently cheap to render cultivation profitable. Tea was grown commercially in Brazil, on a small scale, from 1814 to 1837.

With the enormous growth of the industry in India and Ceylon, which now have between them about 1,000,000 acres in tea, the export of tea from China has gradually fallen off, and the merchants have left Foochow for Calcutta and Colombo. Thus, the figures of consumption in England for a few different years may be quoted, as clearly illustrating this statement:

	China	India	Ceylon
1849	50,021,576 lbs.	—	—
1859	76,303,661	—	—
1869	101,080,491	10,716,000 lbs.	—
1879	126,340,000	34,092,000	—
1889	61,100,000	96,028,491	28,500,000 lbs.
1899	24,000,000	134,000,000	85,137,945

In 1910-11, Ceylon exported 183,905,153 lbs. of tea, of which 108,356,360 went to the United Kingdom.

The rise of the tea industry of Ceylon affords one of the most remarkable instances of rapid development of an agricultural pursuit, especially when the previous history of the planting industry in the island is remembered. In 1875 there were barely 1000 acres planted with tea. During the next ten years of depression, due to the failure of coffee, this acreage increased to 102,000, by 1889 it attained 205,000, by 1893, 305,000, and it is now about 405,000. A good deal of interplanting of rubber in the tea has gone on in the lower districts, but this has been compensated by new planting in the higher. The island imported its tea in the early days of tea planting, but in 1883 the export exceeded 1,600,000 lbs., in 1887 it was 13,813,872 lbs., in 1896, 108,141,412 lbs., and in 1910–11 no less (including green tea) than 183,905,153 lbs. For the present, at any rate, the growth of the industry seems to have practically reached its upper limit (1920, 184,846,683 lbs.).

Tea is now the chief industry in the mountain districts of Ceylon, the Nilgiri Mountains of South India, the great valleys of Assam, the hills at Darjiling, and elsewhere in India, to say nothing of the increasing industry in Java. In Ceylon, above the elevation of 2500 feet, it forms almost the only cultivation, and affords one of the most striking instances in the world of a large stretch of country covered with one crop.

Photo by A. W. A. Plate

V. Tea Estate in Ceylon

Several varieties of the tea plant are known; the China variety is but little cultivated except in China, and the usual ones cultivated on estates are the "Assam Indigenous," and the "Hybrid," a cross between this and the China. Both of these have larger leaves than the China variety, and yield more crop. The tea plant, a small tree when left to itself, is cultivated on estates in large fields, in which the plants are placed about four feet apart, and severely pruned at intervals of eighteen months to four years according to the elevation (low or high) of the estate above the sea, down to a height of 1½ feet. They thus form squat bushes about three feet high, and with flat spreading tops, so that it is easy for the coolies to get at the young shoots that are constantly appearing on the tops of the bushes. These shoots, taken together, are termed the "flush," and the object of cultivation and pruning is to ensure large, frequent and regular flushing. In the colder climates of China and Assam flushing ceases in winter, but in Ceylon or Java it goes on all the year round.

Tea manufacture consists essentially in the plucking of the young shoots of the flush and their subsequent treatment by "withering," "rolling," "fermenting," and "drying" or "firing," to form tea. In Ceylon the flush is plucked every eight to twelve days by women and children working in gangs under overseers. They soon become remarkably quick and expert at the work. Plucking is designated as "fine" when the bud at the tip of the young shoot and the two young leaves just below it are taken, "medium" when the bud and three, "coarse" when the bud and four leaves are taken. The coarser the plucking the poorer the average quality of the tea produced, though the greater the quantity. Fine plucking produces the various teas known as pekoes, while the older leaves give souchongs and congous. Pekoes consisting only of the buds or tips are known as "flowery," those containing also the first young leaf as "orange" pekoes.

The coolies bring in their leaf plucked to the factory, usually a large well-equipped building, containing the most modern machinery, and worked by water or steam power. The "leaf" is examined and weighed, and the amount plucked by each coolie recorded, the wages depending partly on the amount plucked.

After the leaf has been weighed it is taken to the upper floor of the factory and thinly spread out on light openwork shelves of canvas known as tats, to wither. In good weather it becomes limp and flaccid in about 18 hours, but in wet weather artificial heat is employed and a current of warm dry air drawn through the withering loft. The properly withered leaf is next thrown down through shoots into the rollers or rolling machines on the ground floor. A roller consists essentially of a table with a central depression to hold the leaf, and a hopper above it, the two moving over one another with an eccentric motion. Pressure to any required extent can be put upon the mass of leaf that is being rolled, and at the end of an hour or so the door in the bottom of the table is opened, and the " roll " falls out, the leaves all twisted and clinging together in masses, which are then broken up in a machine called a roll-breaker, to which is usually attached a sifter that separates the coarser leaf from the finer. After this the leaf is piled in drawers or on mats to ferment or oxidise, with free access of air. This process is omitted in the manufacture of green tea. In a couple of hours or so, depending upon the weather, the leaf assumes a coppery colour, and gives out a peculiar smell. Experience is required to determine the exact point at which to stop the fermentation and place it in the firing or drying machines. There are many types of these machines, but all act by passing a current of hot dry air through the damp fermented leaf till it is dry and brittle, when it is removed and sorted into grades by a machine composed of a series of moving sieves of different sizes of mesh. Finally it is bulked (i.e. the whole mass of each grade made on one or more days is thoroughly mixed together, so as to secure as great uniformity of quality as is possible), packed in lead-lined boxes of about 100 lbs., soldered up, labelled with the name of the estate, and despatched to the port for shipment.

The grades of tea usually prepared in Ceylon and India are known (in order of quality and value) as orange pekoe, pekoe, pekoe-souchong, souchong, congou, and dust.

Photo by A. W. A. Plate

VI. Plucking Tea

Green tea, made in the same general way as black, but withered by means of steaming, and prepared without fermentation, is graded as young hyson, hyson No. 1, hyson No. 2, gunpowder, and dust. Green teas are mainly made for the American market, where the common black teas made for the English and Australian markets are not popular.

Until about 1900 the price of tea fell fairly steadily, and cheapening of production did not keep pace with it, so that the profit also fell off. That it has not continued to fall must be attributed to two causes, the cessation of extension of the cultivation, and the increased consumption in markets outside of the United Kingdom, such as Australia, Russia, America. This has largely been the work of the export cess formerly levied by the Ceylon Government at the request of the planters, and applied to advertising Ceylon tea in new markets. This cess was 30 cents of a rupee (or 5d.) per cwt. of tea exported, too small an amount to be noticeable, but making a very handsome total upon the whole export.

The whole history of the tea industry is thus a conspicuous instance of the success of good methods and modern machinery against primitive hand methods, such as are still employed in China, a country which, though possessing the cheapest labour in the world, has been quite unable to hold its own against the competition of India and Ceylon. Somewhat the same story has been enacted in the cases of cinchona, coffee, and cardamoms, and is now about to be enacted in the case of rubber.

The general tendency in the case of tea would seem to be towards the further cheapening of production by grouping together of estates and opening of very large factories, towards the further opening up of important foreign markets, such as America and Russia, perhaps by the manufacture of oolongs and other special kinds of teas to suit their tastes, and towards the abandonment of areas which have proved, now that the great rush is over, quite unsuitable for the cultivation of tea. Agriculture in the tropics has in the past been conducted too much at hazard, and the suitability of the soils and climates to the production of particular crops has been too much neglected, but in the future this will have to be more carefully regarded.

Other directions in which improvement is to be looked for are in the general application of green manuring, in the more scientific use of bulk manures for flavour, in the selection of the best seeds for propagation, and in the manufacture.

Maté or **Paraguay Tea.** This plant (*Ilex paraguayensis*) furnishes one of the staple drinks of South America: it contains a considerable proportion of caffein, the alkaloid to which coffee owes its stimulating properties. Many attempts have been made to introduce this drink in northern countries, but the mistake has been made of trying to introduce it as maté, and no success has been attained, as was the case with kola. What should be done is to mix it in small proportion with tea or coffee, calling the mixture by some fancy name including tea or coffee in the title, and as the taste for the mixture grows increase the proportion of maté.

The consumption in South America, where the plant is native in southern Brazil, Paraguay, and Uruguay, is enormous. Brazil exports about 190,000,000 lbs. a year, besides consuming a good deal locally; and Paraguay also a very large amount, most of it going to Argentina.

The plant is but rarely cultivated, but occurs wild in great abundance. The young branches are cut, and dried over a fire of aromatic wood, until the leaves are crisp, when they are broken off and packed to go to the grinding mill, where they are ground into a fine powder in a large iron pan, and packed for market.

VII (a). Withering Tea

VII (b). Rolling Tea

CHAPTER IV

COFFEE, CACAO OR CHOCOLATE, KOLA, ETC.

Coffee. This plant is now mainly cultivated in Brazil and the rest of tropical America, which give more than half the supply, Java, and South India, but thirty or forty years ago was the mainstay of export agriculture in Ceylon, in which island there were about 300,000 acres devoted to it. Its history in Ceylon is of some interest. Next to the old sugar cultivation of the West Indies, coffee cultivation was the first industry in the tropics that was found worth attention by Europeans (other than Governments)—the first, if slave labour be left out of account. It was first taken up in Ceylon in the early thirties. From then till about 1845 there was a tremendous "boom" in it, and it was engaged in by numerous persons who had no knowledge whatever of tropical cultivation, with the inevitable collapse, as described in more detail in another place. Then came a period of resuscitation and renewed prosperity under more skilled superintendence, lasting till about 1870, when the first signs of the insidious leaf-disease, *Hemileia vastatrix*, a parasitic fungus feeding upon the leaves of the coffee bush, began to appear. Numerous remedies were suggested and tried, but all without avail, and the disease spread and spread over the great sheet of coffee cultivation in the mountains, and was closely followed by a bad attack of "green bug," until in the eighties the cultivation was practically entirely ruined, and the numerous European planters reduced almost to beggary. It is doubtful if the world can produce a more striking instance of the complete destruction of an industry by the attacks of disease, though it is certain that if tea had not then come in, and proved very profitable, coffee would not have died out so completely as has been the case.

At the present time, though rubber may eventually surpass it, coffee is the greatest exportation industry of the tropics. Brazil alone exported in 1920 a value of £52,500,000, the produce of an area of 3,300,000 acres, chiefly in the states of São Paulo and Minas Geraes, where perhaps 1,000,000 men, chiefly Italian and Portuguese, are employed upon the coffee plantations. Other countries of South and Central America, notably Venezuela and Guatemala, also export large quantities of coffee, while India, Java, and other countries of the Old World occupy much lower places, although their production has of late been increasing. Although Brazil at present supplies the greater part of the coffee consumed, the finest qualities come from the higher mountain districts of Java, Jamaica, Mexico, Arabia, etc. The total area cultivated in coffee is about 5,000,000 acres.

The chief species of coffee cultivated is the Arabian (*Coffea arabica*), which gives the finest quality of coffee. *Coffea robusta*, an African species, has of late years come prominently to the front as a producer of good coffee at elevations lower than those at which Arabian succeeds, and as it possesses the marked advantage of producing a noticeable crop at two years old, it has come into great favour in Java, Sumatra, and elsewhere. Liberian coffee (*C. liberica*) is also a good deal cultivated in countries with low-lying, humid areas, like the Federated Malay States and other flat countries. There are many other species of coffee known, and some of them are proving useful in hybridisation, which gives promise of producing valuable results.

Coffee grows in very different climates and soils, but in general the climate should allow of dry weather for the ripening of the crop, and the soil should be deep and water-retaining. In Brazil suitable soils are to a large extent picked out by observing whether certain trees, such as *Apeiba Tibourbou*, are to be found growing well upon them. The best coffee soils in the state of São Paulo have a depth sometimes exceeding 20 yards. The rainfalls of coffee countries vary from 30 to 150 inches. Frost is dangerous, especially if accompanied by wind.

VIII. Arabian Coffee, cultivated under shade, in Java

The bushes are usually placed about 10 feet apart in Java, and more in Brazil. In many countries, but not in Brazil, they are shaded by growing among them other trees, generally species of Erythrina, under which the leaf-disease, unknown in Brazil, is less troublesome. In Brazil they are merely lightly shaded during the first two years of growth.

In many countries the tops of the bushes (other than Liberian) are pruned off in order to give them a spreading habit and render it easier to pick the fruit, but in Brazil they are allowed to grow to a height of 15 feet or more. In the same way, in Java, etc., they are very carefully pruned as they grow up, the primary branches being left, but the secondaries removed for the first six inches from the stem, and beyond that one at each node, on each side in turn, so that if at one node the branch project north, at the next it will project south.

Coffee comes into bearing at 2—5 years old, *Coffea robusta* bearing sooner than *C. arabica*, and the countries of tropical Asia bearing sooner than Brazil, where however the bushes keep longer in good condition. In climates with a marked dry season, the bushes usually flower simultaneously, and the large snowy flowers present a very beautiful sight. The fruits are red berries ripening some time afterwards, and must be picked soon after they are ripe, or even, to obtain the best results, each one as it becomes ripe.

The average yield of dried seeds in Brazil is at the rate of $\frac{3}{4}$ lb. (on old soil near Rio de Janeiro) to 15 lb. (on virgin soil in the finest districts of São Paulo) per bush. But it is better to take the average yield per acre, and this in Brazil upon good, new, land reaches as high as 2900 lb. About half that amount was the average in Ceylon in the old coffee days, and in general tropical Asia gives rather smaller yields as compared to southern Brazil. The crop varies considerably from one year to another. A "bumper" crop, which is usually obtained once in every seven years or thereabouts, generally damages the plants, and is succeeded by poor crops for some years.

The collection of coffee in tropical Asia is generally by careful picking of the individual berries, which are thus obtained in the best condition and without intermixture of leaves and other debris, but in Brazil, where labour is more costly, they are generally stripped from the branches by drawing the hand along, and fall upon the ground below, from which they are collected, a cloth being sometimes laid down for them to fall upon, and the intermingled debris is subsequently removed.

The fruit, or "cherry" as it is termed by coffee planters, is a fleshy fruit containing two seeds placed face to face in a common envelope of somewhat horny consistency, which is termed the "parchment." The cherries are in some cases simply dried in the sun like cacao seeds, being piled together again at nights and spread out in the morning until fully dried, but in more careful preparation they are treated by what is often called the wet method.

The ripe fruits are first washed through a "pulper," a machine with a barrel, covered with teeth like that of a musical box, or with semi-circular projections, revolving against a fixed beam. This crushes the pulp on the fruits, and they pass through into a stream of water, where it is washed away. The pairs of seeds are then placed in a vessel to ferment for a couple of days, the remains of the pulp are easily washed off, and they are dried. The dried fruits then form what is termed "parchment," the two seeds being enclosed face to face in a parchment-like covering. In this condition they may be kept a long time, but they are generally put through what is called a "huller," in which a revolving heavy wheel breaks up the parchment layer, and sets free the seeds, which are freed from the broken parchment by winnowing. They are then bagged and sent to Europe. Five pounds of the fresh fruit finally give about one of dry coffee.

A few years ago, in a year of "bumper" crop, Brazil, which then had a greater monopoly of the market than she now has, took the bold step of "valorising" coffee, i.e. the Government took off the market the excess of production, and has sold it in later years of smaller yield. But this of course only postponed the evil day of over-production, which is bound to arrive when the next Brazilian bumper crop comes, while Java and other countries have vastly extended their area under coffee.

The chances of improvement in coffee cultivation seem to

lie to a large extent in scientific treatment. Careful study of the different hybrids is required, and also of the methods of grafting one kind of coffee on another, or possibly even on other members of the same natural family. The successful acclimatisation of Liberian coffee in Java at high levels, even to 3000 feet, by taking the seed up a few hundred feet at each generation, also indicates a line which may be useful in hybridisation. Careful selection of seed of the best bearers both as to quality and as to quantity is also urgently needed, and it is possible that even selection of the quickest bearers might prove of advantage, by producing a breed that would yield a crop earlier than those at present cultivated. Green manuring, again, would probably prove of use.

Cacao, Cocoa, or Chocolate. The cacao tree, *Theobroma Cacao*, is probably a native of Venezuela and northern South America, and is still largely in cultivation there, but is now probably almost the most widely cultivated of those tropical products in which there is an export trade. The following figures give the export from different countries for the year 1919:

Gold Coast	176,000 tons	Ecuador	40,000 tons
Other British		San Domingo	22,000
Colonies	70,000	Venezuela	15,000
Brazil	62,500	Elsewhere	27,000
St Thomas	46,500	Total	460,500 tons

These are large figures, but, allowing 7 or 8 acres to produce a ton, it will be seen that they do not represent very large areas.

The most remarkable feature in this table is the rapid rise to first place of the Gold Coast, which in 1904 was eighth, and now produces about 38 $\%$ of the supply.

The general principles of the cultivation of cacao are much the same in all countries, and therefore the methods followed in Ceylon, whose cacao in general obtains the highest prices, may be described here, with notes on the important points of difference in other countries.

Cacao is a small tree or large shrub, from 12 to 25 feet in height, and much branched. It has large leaves, which when young are reddish in colour, and hang downwards. It flowers in vast profusion, not on the twigs, as one would expect, but upon very short branches produced on the old and stout stems. The flowers are succeeded by a considerable number of oval reddish, greenish, or yellowish fruits, about 6 to 11 inches long, with rather fleshy outer walls, and containing about 30 bean-like seeds, each enclosed in a mucilaginous outer coat.

There are numerous varieties of cacao in existence, but these may in general be classed under two main types, conveniently known by their Spanish names of Criollo and Forastero[1]. The former are characterised by plump pale-coloured seeds of fine quality, making up a large bulk in comparison with the external size of the pod, the shell being relatively thin. The tree itself is usually small and somewhat delicate. On account of the pale colour, these seeds are specially valued in Europe and America for the manufacture of eating chocolate, and considerably higher prices are paid for them than for the Forastero. The very high prices obtained for many years by the Ceylon cacao were due mainly to its being the seed of this variety, and now that it has been very largely replaced by Forastero, the average prices of Ceylon cacao have gone down.

The term Forastero includes all the varieties other than the Criollos. The chief ones, in descending order of merit, are Cundeamor, Liso or Trinitario, Amelonado, and Calabacillo. The seeds of these varieties are more or less purple in colour, and the shell of the fruit is thicker and harder. In consequence of the purple colour, the seeds sell for lower prices, but this is to some extent made up by the better and hardier growth.

Other species of cacao, e.g. *Theobroma pentagona*, are also occasionally used as cacao producers.

The cacao plant must be cultivated, generally speaking, under a certain amount of shade, more especially to protect it from wind, which produces disastrous results. The favourite

---

[1] Lock, R. H., *On the varieties of Cacao existing in the Royal Botanic Gardens and Experimental Station at Peradeniya*, Circ. & A. J., R. B. G., Peradeniya, II, 24 Oct. 1904, p. 385.

IX. Criollo Cacao, in fruit

(Original in possession of the Kolonial Wirthschaftliche Komitee, Berlin)

shade trees have hitherto been species of Erythrina, known in the West Indies as Madre del Cacao, or Bois Immortelle, in the East as dadap, but in recent years some variety is coming in. The shade trees are usually planted at about 50 feet apart, and the cacao under them at 12 or 15 feet apart. Some of the West Indian Islands with little wind (on the leeward side) are able to dispense with shade altogether.

The tree is carefully started in nurseries, and planted out at about six months old, the shade trees being at first closer together and being gradually thinned out, providing much nitrogen for the soil in this way. The suckers which appear on the stem are pruned off, unless one is wanted to replace a stem that may have been injured by disease or otherwise.

The tree is apparently somewhat narrowly limited in range of temperature that will suit its growth, for it only succeeds in Ceylon at elevations from 200 to 2500 feet, and not very well at either of these extremes. In more continental climates it is grown at higher elevations, e.g. 3500 feet in Uganda, and it is said even to 5000 or over in Ecuador.

The tree begins to bear fruit in about its fourth year, and the yield increases for some years. A fair average yield of dried cacao "beans" is about 3 cwt. per acre per annum, but from 5 to 8 cwt. is not uncommon with Forastero kinds.

The ripe fruits are picked by means of a tool not unlike a reaping hook, it being important that they should be cleanly severed from the stem, and they are then opened by means of knives or otherwise and the mucilaginous seeds shaken out. The treatment of these seeds differs slightly in different countries. In Ceylon they are piled in heaps and covered with sand and plantain leaves, or placed in tubs or vats and similarly covered, in order to ferment. The heaps are turned over at intervals, and at the end of from 2 to 4 or even 10 days the fermentation is complete[1], when the seeds are taken out, and the thin watery fermented mass of outer pulp is washed off by rinsing in water. Fermentation also ensures the penetration of water into the interior of the seeds, causing them to swell out and giving them a plump and "bold" appearance.

[1] It takes least time with the best varieties.

The fermented and washed beans have next to be dried, which is done by spreading them out on mats in the sun for a few hours daily, and keeping them heaped up for the rest of the time. A few days of this treatment causes them to dry in the same plump and bold outline which they had while still wet. In very wet or sunless weather the beans are dried by artificial heat in closed chambers, hot air being drawn over them in various ways, but the results are not in general so good as those obtained by drying in the sun.

In some places the beans are simply dried without any fermentation, but this gives a poor product. In the West Indies the washing is often dispensed with. In Venezuela the cacao is "clayed," the wet beans from the fermentation being sprinkled with dried and powdered red clay, and afterwards rubbed between the hands to remove the mucilage.

Once dry, the beans are simply bagged and exported to Europe. Lately, however, a manufactory of prepared cacao and chocolate has been opened in Ceylon.

The cultivation of cacao is thus a fairly simple one, and as no manufacture is required upon the spot, it commends itself to "native" proprietors, and also to planters in countries where labour is not very plentiful. This is perhaps or probably the reason why its cultivation has grown so enormously in West Africa during the last ten years.

In recent years the cultivation of cacao has shown signs of becoming more scientific. In 1897 and later there was a considerable outbreak in Ceylon of a canker attacking the stems. Warned by the fate of coffee in the island, the planters of cacao were alarmed, and early measures for the eradication of the canker were taken, under the advice of the Botanical department. These have been almost entirely successful, except in so far as the cultivation of the old Criollo cacao, which gave to the Ceylon product its very good name and high prices, has been largely replaced by that of the Forastero varieties, whose purple seeds command a lower price. Treatment of the disease was at first almost entirely by excision of the diseased parts, but of late spraying has come in, the fruits, which are extremely liable to attack, being sprayed with Bordeaux mixture or other com-

X (a). Drying Cacao in the Sun (Ceylon)

X (b). Cacao drying house in Surinam with moveable platforms to roll out
(*Original in possession of the Kolonial Wirthschaftliche Komitee, Berlin*)

pound. This is about the first case of spraying, now so very much in use in colder countries, being employed on a large scale in the tropics. Science is also coming in in the use of green manures, various leguminous plants being planted between the rows of cacao, and subsequently being ploughed or dug in, increasing the nitrogen available at small cost.

With the great extension of cacao cultivation, which is now taken up in nearly all tropical countries, there will presently be a fairly severe competition, and prices will probably be very low. Improvement must therefore be sought for by those countries which would keep ahead in this matter. Some of the directions in which this improvement may be looked for are in the selection of better varieties for cultivation, e.g. even in the simple substitution of Criollo for Forastero, or the selection of seed from trees that regularly bear large numbers of good pods (for there are well-marked differences in this respect). Another moderately easy thing to manage, and one which repays itself, is the careful grading of the seeds sent to market. If Criollo (pale pink or brown) and Forastero (purple) seeds are sent into the market mixed, the price paid for them will of course be the lower price, that of the Forastero, whereas if they be separated, the Criollo seeds will fetch a much higher price. Though at first the two kinds of seeds look alike, it will soon be found possible to distinguish them, and coolies can be trained to separate the two kinds of seeds with a fair amount of certainty. Prevention of disease, by spraying and in other ways, is another thing that requires careful attention, cacao being very liable to various diseases.

Kola or Cola. Another very important cultivation, more perhaps from the point of view of its local uses than from that of export, though the latter is large, is that of the Kola nut, which is extensively cultivated in West Africa from Loango on the south to southern Senegambia on the north. The consumption of these nuts is one of the great features of West African life, they being used both as a food and as a stimulant. They are sent in token of reconciliation, are used like olives before a meal, are said to make bad water drinkable, are a cure for alcoholism, a stimulus to cheerfulness; in fact they take the place of tobacco and other things in other countries.

The Kola tree (*Cola acuminata*, and perhaps other species) has been introduced into other countries in the tropics, e.g. into Ceylon, but has not proved sufficiently profitable to form the basis of any important industry, and the export is as yet practically entirely from West Africa. The tree is closely related to the cacao, and grows about 20 to 45 feet high, with panicles of flowers which give rise to strings of fruits, each fruit having two to six rays, each ray a pod containing a few seeds, for which the tree is cultivated. The essential principle in these is caffein, and they contain about $2\frac{1}{2}°/_{\circ}$ of it, or a good deal more than coffee does. The nut containing also a full third of its weight of starch, besides other matters, forms a good food stuff, as does cacao, and were it not for its unpleasant flavour would probably compete very closely with the latter; so far, however, it has only come into use when mixed with cacao, and in certain drinks.

The tree is rarely planted in plantations, but is cleared in the forest, or forms part of the mixed cultivation of the West Africans. It begins to bear at about seven years old, and produces perhaps about 50 fruits a year on the average. The principal crop is in December, and there is a second in April.

The seeds are gathered, and left for a few days, when the seed coats can be easily rubbed off, and they are then packed in leaves, and kept damp, so as to travel as fresh as possible. For export they are carefully dried in the sun. The value of the exports from the Gold Coast Colony in 1919 was about £250,000.

By mixing it with cacao, a considerable quantity of kola has been gradually brought into consumption in England.

Guaraná. This plant (*Paullinia Cupana* is a good deal used in South America, but is hardly exported. The tree is not unlike the cacao tree. The fruits are collected, and laid in water to loosen the skin, which is then removed and the fruits dried by the fire. An infusion like chocolate is made from them. They contain a high percentage of cafein, and would be useful for mixing with other drinks, as they have but little flavour. Excellent aerated drinks are made from them in Brazil.

CHAPTER V

COCONUTS AND OTHER PALMS

Coconuts. The coconut[1] palm, *Cocos nucifera*, is the most widely cultivated plant in the tropics, but, except in Ceylon, the Philippine Islands, South India, Trinidad and parts of Polynesia, not as a rule upon a large scale for export of the products, but in the mixed cultivation of the peasants. There is probably no single plant capable of so large a variety of uses, whether locally or for export. So old and so universal is the cultivation in the tropics, that even yet the original native country of the palm is uncertain, though opinion seems to favour the western islands of Polynesia from which it has been carried by the currents of the ocean to Malaya, Ceylon, India, Africa, etc. The fruit being enclosed in a thick fibrous coating, can be carried by the sea for a very long time without losing the power of germination, and hence this palm is one of the earliest things to appear on any newly formed land, such as a coral reef, in the tropics.

While in a small way the cultivation is important in America and in Africa, it is to Ceylon and other eastern lands that one must look for large and important plantations. The palm flourishes best in the damper coastal regions, but is also cultivated inland, and up to elevations of 2500 feet or over. The cultivation is mainly in native hands, though in recent years many Europeans have invested in what is sometimes called the consols of planting. The palm is the most common

---

[1] I adopt the correct spelling of this word. It is much to be regretted that the spelling cocoanut should have crept in, as it leads to much confusion with cocoa or cacao. Matters are further complicated by the existence of coca, cocoes, coco-plum, coco-yam, etc.

and regular constituent of the mixed cultivations already mentioned, and described in Chapter XIV below.

The usual idea about a palm is that it grows vertically upwards and is crowned by a tuft of leaves. This, however, is not quite true about the coconut, the stem of which is practically never erect, but grows upwards in a more or less graceful curve. Along the sea coast the stems of the outermost palms project over the water, and this is often given as the reason of the curve, but in actual fact it would seem to be a case of the stem bending towards the light, as the outer stems of a clump usually all bend outwards, whether over water or not.

On properly managed estates the palms are planted in regular rows, and at about 25 feet apart, whereas in the ordinary native garden they are planted anyhow, usually mixed with other trees, or if planted alone then much too closely. The palm begins to bear fruit about the fifth year, and bears for seventy or more years thereafter. The crop varies very much, but perhaps on the average is from 40 to 75 nuts per tree per annum on an ordinary estate.

The coconut, as might be expected, occurs in a great many varieties with rather small differences. The two chief and most conspicuous groups of varieties are those with green nuts, known in Ceylon as ordinary nuts, and those with yellow nuts, known in Ceylon as king coconuts. Some kinds have a larger yield of fibre, some give larger nuts.

On a good estate the trees are planted out from nurseries, but in the villagers' gardens are often planted out as seeds. In Ceylon and other equatorial countries the latter get but little cultivation till they arrive at maturity, a fact which appeals with some force to the ordinary villager, but in India, etc., greater care is taken of them, especially in the north about Bombay, etc.

The tropical villager obtains from this palm many of the necessaries of life. The large leaves are woven into "cadjans" for thatching, into mats, baskets, etc.; their stalks and midribs make fences, brooms, yokes, and many other utensils. The trunk affords rafters, beams, canoes, troughs, and many other articles of furniture, etc. The bud or "cabbage" at the apex

XI.   Coconuts on the Ceylon Coast

of the stem (of course there is only one, and when this is removed the palm dies, so that it is not as a rule taken till the palm is old) makes an excellent vegetable and is also made into preserves, etc. When the palm is flowering, the main flower stalk can be tapped for "toddy," a drink like the Mexican "pulque," containing much sugar. Evaporation of the toddy furnishes a coarse but good sugar known as jaggery ; its fermentation gives an alcoholic drink, from which distillation produces the strong spirit known as arrack, while further fermentation produces vinegar.

The fruits while young contain a pint or more of cool sweetish watery fluid, which affords a most refreshing drink. As the nut ripens the water decreases and the kernel hardens. The nuts are gathered at about ten months old. Their kernels are eaten raw or in curries and in other ways, milk is expressed from them for flavouring curries and other purposes, and oil is extracted from them by boiling. The commercial oil, in which there is an enormous trade for soapmaking and other uses, is obtained by first drying the kernels in the sun or by other artificial means till they form what is known as "copra," and then pressing this copra in mills. About two-thirds of the weight is obtained as oil, and the refuse, "cake" or poonac, forms a valuable fattening food for cattle or poultry. The oil is occasionally used for lighting, but its great use, especially in Europe and America, is for soapmaking; it also forms a good hairdressing, and is largely used for the manufacture of candles, as it separates under pressure into a hard wax-like body, stearine, and a liquid oleine. The shell of the nut, after the kernel is taken out, forms drinking cups, bowls, spoons, handles, and many other things: it also makes an excellent smokeless fuel, and yields a good charcoal.

In recent years a large industry has sprung up in Ceylon in desiccated coconut, i.e. the kernel of the nut with some of the oil expressed, sliced and dried in special desiccators. The product is soldered up in lead-lined boxes, and exported for use in confectionery.

The thick outer husk of the coconut, rarely seen in Europe or in North America, contains a large number of long stout

fibres running lengthwise. The villagers obtain these by splitting the husks, rotting them in water, and then beating out
the softer tissue from between the fibres. There are also many
large mills where special machinery is used for preparing coir,
as this fibre is called. The uses of coir are many: the fibres
are graded according to their stoutness, and used for making
brushes, yarn, rope, mats, and many other purposes. There is
a large export from Ceylon and other tropical countries.

Though very many tropical countries have more or less
export trade in the products of the coconut, Ceylon, both for
home consumption and for export, stands almost at the top of
the trade, and the figures of the chief coconut product exports
during 1919 may be quoted:

Coconut oil	675,000 cwt.	Desiccated coconut	675,000 cwt.
Copra	1,759,000 cwt.		

Besides large quanties of poonac, coir, coconuts, arrack, etc. The export
from the Philippines in 1920 was over 100,000 tons.

The trade in coconut products continues to increase rapidly
and, though many new countries are now taking part in it, and
the extension of planting in Ceylon never ceases, the prices
obtained have not fallen but risen. New uses are constantly
being discovered for the oil, etc. The complete removal from
the oil of its "coconutty" smell has now almost been accomplished, and butter-like bodies can be made from it, which have
already an extensive use in cooking, and will probably come
more and more into use as they are perfected.

There are many directions also in which the cultivation of
the coconut is open to improvement. For instance, as in cacao,
the use of green manures will probably be found to give better
crops at less cost, provided the manuring plants be not
attractive to rats, as some that have been tried or suggested,
e.g. ground-nuts, are. More careful cultivation is required, and
in native gardens the distance apart of the palms should often
be much increased. This is a difficult point to teach to a native
of the tropics; he almost always has the idea that the more
plants he can get on to his ground, the larger return he will get.
A striking instance of this came under my notice some years

XII. Making Copra in Samoa

(*Original in possession of the Kolonial Wirthschaftliche Komitee, Berlin*)

ago. An estate near to Peradeniya, supposed to be a cacao estate, had been continually planted up with coconuts, areca nuts, pepper, crotons, and other products, till in 1902 the average number of trees per acre was no less than 512. The estate then gave ½ cwt. of dry cacao per acre, and a small quantity of the other products, and was losing money at the rate of Rs. 40 per acre per annum. In 1902 a system of cutting out the extra trees was adopted, and now the estate contains only about 300 trees per acre, almost all cacao, the cacao crop is 3½ cwt. per acre, and the estate is profitable.

Another direction in which great care is required is in the selection of nuts for seed; the very best nuts, i.e. regarded from the point of view of the object of the plantation, whether for copra, for nuts, for desiccated coconut, for oil, or for other purposes, should always be picked for seed, to improve the next generation. On the whole this has been done in Ceylon though not in the Seychelle Islands, and a recent lot of Ceylon nuts sent there was found to exceed the local nuts sometimes in the proportion of three to one. It is also possible that careful hybridisation might improve the varieties of the palm in culti-vation. Different varieties should be tried in the same place, for it is quite possible that a better return might, for example, be obtained by changing the variety cultivated, e.g. by abandon-ing the cultivation of oil nuts, and taking to good fibre nuts. It is also possible that quickly maturing nuts might be selected, which would in time considerably reduce the period of waiting for the palms to flower (now about five or six years).

A tendency in coconut cultivation just now seems to be the opening of very large plantations under European management. Such plantations can turn out large and uniform supplies of copra, for instance, whereas the copra obtained from the innumerable small native plantations is of very variable quality.

Palmyra Palm. Another palm of considerable importance is the Palmyra palm (*Borassus flabellifer*) supposed to be a native of both tropical Africa and tropical Asia, and now very extensively cultivated in tropical India and Ceylon, especially in districts which are a trifle dry for the coconut. It is a tall straight-growing palm, fruiting only at one season of the year. It has innumerable native and local uses, an old Tamil song enumerating 801, but from the point of view of export trade, the most important product of the palm is the fibres at the bases of the leaves, which are exported under the name of Palmyra fibre, and used for making brushes, hard brooms, and for other purposes. As far as local uses are concerned, the greatest is the preparation of sugar or jaggery, and of toddy for drinking, whilst arrack is also made. The fruit is edible, the large fan-shaped leaves are used as thatch, and for fencing, the leaves cut into strips are employed in weaving baskets, toys, matting, etc., the stems are used as building posts and rafters, and as piles in salt water, for which purpose they are very well adapted. In many other ways this palm is almost as useful as the coconut.

Areca Palm. This is another palm the cultivation of which is of great importance in the East, for nearly every native "chews betel," i.e. he chews a mixture of areca nut, lime, and various flavouring matters, such as tobacco or cardamoms, wrapped up in a leaf of the betel pepper, *Piper Betle.* This act turns the saliva red like blood, and is somewhat disgusting to watch, but it must not be hastily condemned. For one thing it gives the rice-feeding native some lime in his diet, an item which is often lacking in it. Now that betel chewing is being to some extent replaced by smoking, this question of how to provide lime becomes more pressing. The cultivation of this palm is carried on upon a large scale in Ceylon, India, Java, etc., usually in the mixed garden cultivation of the villagers, but sometimes in regular plantations. The palm bears at about the sixth year, and when in full fruit each gives about 300 nuts a year.

Kitul or Toddy Palm. This palm (*Caryota urens*) is cultivated in the mixed garden cultivation of the natives of Ceylon and wherever else it is indigenous. The flower stalk is tapped for toddy, just as in the coconut, and sugar is also made from it. From the bases of the leaves a fibre is got as in the Palmyra palm.

Other palms are also used, e.g. those mentioned under sugar in a previous chapter, the talipot (*Corypha umbraculifera*) the leaves of which provide umbrellas, books, and other things, the royal and cabbage palms of Cuba (*Oreodoxa regia* and *oleracea*), the oil palm of West Africa (below), and many others.

CHAPTER VI

SPICES

Cinnamon. This spice was the earliest article of export from Ceylon upon any important scale, and was much the most famous of the island's early exports to Europe. Until 1833 its cultivation was a Government monopoly, first under the Dutch and afterwards under the British Government. "The trade was at its height when Nees wrote a disquisition upon it in 1823; but opinion was already arraying itself against the rigidly exclusive system under which it was conducted. This was looked upon as the more unjustifiable, owing to the popular belief that the monopoly was one created by nature; and that prohibitions became vexatious where competition was impossible. Accordingly in 1832 the odious monopoly was abandoned; the Government ceased to be the sole exporters of cinnamon, and thenceforward the merchants of Colombo and Galle were permitted to take a share in the trade, on paying to the crown an export duty of three shillings a pound, which was afterwards reduced to one.

"The adoption of the first step inevitably necessitated a second. The merchants felt, and with justice, that the struggle was unequal so long as the Government, with its great estates and large capital, was their opposing competitor; and hence, in 1840, the final expedient was adopted by the crown of divesting itself altogether of its property in the plantations."

Since that period the cultivation has greatly extended, chiefly on the light sandy soils near the southwest coast, where the spice is native; and though various other countries grow trifling quantities, no serious competitor has yet arisen for Ceylon. At the present time about 35,000 acres are in cultivation. Left to itself, the cinnamon plant (*Cinnamomum*

XIII (a). Preparing Cinnamon

XIII (b). Picking Cardamons

zeylanicum) would form a small tree, but in cultivation it is kept coppiced, sending up long willowy shoots, whose bark, peeled off and dried and rolled into quills, forms the spice of commerce. The cinnamon peelers form a separate caste among the Sinhalese. The finer quills are made up into bales, while an inferior grade is shipped under the name "chips."

A considerable quantity of cinnamon oil is distilled in the island from broken quills and larger fragments of bark. Another oil, with something of the smell of oil of cloves, is distilled from the leaves, but only rarely, while camphor is obtained from the roots.

Cinnamon is used mainly in confectionery, incense, etc. A considerable proportion of the exported chips are used in Europe for the distillation of oil. The Seychelles are now producing a good deal of oil. The Ceylon exports in recent years have been:

1911	51,086 cwt.
1920	34,846

The cultivation and harvesting of cinnamon being very simple, and Ceylon having a practical monopoly of the trade, which is no longer seriously increasing, it is somewhat difficult to make any recommendations for the improvement of this cultivation. Green manuring may probably prove of considerable use, and more careful planting and cultivation are required. A careful study of the formation of the oil and its best method of distillation are also needed. It would seem, on the face of it, rather absurd that so much oil should have to be made in Europe, and· that all the labour of making up the chips should in a sense be wasted. It is quite possible that oil may be profitably obtained from the green twigs.

Pepper. This was the great staple of the spice trade of the Middle Ages, and was then exported solely from Malabar. Five ships a year were loaded with it in the days of Portuguese supremacy. Gradually the cultivation in India (and Ceylon) died away, and the Straits Settlements took the chief place. At the present time there is a very considerable trade in this spice, of which over 20,000 tons are annually exported from Singapore, chiefly the produce of the Straits Settlements and Federated Malay States, but also of some of the Dutch Islands, especially the islands of Rhio, opposite Singapore.

The common pepper, *Piper nigrum*, is a native of south-eastern Asia, and is a climbing plant which if left alone grows to a height of about twenty feet. It is cultivated in damp climates, with a rainfall of 80 inches, or over, in the shade of large trees, at distances of about seven feet apart, being planted as cuttings. Sometimes the cuttings are trained upon artificial supports, sometimes they are trained up the living trees which were left for shade. The vine does not flower for about three years, and comes into full bearing some years later. The fruit, which is the part to be gathered, is a string of small berries, greenish at first, then reddish, and finally yellow. Gathered and dried as they are, these form black pepper, but if the outer skins are removed (in various ways in different countries) before they are dried, they form white pepper. The yield is said to be very variable, differing in different years, and varying from half a pound to seven pounds a plant.

This difference in the yield points out one way in which it is very probable that the yield of pepper can be improved, namely by a careful selection of seed from the best bearers. A careful study of the manuring of pepper is also required, with a view to finding out which manures give the best returns.

Betel-Pepper (*Piper Betle*) is largely cultivated in Ceylon, India, Java, and other Eastern countries for its leaves, which are chewed with lime and with the fruits of Areca palms in the universal masticatory. The chewing of the leaves, which contain an oil, is said to be good for the health, and the lime provides an item which is often somewhat lacking in the diet of a rice-feeding people.

The plants are grown as cuttings, sometimes against poles, sometimes against planted supports. The ground is very care-fully and deeply tilled, and manuring is carried out with great care. In Ceylon it is done only with the leaves of *Croton lacciferum*, other manures being rejected. The leaves are picked after the first year, and in different places the plant is allowed to go on from one to six or more years in bearing.

The cultivation is very profitable, but there is a large outlay before any return can be obtained, and considerable risks are run from attacks of disease.

Cardamoms. Though an important industry in Ceylon and Southern India, this is as yet a comparatively unknown spice in Europe or America. It is chiefly used in India for confectionery, cooking, and masticating, but is steadily coming into use elsewhere, and deserves to be more widely known. About 7000 acres are now devoted to the growth of this spice in Ceylon, and about the same in Southern India. In Ceylon it is chiefly grown in the mountain districts north of Kandy, at an elevation of 3000 to 4000 feet.

The plant itself (*Elettaria Cardamomum*) belongs to the ginger family, and is not unlike ginger in appearance, but very much larger, growing to a height of about 5 to 10 feet. It is cultivated in clumps under the shade of the trees of the forest, which has its undergrowth thinned out to make room for it. The flowers are borne in little racemes, and are succeeded by little capsule fruits, which are picked, spread out in trays or on barbecues (or drying grounds), and slowly dried and bleached. The essential part of the spice is the seed contained in the capsules, but the latter are always dried with the seeds, and so far as possible without splitting. If the seeds were sold without the capsule, they could be easily adulterated with other similar and less valuable seeds. Lately a considerable demand for green or unbleached cardamoms has sprung up.

The exports of cardamoms from Ceylon in recent years, have been

1901	559,704 lbs.	1905	829,276 lbs.
1902	615,922		
1903	909,418	1910	639,007
1904	995,680	1920	374,216

Until fifteen years ago the cultivation of this spice was very profitable, and of course there was a rush into planting it, with results which may be anticipated. A cess has now been established in Ceylon, similar to that on tea, every pound of cardamoms exported having to pay one cent[1], and with the produce of this cess it is intended to advertise the spice and to endeavour to open new markets for its consumption. It is as yet too early to speak of the success or otherwise of this measure, but in the meantime, there has been a drop from the enormous figures of export of 1904.

Nutmegs. The nutmeg plant (*Myristica moschata* Thunb., *M. fragrans* Houtt.) is a native of the Molucca islands, formerly known as the Spice islands. For a long time the Dutch were able to maintain a monopoly of this spice, as of others, burning any excessive supply; but it was finally carried by the French to Mauritius and Cayenne, and has gradually become distributed over the world. It is said that one of the ways in which it was first carried from the Moluccas was by the large fruit-eating pigeons, which swallow the whole seed, large as it is, for the sake of the mace, and afterwards throw it up.

The nutmeg plant forms a small tree, from 30 to 50 feet in height, and is best cultivated in a loamy soil, at a height not over 1500 or 1800 feet above the sea. It is raised from seed, and the trees are planted about 30 feet apart. The great disadvantage in cultivating the nutmeg is that it is dioecious, i.e. that it bears male flowers on one tree, and female on another. Consequently the planter is liable to find, after waiting about seven years for the trees to flower, that he has got far too many male trees, which of course are useless for fruit. On the average, perhaps, about half the trees will prove male, when really one in about five or six is sufficient. Attempts have of late been made to graft male shoots on to the female trees, but of course this does not get over the difficulty of distinguishing the trees when young.

The tree bears when about seven years old, and, to judge from those in the Peradeniya gardens in Ceylon, until at least a hundred years old. The fruit is like a large yellowish plum, with a fleshy rind, which when fully ripe splits into two halves,

---

[1] I.e. every hundredweight Re. 1.12 or 1s. 6d.

exposing the large brown nutmeg in the middle, enclosed in an irregular coating of red mace, which runs in thick branching lines over the nutmeg. The mace is separated from the nutmeg, and both are dried and exported, the tree thus yielding two spices, of which the mace is perhaps the more in demand, so that some years ago an order was sent to a Ceylon planting company from the London office, that they were to grow more mace, and fewer nutmegs. The fleshy rind of the fruit makes an excellent jelly.

Cloves. The clove, *Eugenia caryophyllata* (or in the older books *Caryophyllus aromaticus*), is also a native of the Moluccas, and for a long time the Dutch were able to maintain a monopoly there, destroying the trees everywhere else. Finally, however, the French carried it to Cayenne, and from thence it got to the West Indies, and now is all over the world.

The plant is a small tree, about thirty feet high, and is cultivated like the nutmeg, in loamy soil, not too near to the sea, and up to elevations of perhaps 1500 feet. It begins to yield at the sixth year. The spice is the unexpanded buds, which occur in little clusters at the ends of the branches, and are carefully knocked off with bamboos, or picked. They are dried in the sun, and exported.

Pimento or Allspice. This plant, *Pimenta officinalis*, is a native of Jamaica and other West Indian islands, but the trade in it is practically entirely in the hands of Jamaica. The plant grows into a small tree, and the unripe fruits are picked and dried. They are of the size of a small pea, and have a sort of combination of the flavours of cinnamon, cloves, and nutmegs, whence the name allspice.

From the leaves of the pimento, and from an allied species of Pimenta, *P. acris*, an essential oil—bay-oil—is distilled, and this is afterwards mixed with rum to form the well-known bay-rum.

Ginger. This plant, *Zingiber officinale*, is a native of south-eastern Asia, but is now more cultivated in Jamaica than almost anywhere else, though of late bananas are being planted on much of the land formerly occupied by ginger, and give an equal or better return with less work. It is a small herb, with a stout underground rhizome or root-stock, known to planters as a *race*, which is the actual spice. The plant grows to about one to three feet high, and the flowers come off on separate branches from the root-stock. The plant must be grown in good soil, at moderate elevations, and bears within the year. The races are carefully dug up, placed in boiling water for a few minutes, and then dried in the sun. More often they are carefully cleaned, and the whole of the dark outer skin removed with a knife, and dried after washing, without boiling. The produce of the latter method is known as uncoated, scraped, or white ginger, in contradistinction to the coated, unscraped, or black ginger prepared by the first method.

Careful selection is required in this plant, to pick out the races giving the largest return, and the best flavoured ginger.

Vanilla. This plant (*Vanilla planifolia*) is wild in Mexico, and the Aztecs were found to be using it to flavour chocolate at the date of the Spanish conquest. It is a climbing orchid, and the flavour is found in the ripe pods. It is usually cultivated under small trees, e.g. physic nuts (*Jatropha Curcas*) up which it climbs, and bamboos are placed across between the trees at a height of about six feet, upon which the orchids are then trained. The flowers require to be artificially fertilised, and the pods, when ripe, are gathered, placed for half a minute in hot, nearly boiling water, and then exposed to the sun, being rolled up tightly to ferment every night until dry. When brown and pliable they are ready, and are then straightened out and tied together in bundles.

Vanilla is cultivated in a great many tropical countries, the world's production being about 1,500,000 lbs., of which the bulk comes from the French tropical colonies, especially Tahiti and Réunion.

CHAPTER VII

FRUITS AND VEGETABLES

Fruits. The tropical zone furnishes a very large number of wild fruits to which the late Dr Trimen's judgment—that they are edible but not worth eating—may in general be applied. At the same time they are by no means usually so inedible as the wild fruits of the north, from which the plum, the apple, the gooseberry, etc. have been produced, and there is consequently reason to hope that in the future we may get some very fine fruits from the tropics, when selection has been properly applied. What has been done in the past with the mango, the pineapple, the plantain, gives good ground for hope in this respect, the more now that we are beginning, thanks to the work of Mendel, Bateson, and others, to understand the principles upon which to work.

Though fruit is everywhere cultivated, there is no actual export trade in it except in a few places. Many parts of northern India grow fruit for the Calcutta and other markets ; in Ceylon there are considerable areas of bananas for the supply of the towns, and in southern Brazil there are extensive orchards of oranges, mangoes, pears, apples, pineapples, strawberries, and other fruits for the supply of Rio de Janeiro, São Paulo, and other towns. There is an actual export trade in fruit upon a noteworthy scale only in Central America, where the West Indies, Nicaragua, etc., grow fruit, chiefly bananas, for the United States and Europe, Jamaica in 1919 exporting £1,218,000 worth of fruit.

The most popular fruit with the people of colder climates is of course the plantain or banana (*Musa paradisiaca*), which is now consumed in very large quantities, and is largely cultivated for the market in Nicaragua, the West Indies and the Canary

Islands. The plant grows from suckers which are planted out at regular intervals. Each produces what appears to be an erect stem about 8 to 12 feet high, but in reality this is made up of the bases of the leaves coiled round one another, and the real stem is a root-stock below the ground. Presently the flowering shoot comes right up through the coiled leaf bases, and produces a drooping spike of flowers at the top of the plant. The fruits are produced independently of the fertilisation of the flowers, and though in the wild plantain they are full of seeds, in the cultivated one they produce seed but rarely, and then only one or two infertile ones. The flower head that crowns the stalk is often cooked as a vegetable.

There are many varieties of the banana, but as a rule only one kind is seen in England, this being the one which produces most freely, and at the same time stands being carried long distances, while it ripens on the way. Many of the other varieties are preferable to this one, being more soft and mealy. One of the favourite ones in the east is a dull red colour and very large.

The name banana, by which this fruit is known in England and the United States, is confined in the tropics to the West Indies, while in India and Ceylon it is termed the plantain, a name applied in the west only to the cooking variety.

The pineapple (*Ananassa sativa*) is another very popular fruit in the north, and at one time hothouse pines were highly favoured. Now, however, with the large cultivation that goes on in the tropics, the fruit has cheapened so much that hothouse culture has almost died out. It is cultivated on open land, and very carefully packed for export, each fruit in a separate compartment of a crate. Another very considerable trade is that in tinned pineapples from Singapore, which is in the hands of the Chinese in that port.

The pine occurs in many varieties. The largest is perhaps the Smooth Cayenne as grown in Ceylon, where on good rich soils it has reached a weight of 23½ lbs., with an excellent flavour.

The mango (*Mangifera indica*) is of course an Indian fruit, and the really delicately flavoured mangoes can as a rule only be got in a few favoured places in India, but of late the fruit has been grown in the West Indies, and a few have been sold in London and elsewhere. A small trade also goes on between Bombay and London in the same fruit. The chief difficulty is the packing of the very rich and juicy fruit to stand the long voyage, and probably this will for some time stand in the way of introducing really good mangoes to Europe.

As cultivated from time immemorial in the east, the mango is one of the commonest fruits, and occurs in perhaps as many as 100 varieties. Of these only a few are really good to the European taste, most of them having about them more or less of the stringiness and flavour of the wild mango, which made some one describe the fruit as tasting like a ball of cotton dipped in turpentine. The differences between these varieties are perhaps greater than in almost any other fruit, and no two fruits could be imagined more distinct in look and even in taste than the little red " plum " mangoes which look just like Victoria plums, and the large green "rupee" mangoes weighing some pounds each.

The exquisite taste of a really good mango, as one may at times get it in India or Brazil, is a revelation, and it is much to be desired that this fruit should appear in European commerce in really good condition.

The mango is usually cultivated casually among other trees in the common mixed cultivation of native gardens, but in some places, especially in Western India, there are real orchards of nothing but mangoes, the trees growing to about 20 feet in height. These orchards are very carefully tended, and contain nothing but the best varieties, carefully grafted on to hardy stocks.

The orange (*Citrus Aurantium*), though of course really a sub-tropical cultivation, is another fruit very largely cultivated throughout the tropics, but is only exported from the West Indies, where the industry has grown to considerable size. The finest orange in the world is probably that grown at Bahia in Brazil (whence, among other forms, came the famous "Washington Navel"). The West Indian orange is very good; the trees yield very heavily, up to 3000 or 4000 oranges a tree a year, it is said, and the industry is now a very considerable one.

In Ceylon and the other eastern countries the cultivation of oranges for market is not engaged in, and the local oranges are in general rather poor (except in north-east India). Furthermore, in recent years Australian and Italian oranges have been imported in large quantities, and this has still further discouraged any local attempts to grow them.

The lime (*Citrus medica* var. *acida*) comes next to the orange in importance, and there is a considerable industry in Dominica and other West Indian islands in exporting the preserved juice to Europe and America. As this juice, pleasant though it is, has only a very slight resemblance indeed to the juice of the fresh limes, it would seem as if it might be worth while exporting the latter themselves to Europe, where people might then make fresh "lime and soda"—a very popular drink in the east.

The lime is a near relative of the orange, and grows on very similar trees, and is in general cultivated in the same manner.

Of late the trade in lime juice is showing a change. Instead of exporting the concentrated juice, it is carefully neutralised with fine prepared chalk, and the resulting citrate of calcium dried and exported in airtight receptacles. From this citric acid is made in Europe and America.

A few other fruits require mention here, as, though they are not exported to Europe or America, they are of enormous importance within the tropics, furnishing a large proportion of their food to the inhabitants. Thus the jak fruit (*Artocarpus integrifolia*), a huge fleshy fruit which may weigh 30 lbs. or over, is universally cultivated in Ceylon and southern India, and common in other tropical countries. The disagreeable smell of the fruit renders it unpalatable to Europeans, but it is one of the staples of life to the ordinary villager. Its place is largely taken in the Malay countries by the durian (*Durio zibethinus*), a fruit with an exceedingly disagreeable and penetrating smell of mustard oil, but one of which most people who can get over their dislike for the smell (which is mainly in the rind, whereas one eats the coats of the seeds) become almost inordinately fond, the flavour being very good, and varying a good deal from fruit to fruit. Wallace in his *Malay Archipelago* says that it is worth a journey to the east to eat this fruit. The objections of smell do not apply to the breadfruit (*Artocarpus incisa*), which is one of the staples of life in the coastal districts of the equatorial regions, and which, when properly cooked, is very good eating. There is a possibility that this fruit would meet with favour in Europe.

These fruits, providing a great deal of nutriment, are almost "food products," but there are others eaten more for their flavour, and some of these are very good, and would be worth taking pains with, and introducing into the markets of the north. Among the best of these is the mangosteen (*Garcinia Mangostana*); the white fleshy coat of the seed of this is one of the most delicately flavoured of fruits. The cherimoyer of Peru (*Anona Cherimolia*) is also exquisitely flavoured, and the other species of *Anona*, such as *A. squamosa* the sweet-sop or sugar apple, *A. muricata* the sour-sop, *A. reticulata* the custard apple, all of which are sometimes seen in European markets, are also very pleasantly flavoured. Another tropical fruit which is becoming popular in the north is the Aguacate, Avocado, or Alligator pear (*Persea gratissima*), which occurs in many varieties, especially in tropical America, of which it is a native, and which makes an excellent salad with pepper and vinegar. Yet another very good fruit, which is rather subtropical than tropical, growing best at high elevation above the sea, is the Passion fruit (*Passiflora edulis*), which can also be cultivated in warm temperate climates. The fruits, scraped out into a tumbler with the addition of a pinch of bicarbonate of soda and some sugar, make a most refreshing drink. Another very good fruit is the chiku or sapodilla (*Achras Sapota*), and others worthy of mention are the guava (*Psidium Guava*), the rozelle (*Hibiscus Sabdariffa*, used in jellies, etc.), the jambu (species of *Eugenia*), the mountain papaw (*Carica candamarcensis*), and the tree tomato (*Cyphomandra betacea*). And of nuts may be specially mentioned the cashew (*Anacardium occidentale*), which when roasted is perhaps the best of all nuts. It is often known in the east as the coffin nail or promotion nut, but there is no reason to suppose that it is specially indigestible unless eaten in large quantity.

Another fruit which is of importance, and requires a paragraph to itself, is the papaw (*Carica Papaya*), which bears a large fruit not unlike a melon, but with a peculiar and not unpleasant flavour of its own. It is one of the great staples of native mixed cultivation in the tropics. The leaves and the unripe fruits of this plant contain a milky juice, in which is the ferment papain. Meat wrapped in a leaf and buried becomes partly digested and much more tender, and of recent years the ferment has come a good deal into use in the north for people of weak digestion. It is obtained by bleeding the unripe fruits, and purifying the product. Until lately, the trade was mainly in the hands of the peasantry of the West Indian island of Montserrat, and the capture of it by Ceylon, where it is a mere bagatelle, will likely involve them in some suffering. This phenomenon again illustrates the advantage possessed by a country with cheap labour and European supervision over one in which an industry is merely in the hands of the peasants.

Vegetables. Speaking generally the tropics are poor in really good vegetables, the best available, from the European point of view, being the actual European vegetables grown at high levels in the mountains or imported from Europe, America, or Australia. Thus, in Ceylon, at 6200 feet and in south Brazil at 2500 feet, the cabbage, cauliflower, carrot, turnip, potato, celery, lettuce, leek, parsley, and other vegetables are commonly cultivated by market gardeners and sent down to the low levels by the night mail trains. It is true that these vegetables can be grown at lower levels, but their cultivation takes much more care and trouble, and cannot be commercially carried on.

A very great variety of vegetables is grown by the inhabitants of tropical countries, e.g. the yams, etc., described in Chapter I, and other tubers, such as those of Canna, Tacca, Curcuma, etc.; pulses such as *Phaseolus lunatus* and other species, *Dolichos Lablab, Lens esculenta*, the lentil, *Arachis hypogaea*, the ground-nut, and many more; gourds and pumpkins of all kinds; onions, beet, radish, cabbage and other

"European" vegetables; and many spicily flavoured "curry-stuffs." It would lead too far to enter into details about all these.

The most striking instance of vegetable production is probably to be seen in Java, where the rice fields are cultivated in vegetables after the rice crop is reaped, and where vegetables are good, cheap and abundant.

In general native vegetables are poor of their kind, probably owing to the crossing with poor sorts that continually goes on.

There are several quite good kinds of tropical vegetables cultivated in the lower levels, but the ingrained conservatism of the European residents in the tropics prevents their cordial acceptance. Such for instance are the sweet potato, the various beans, pumpkins, gourds, yams (many of which are really excellent if properly cooked), onions, egg-fruits or brinjals, okras or bandakais, etc. It is true that none of these, except the sweet potato, the brinjal, the onion, and perhaps some of the yams, are quite up to the ordinary European standard, but much more might be made of them than is made, especially if better methods of cooking them were devised.

There is a great want, from the point of view of the European residents in the tropics, of good and varied vegetables for eating. People constantly ask, in all eastern countries at any rate, why this demand is not supplied, and blame the native for not being sufficiently awake to his own interests to supply it. In actual fact, however, the small European population creates but a very small demand, and it is rare to find Europeans who are willing to pay a higher price for a better article. The cultivator who starts to grow fancy fruits or vegetables for the local markets takes considerable risks. On the other hand, a good many Europeans are willing to go to some expense and trouble to grow such things in their own gardens. At high elevations, seeds of the best kinds of vegetables can be imported every year from Europe, and cultivated with success, but this is rarely the case in the low country. If the right time of year be chosen for sowing, a surprising number of European vegetables will give a fair crop there, but for all the year round supplies reliance must necessarily be placed upon the native vegetables. Hence the obvious policy to pursue is to improve these. Hitherto the usual way in which this has been attempted has been to introduce other varieties from abroad, but in general there is but little to choose between the varieties from different tropical countries if the differences in methods of cultivation and effects of soil be left out of account, while varieties of tropical or subtropical vegetables soon deteriorate in the hot climate, if introduced from colder countries. Furthermore, it is obvious that there are very well marked limits to this kind of work; every variety from every tropical country may soon be introduced into any given country, and then the work must come to an end. What is wanted is systematic selection and improvement, a work of time, trouble and expense, but the only way in which good results can be obtained, and good and suitable varieties produced. A vast difference would be apparent in the quality of tropical produce if careful selection of seed were attended to. The European seedsman keeps up the qualities of his varieties by careful selection, while the same varieties in the hands of his customers deteriorate in every generation. Local races should be improved by selection, by scientific crossing with imported races possessing desirable characters, and by careful attention to good cultivation. Even wild edible plants and fruits, so often contemned as "jungle stuff," may in this way become valuable products. In Ceylon, a few years ago, Mr R. H. Lock, by careful crossing with the European pea, so much improved the native pea that it was almost a new vegetable.

CHAPTER VIII

TOBACCO, OPIUM, HEMP

Tobacco. The tobacco plant (*Nicotiana Tabacum* and other species), a native of warmer America, is now one of the most widely cultivated plants in the world, for, being only of short duration, it can be grown in the summer season of the temperate zones, and is as a matter of fact very largely cultivated in the eastern United States, Egypt, Persia, etc. The most prosperous tobacco-growing countries are however probably Sumatra and Cuba, while large quantities are also grown in Borneo, Java, the Philippines, Brazil, South India, Ceylon, and other places. Tobaccos for cigars, for pipe-smoking, for cigarettes, and for chewing, are grown in different localities, some suiting one kind better, some another.

The custom of smoking was first noticed by Columbus, and was introduced into Spain by the early explorers. A hundred years later it was brought to England by Sir Walter Raleigh, and, though at first it excited alarm, it was not long before the habit spread. The great plague gave a considerable impetus to smoking, smokers being supposed to be immune. After this began the period of repression, when great efforts were made to put down the habit by penal laws and severe punishments, in Russia people being even knouted for the offence of smoking. But all was in vain, and the habit continually spread, until now it is almost universal.

Tobacco is grown from seed, and planted out from nurseries upon rich, light soils, in which there must be plenty of lime, potash and decaying organic matter. In Sumatra the custom at one time was to fell fresh forest for each crop, but now it is found that 8—10 years lying fallow will render the ground suitable once more, and an estate is made of about 8—10 times the area cultivated in any one year. The rows are about three feet apart, and the plants are separated by about 18 inches in the rows. When, in a few months, the flower buds begin to appear at the top of the stems, they are nipped off, so as to leave the plant with from 10 to 15 leaves; lateral flower buds appear soon after, and must be similarly treated. In three months or so the leaves are ripe, and they are then treated in different ways in different countries. One of the best ways of treatment is that adopted in the West Indies. The plants are cut down and allowed to wither for a short time, and are then carried to the drying house, where they are cut up into short lengths, each length having one pair of leaves. These are hung on sticks and placed in the sun to wither, and are then hung in the drying house for three days, with the leaves touching one another, and then hung more widely apart. When the midribs are perfectly dry, say in 30 days, the leaves are cut off from the stalks, and packed in large heaps, several feet in depth, to ferment, and changed in position in the heap every day or two. After thirty or forty days, all the heat will have gone, and the leaves will now be cured and ready for export.

In Sumatra much the same plan is followed. The leaves are cut at about 1 p.m., when they are dry and supple. They are dried for 20—30 days, and then sorted into bundles of different qualities and fermented. Bamboos are put into the fermentation heaps and by the aid of thermometers placed in them the fermentation is regulated.

Of late years some successful work has been done, especially in temperate-zone countries, in growing tobacco under shade, it being grown in light sheds roofed with cheese-cloth. By this means larger plants are produced, there is less damage by insects, etc., and a fine quality of wrapper leaf is obtained.

Great efforts are constantly being made to introduce the cultivation of tobacco, which on the whole is one of the most profitable in the tropics, though somewhat risky, into new countries, but there are many difficulties. The soil is often unsuitable through containing too little lime or potash or

XIV (a). A Tobacco Field in Sumatra

XIV (b). Fermenting Tobacco in Sumatra

for other reasons, or the plants may not grow well through being in a somewhat unsuitable climate. To get enough leaf to cure properly, a comparatively large area has to be grown in tobacco, say 50 acres, and the curing is a matter requiring considerable experience and skill.

In northern Ceylon there is a considerable industry in preparing tobacco, not for the European or American market, to which the tobacco of most countries goes, but for South India, where the preference is for a coarse rank tobacco. Many thousands of acres are given up to this crop in the extreme north of Ceylon. As a rule, each villager only grows a very small area. The tobacco grown has extremely large leaves, and is very rapidly cured, so as to form a rank and heavy brand, which can rarely be smoked with pleasure by any white man. The trade in this tobacco is, however, fairly profitable. Attempts have at different times been made to get a tobacco from Ceylon suitable for the European market, but the difficulties are many, not the least being that the villagers grow areas too small to give enough tobacco for a proper cure, and consequently anyone trying to cure properly would have to buy the tobacco from a large number of villagers.

Opium. The cultivation of the opium poppy (*Papaver somniferum*) has until lately been largely carried on in Bengal, and in other parts of India. The object of its cultivation is mainly for export to China, where the drug is largely smoked. Opium, whose effect depends on the presence of morphine and other alkaloids, is one of the most useful but, at the same time, most dangerous drugs, and the habit of opium smoking, which produces very pleasant dreamy sensations, is one that rapidly grows upon its victims. Opium was the primary cause of the China war of 1860, a Chinese customs official, anxious to prevent its importation into that country, having destroyed about £2,000,000 worth of it on landing.

The cultivated opium poppy is apparently a form of *Papaver setigerum*, a Mediterranean species, and the finest opium for medicinal purposes comes to this day from Asia Minor. The plant comes into flower about three months after sowing, and the petals are removed when fully matured, and kept to form the packing round the opium. The seed-capsule is ready for treatment in about another ten days, and is lanced with a series of parallel knives about 1/30 of an inch apart. The opium which runs out—the. milk of the plant—is collected next day with a kind of scoop, and made up in factories into cakes of about 21 lbs., wrapped in a thick coating of the petals.

Hemp. It is best to consider this plant along with opium, for in the tropics it only yields the drug, whereas in temperate climates it gives a very excellent fibre, but no drug. The plant (*Cannabis sativa*) is a native of the northern tropics and the subtropics of Asia, and is largely cultivated in India for the drug, and in southern Europe, China, etc. for the fibre. It is especially cultivated in Bengal, and the area devoted to it is very large.

In Bengal nurseries are prepared in May, the plants are sown in August, and planted out in September, six or eight inches apart. They mature from January onwards. The male flowers are removed in November, for, if the female flowers are fertilised, there is no formation of the drug.

The drug is a resinous exudation found upon almost all parts of the plant, and is marketed in three forms, ganja, charas, and bhang, the resins of the flowers, the young shoots, and the mature leaves respectively. Ganja is prepared from the flowering shoots (female) by packing them together and tramping them down. Charas is prepared in climates further north than ganja, and the flowering twigs are beaten over a cloth, when the resin drops off as a fine powder. Bhang consists of the actual mature leaves, mainly gathered from the wild plants, and is used in the preparation of the intoxicating drink hashish, or in the making of sweetmeats. The handling of bhang is therefore very difficult to regulate, whereas that of ganja or charas, which are made from the cultivated plant, is subject to strict laws, and no one is allowed to sell without a license. The action of the drug is not unlike that of opium.

CHAPTER IX

CINCHONA AND OTHER DRUGS

Cinchona. The Cinchona tree (*Cinchona succirubra, officinalis, Ledgeriana,* and other species), whose bark, often known to this day as Peruvian bark, yields the drug quinine, besides the other less valuable alkaloids cinchonidine, etc., is a native of the Andes of Peru. The drug, in the form of the powdered bark, was first introduced to Europe in the sixteenth century by the Jesuits, and its value became well known when in 1638 the Countess of Chinchon was cured of a fever by its aid.

For a very long time the drug was entirely obtained from the wild trees in Peru, which were felled and their bark removed, but about 1860 it was realised that these wild trees were getting into serious danger of extermination, and an expedition, headed by the late Sir Clements Markham, was sent to Peru, and after toilsome and often dangerous journeying, secured a large supply of young plants and seed, which was successfully introduced into India and Ceylon. Quinine at that time was worth about twelve shillings an ounce, and the history of its cheapening to one shilling must be mainly credited to Ceylon.

The tree was cultivated for many years at Hakgala, the Government mountain garden in Ceylon, at a height of about 5600 feet above the sea level, but in the days when coffee was prosperous no one could be persuaded to have anything to do with the plants, and it was only after about ten years, as coffee began to be depressed by the attacks of the leaf disease, that anyone was induced to plant them, although at first they were given away. Later, as the collapse of coffee began to drive the planters to look out for something else, cinchona was tried,

cautiously at first, but with a rush so soon as the profits realised
by the first planters became known. A large area was rapidly
covered with the tree, and prices of quinine fell rapidly, till at
last they reached one shilling an ounce. The figures of export
from Ceylon, with the average prices of quinine, may be quoted
here, as they show what went on better than any description:

	Export of bark	Price of Quinine an ounce
1875	19,152 lbs.	6s. 9d.
1880	1,208,000	12s. 0d.
1885	11,678,000	2s. 3d.
1886	15,365,000 (maximum)	
1890	8,729,000	1s. 1d.
1895	920,000	1s. 1d.
1900	591,000	1s. 1d.
1905	171,485	1s. 1d.

The reduction of the price to such an enormous extent
made the cultivation in Ceylon unprofitable, and it was rapidly
given up, the more so as tea was at the same time coming in,
and proving to be very remunerative. At the present time,
there is but little cinchona cultivated in Ceylon, probably about
150 acres in all.

In India the cultivation was but little taken up by private
individuals, but was largely gone in for by the Government,
especially in the Nilgiri Mountains in Madras, and in the
Himalaya near Darjeeling. The Indian Government has not
entered the open market as a competitor, but manufactures its
own quinine for sale to the people of India, who by an admirable
arrangement introduced by the late Sir George King, Superintendent of the Calcutta Botanic Gardens, are enabled to buy
packets containing one dose of 7 grains at the price of one pice
(i.e. one farthing) at any post office in India. This has done a
great deal against that scourge of the poorer people of India,
malaria.

At the same time that Ceylon was giving up cinchona,
Java was taking it up, in the slow but persistent way that
characterises the Dutch planters, and at the same time, by
the aid of science, taking steps to improve the yield of the
alkaloids in the bark by a careful selection. This selection has

XV. Cinchona succirubra in Java; 30 years old

(*Original in possession of the Kolonial Wirthschaftliche Komitee, Berlin*)

gone on for a great many years, and the result has been that
the best Java barks of *Cinchona Ledgeriana* now contain as
much as 15—17 per cent. of their weight of the drug, while
the Ceylon barks rarely exceed 8 per cent. This of course
means that a far less quantity of the heavy bark has to be
grown and sent to Europe to obtain the same monetary return,
and consequently nowadays Java has a practical monopoly of
the cinchona market, from which there seems little likelihood
of ousting her, though it must be pointed out that the profits
in this cultivation are now but small, even in Java.

The plant is grown from seeds, and forms a small tree
which grows best in the mountains of the tropics at elevations
of 4000 feet or more, in wet districts. The plants are usually
put out at distances of three or four feet, and after three or
four years are thinned out. The most usual ways of obtaining
the bark are coppicing and shaving. In the former case the
trees are cut down, and the stocks are allowed to grow up
again. In the latter case the bark is shaved with a spokeshave
nearly, but not quite, down to the cambium. If the latter be
not injured, the bark will quickly grow again. It is sometimes
tied up in moss to encourage renewal.

The most promising directions in which improvement may
be looked for in cinchona cultivation are in the continual improvement of the barks by selection of the richest in each
generation, in green manuring, and in grafting the less hardy
species, which also happen to be the richer in alkaloid, upon
the more hardy, such as *Cinchona succirubra*. This is now
largely done in Java, with very good results.

Coca. This plant (*Erythroxylon Coca*) is also a native of
the Andes, and the Indians use the leaves largely as a masticatory, the chewing of coca leaves enabling them to resist
fatigue. In recent years the plant has also come into use
in Europe and America, the drug cocaine, obtained from the
leaves, proving to be a most valuable local anaesthetic. It has
also powerful stimulating properties, and the "cocaine habit,"
whether in the direction of drinking wines medicated with
cocaine, or in other ways consuming the drug, has assumed

considerable proportions. Until lately obtained entirely from
the wild plants of Peru, etc., the drug is now largely got from
the cultivated plants of Ceylon, Java and elsewhere. The
plant in cultivation forms a small bush, not unlike tea, and
the mature (not the young) leaves are picked and dried, and
exported. The Eastern leaf is now practically the standard of
the market.

Ipecacuanha. This plant (*Cephaelis Ipecacuanha*) is a
little herbaceous plant grown in Brazil, the Federated Malay
States, and elsewhere. The roots form the drug, and are like
rows of beads.

Jalap. The jalap plant (*Ipomoea purga*) is a native of
Mexico, occurring especially near the town of Xalapa, from
which it takes its name. The plant is a small climber, with
large tuberous roots, which when rooted up and dried form the
drug.

Cubebs. The cubeb plant (*Piper Cubeba*) is a native of
Java, and is grown very like ordinary pepper. The dried fruits
form the drug.

Sarsaparilla. *Smilax officinalis* and other species of
Smilax are natives of Central America, and are cultivated
to some extent in Jamaica. They are slender climbers, and
the drug consists of the cord-like roots.

Castor-oil. This is extracted from the seeds of *Ricinus
communis,* a native of the eastern tropics, and cultivated to
some extent in India and elsewhere. It forms a very common
weed in Ceylon, the West Indies, and other countries. Its
cultivation is very easy, but unremunerative, experiments in
Ceylon having shown that only about 4 to 5 cwts. of seed per
acre can be looked for, the seed being worth only a few rupees
a hundredweight.

CHAPTER X

FIBRE-YIELDING PLANTS

Cotton. So far as the tropics are concerned, this cultivation is mainly restricted to India, in which country it is a great staple, and to Brazil, the West Indies, and parts of tropical Africa. Its extension in the latter two has been largely due to the efforts of the British Cotton-Growing Association, ably seconded by those of the Imperial Department of Agriculture for the West Indies, and the other local departments of agriculture. In Brazil, with the high price of cotton during recent years, and the efforts of the Government, a great stimulus has been given to its culture, and it looks as if that country, the native home of so many kinds of cotton, might become the chief tropical centre of cultivation.

Cotton has been cultivated in India from prehistoric times, and at one time Indian manufactured cotton goods were mainly used in Europe. When America was discovered, the Mexicans and Peruvians were found to be using their native cottons, but this industry died out under the Spanish conquests. Later on, cotton cultivation was begun in the southern United States, and by the end of the 18th century there was a considerable export to Great Britain. By 1860, with the continual improvement that was going on in length of fibre and other qualities, the supremacy of American cotton upon the market was assured. Then followed the Civil War, which for the time cut off American supplies, and the Indian cotton, hitherto only received to the extent of about 400,000 bales annually, was sent to England at the rate of about 1,500,000 bales a year. With the better prices, India unfortunately took to adulteration, and after the close of the war, America rapidly regained her premier position, and Indian cotton sank to the bottom of the market grades.

The cotton earliest cultivated in India would appear to have been a tree cotton, probably *Gossypium arboreum.* At the present time, although it occurs almost everywhere in single specimens, and its fibre is used for making the sacred string of the Brahmin and the wicks of temple lamps, this species is not cultivated; the forms of cotton—all annual— grown in India are referred by Watt[1] to *G. Nanking, G. obtusifolium,* and others. The Levant cotton, according to the same authority, is *G. herbaceum,* and this, with *G. hirsutum,* and especially *G. mexicanum,* and perhaps others, are cultivated in the United States, while *G. peruvianum* is grown in Peru, Egypt, etc. All these are cottons with a closely adherent "fuzz" on the seed, while *G. barbadense,* the parent of the Sea Island cotton, and others, have none, the fibre or lint coming clean off, and leaving a naked seed.

While at first it was the perennial species of cotton that were cultivated—indeed no wild annual species is known—the growth of cotton as an annual, yielding its crop in the same year in which it is sown, and much less liable to disease (owing to the periods of fallow), has steadily come in, and now it is but rare for a tree cotton to be cultivated. At the same time, the growth of the annual forms allowed of a considerable extension northwards and southwards of the cotton growing area.

India has about 10—12 million acres within the tropics devoted to the growth of cotton, but the yield is very poor, amounting only to about 7 million cwt. Indian cotton appears on the market under many names, such as Oomrawuttee or Hingunghat, Broach, Bengal, Dhollerah, Surat, Tinnevelli, Westerns, etc.

There are many mills for the spinning and weaving of cotton in India, especially in Bombay, and these take more and

---

[1] *The wild and cultivated Cotton Plants of the World.* London, 1907. It is right, however, to point out that many good authorities object to Sir George Watt's conclusions, and that recent experiments in Mendelian breeding are also opposed to them.

more of the local product. As these mills do not want a long but simply a short and uniform staple, the process of improvement of the quality of Indian cottons is naturally handicapped. What is most wanted at present would seem to be a larger yield, for the production is extremely small.

In the 18th century cotton was often grown under irrigation in India, but during more recent times it has commonly been cultivated on lands of good water-retaining capacity. The most marked of these is the "black cotton soil" common in Madras, Berar, etc. This is a heavy black alluvial soil, rather clayey, which cracks, but does not disintegrate, under a hot sun, and retains water exceedingly well. Experiments in Ceylon with similar soils tend to show that this black soil offers no special advantages other than this capacity of holding water, a capacity which must be of great value under an Indian sun.

The cotton crop in India is commonly rotated with others; e.g. in Berar a common sequence is wheat, peas, cotton, linseed, jowari. It is also not infrequently sown with a small admixture of some leguminous crop.

Indian cotton, speaking generally, is about the poorest and dirtiest, and gives the worst yield, of any in the world, and no one who has seen the cotton districts of India can wonder at this. It is a small, low-growing plant, usually not over three feet high. In some parts of India it is sown broadcast, in others planted with a drill, at intervals of 1′ 6″ to 3′ apart, and the crop is put out every year at the beginning of the rainy season. It is kept weeded, but otherwise left to take care of itself, and in a few months it comes into flower, the flowers being succeeded by the pods, or bolls, as they are usually termed. From these, when they burst, the cotton is picked, spread out to dry, and finally ginned. Formerly it was largely ginned by the aid of small and very primitive hand-gins, but now it is often ginned at special factories, established by European firms throughout the cotton districts.

Two kinds of gin are generally employed, the saw gin and the roller gin. In the former the cotton is fed against a grating of fine mesh work, behind which is a revolving drum covered with small projecting teeth, which tear off the cotton from the seeds, the latter being left behind the mesh work. The roller gin has the cotton fed between two roughened rollers, which are so closely placed together that the seed is left behind, while the lint or wool is drawn through. The latter type of gin gives very much better results, tearing the lint much less, but is more expensive to work; it is the only type of gin that can be employed for cotton with long fibres—or long-stapled cotton as it is technically called.

From the gin the cotton goes to the baling press, which compresses it enormously, into bales of about 500 lbs. each, which are then shipped to Japan—which country takes more and more of the short-stapled Indian cotton—or to Europe.

The yield of Indian cotton is astonishingly small, the quality is very poor, and it is commonly more or less dirty. This is due in part to the carelessness of the natives, but largely to the fact that the money-lenders, to whom the villagers usually mortgage their crops, do not allow them to pick it as it becomes ripe, but only in quantities at intervals, and thus a good deal of it falls upon the ground. The prices obtained are as a rule only about say 4d. a pound (pre-war) while the yield is from 60 to 120 lbs. an acre. Thus the financial return is ridiculously small, and in no other country but India could it be looked on as a remunerative crop. The peasant, however, putting his own and his family's labour into the work, and spending comparatively little in actual money upon it, regards the cotton crop, in many districts, as his great financial standby.

At one time Indian cotton held sway upon the market, and there were also special manufactures of it, as, for example, into Dacca muslin, in India itself, but now this is all changed, and the cultivation of cotton in the United States of America has revolutionised the world in this matter, and there seems little prospect, for the present, of America being ousted by India from her position of supremacy, though she may be largely ousted by Brazil.

Much effort is now being devoted, by the new departments of agriculture in India, to getting better cottons to grow successfully in that country. Experiments are being made in

XVI. Interior of Cotton Factory in the West Indies

(Lent by Imperial Dept. of Agriculture, Barbados)

two directions, in the trial of cottons from other countries, and in the breeding of new varieties of longer-stapled cotton suitable to India. The latter efforts must of course take a long time, but in the meantime Egyptian cotton grown in the Sind district of Bombay has been sold in Lancashire at $9\frac{1}{2}d$. a pound, a very good figure.

In the West Indies, on the other hand, it has been found that the climate and soil are excellently suited to the growth of the Sea Island cotton, *Gossypium barbadense*, which indeed is originally a native of the islands, but which is chiefly cultivated upon the coast of South Carolina and in Georgia and Florida. By careful treatment and good cultivation this crop yields from 200 to 300 lbs. per acre, worth from 1s. to 1s. 6d. per lb. so that the maximum return per acre may be as much as £22. 10s. 0d. against about £2 for the Indian, a vast difference, and one sufficient to make a profitable return to anyone putting capital into the cultivation. Sea Island cotton has a special market, and brings the highest prices of any cotton, and it has as yet only been found to succeed in a very small area. But the demand for the very fine qualities is very limited, and the market may be easily flooded. This kind of cotton is ginned with the roller gin, and packed in bags containing about 400 lbs.

The very serious rise in the price of cotton, some years ago, brought considerable trouble to Lancashire, and resulted finally in the formation of a British Cotton-growing Association, whose avowed object was to encourage the growing of cotton within the British Empire, thus rendering Lancashire comparatively independent of the American supply and of the "manipulations" of American dealers. The consumption of cotton in America itself is also growing rapidly, and tending to reduce the amount available for Lancashire.

The most striking feature in the recent cotton situation is the rapid rise in the position of Brazil, which has an enormous area well suited to cotton. She has for a long time been using much cotton in local mills, and during 1920 exported 24,000 tons in addition to the local consumption of about 50,000 tons, much of whose produce is also being exported.

The improvement of cotton cultivation in the tropics is a very difficult matter, and one which cannot be left in the hands of the natives there. Indian cotton has not, so far as one can discover, appreciably deteriorated in the last fifty years, as it is practically wild cotton of several species and hybrids, yet, during that time or a little longer, it has gone from near the top to the bottom of the market prices. A similar plant, taken up by the white man, with careful selection of seed, has given the American Upland cottons, which now form the bulk of the world's supply. Leave the native of the tropics to himself, and he will never select his seed, and without that the quality must remain at the bottom. Either give him a species of cotton, which even when wild is better than his own, or else arrange for Government selection of seed. This may be done in various ways. Probably the best is to have a definite seed farm, on which the selection of seed can be rigidly and carefully attended to, while at the same time definite experiments in hybridisation on Mendelian principles can be made; but another way sometimes adopted is to have inspectors who shall go round the fields of the actual cultivators, and mark the best stocks for seed, the seed of these being subsequently bought and picked by the Government, and exchanged against the cultivators' own seed.

So far as India is concerned, it is probable that, as already stated, it may be wiser at first to aim at an increased yield of the local races, while at the same time carrying on experiments in the production of better qualities for export purposes. Acclimatisation of foreign cottons, so often held up as the most promising way of improvement, is very hazardous. It has been tried on hundreds of occasions in India, and good seed has been distributed to the cultivators, but in a few years at most all trace of it has been lost.

Jute. Next to cotton, this is the most important fibre cultivation in the tropics. A very large area in Bengal is devoted to this crop, and of late it has to some extent been supplanting the cultivation of rice in that province. The jute plant (*Corchorus capsularis* and other species) is a tall, stout annual, growing to a height of about eight feet, and succeeding best in a hot damp climate on the outer margin of the tropics, as in Bengal or São Paulo.

The plants are sown annually, and allowed to grow for three or four months, when they reach their full height, and are then cut with the sickle. They are stood upright for one or two days in a foot or two of water, and are then laid down in the water much as flax is treated in the north of Ireland. The object of first standing the lower parts in water is to give them the start in retting, as they are said to ret more slowly than the higher parts of the stem. The fibre is afterwards beaten out from the decayed softer tissues that lie between. It is thus a stem fibre that is used in jute, and not a fibre surrounding the seed, as in cotton. A good average yield is from 1200 to 3000 lbs. of fibre from an acre of land, a much larger yield than the case of cotton.

The consumption of jute is enormous, it being mainly used in the making of the well-known gunny bags in which cotton, rice, etc., are transported. The fibres are very long and silky, but will not stand exposure to the wet, and it is consequently not used for cordage. It is now extensively used in making cloth, curtains, carpets, and many other things, being very easy to spin. The total export from India averages about 25,000,000 cwt. a year, the product of about 2,000,000 acres of land. In the early part of the last century, Dundee made itself the centre of the jute industry, and large mills were established there, but of late more and more mills have been opened in or near Calcutta, and Dundee is steadily losing its pre-eminence.

The chief directions in which improvement in this cultivation are to be looked for are perhaps in the greater use of the residue, after extraction of the fibre, as manure, in green manuring (possibly), and in the proper rotation of the crop with something else. Fortunately the selection of the seed is not at present an all-important matter, as in the case of cotton, or it would be but a poor look-out for the native cultivators, who at present deal with this fibre. At the same time it is probable that a good deal might be done by selecting seed of the plants that bear the best, longest, and silkiest fibres.

Sunn Hemp. This fibre, the product of *Crotalaria juncea*, is grown upon perhaps 150,000 acres of land in India, as a summer crop. The fibre is somewhat similar to jute, and is obtained in the same way, by retting the stems in water, washing and drying.

Manila Hemp. Attempts without number have been made to grow this very valuable and important fibre in other countries of the tropics, but so far without success, and this industry remains a monopoly of the Philippine Islands, from which 169,260 tons were exported in 1918, valued at £12,000,000. The plant, *Musa textilis*, is a close relative of the banana or plantain, and the fibre is obtained from what look like the stems of the plants, but which are really, as explained under the banana, the rolled-up overlapping bases of the leaves.

The plant grows best on the Pacific slopes of the southern islands of the Philippine Archipelago, but, with the continual demand for this fibre, which is one of the very finest of all, and is almost the only fibre that can for instance be used in the self-binding reaper, now so largely employed, the planted area is continually extending. The plants, which are known in the Philippines as Abacá, are cultivated under shade at a distance of a few feet apart, and when one plant is cut down another is at once put in its place, so that the field contains plants in all stages. The field is weeded about once a week, but otherwise there is but little cultivation and the same land is used unintermittedly. The plants grow to a height of about ten feet, and are considered ripe at about three years old.

The plant is severed at the ground by a blow of a cutlass, the leaves removed, and the "stem" brought in. The rolled-up leaf-bases are then separated, and the outer fibrous layer of each is separated from the fleshy inner layer, the leaves being drawn under an adjustable knife in a very primitive way, but one which has not yet been successfully replaced by any machinery.

A plant gives about a pound of fibre. The fibre is bought by merchants and graded, being packed into bales of about 28 lbs. Its average value is about £50 a ton.

XVII. Sisal hemp in Yucatan

(*Original in possession of the Kolonial Wirthschaftliche Komitee, Berlin*)

Sisal Hemp. The cultivation of this plant (*Agave rigida*, var. *sisalana*) is an industry of some importance in the Bahamas, Mexico, and elsewhere, and it is sometimes used as a catch crop or minor industry in India. It is cultivated in dry places, and can be grown on poor soil. The large fleshy leaves are cut after the third year, retted in water, and the fibre beaten out.

Mauritius Hemp. This plant, *Furcrea gigantea*, is used in Mauritius and elsewhere, like sisal hemp, and others of these Agave-like plants are also used at times.

Palm Fibres. The most important, coir, the fibre of the nut of the coconut palm, has already been mentioned, but there are many palms which furnish valuable fibres from the bases of the leaves, e.g. Raffia (*Raphia* sp.), Piassaba (*Leopoldinia* sp. etc.), Palmyra (*Borassus flabellifer*), Kitul (*Caryota urens*), etc. These fibres are usually coarse, hard, and thick, and are largely used for brushes, etc.

There are many excellent fibres in many plants of the tropics, and people often ask—Why is not this or that fibre in use? Why do you (i.e. agricultural departments) not introduce it? and so on. They forget that a new fibre is perhaps the most difficult of all things to introduce. The market has six or eight good fibres, cotton, jute, flax, coir, hemp, Manila hemp, etc., all of which can be bought at any time in large quantity, are of uniform quality, and fairly cheap. One or other can be used for practically any purpose to which a fibre can be applied, and, before a new fibre can be established, it has to show that it is at least as good and as cheap as (preferably better and cheaper than) one of the old ones, and that it can at once be got in sufficiently large supplies to be used instead of that old one. It is this last condition that makes the establishment of new fibres so particularly hard. Ramie, rhea, or China grass-cloth fibre is at present a case in point. On the whole, perhaps this is the finest of all fibres, being strong, long, and very silky. For many years attempts have been made to introduce this fibre upon the markets, but so far with little success.

w.   8

CHAPTER XI

DYE STUFFS AND TANNING SUBSTANCES

Indigo. Ten years ago this was a very large industry in the central parts of the valley of the Ganges in India, and it is still of minor importance there, in Java, Guatemala, and other countries, but the history of the old madder industry of the south of France is repeating itself with regard to indigo. This dye stuff can now be well and cheaply produced by artificial means, and the competition of the great German dye factories is proving too much for the planters, in spite of the facts that considerable improvements have been introduced, and that the natural dye is still better than the artificial.

A considerable number of species of indigo, *Indigofera leptostachya, sumatrana, tinctoria, Anil,* and others, are used, and they are grown as annual crops, forming small bushes to about three feet high. The dye does not exist in the plant as such, but arises through oxidation, and when the plants are cut, they are steeped in water for about twelve hours, and then the mass is agitated for a few hours till oxidation has fully occurred, when the dye stuff is formed in large quantity.

Recently, when it was almost too late to do anything, a certain amount of attention has been given to the scientific side of indigo cultivation and manufacture in India, but it does not seem probable that much can be done to resuscitate the industry against the competition of the artificial dye. Java, where scientific treatment was begun sooner, seems to be suffering less from the German competition. A combination of countries interested in indigo is required for proper investigation and other measures.

Annatto. This dye, variously known as annatto, anotto, arnatto, roucou, etc., is to some small extent cultivated in Guiana, Ceylon, etc. The plant producing it, *Bixa Orellana*, grows into a small tree, and bears little pods containing seeds, each surrounded by a fleshy reddish-yellow coat. The seeds are collected and placed in hot water to macerate; they are then pounded up with a pestle, strained off from the dye stuff and thrown away, and the dye stuff is dried. There is a small industry in this dye, but it is only small.

Other dyes. Other dye stuffs, of greater or less importance, are obtained from the rhizomes or root-stocks of *Curcuma longa*, the turmeric, from the wood of *Caesalpinia Sapan*, the sapanwood, and from a fair number of other plants, more especially in India and Java, where the natives have known of and cultivated them for a long time.

Tanning Substances. Perhaps the most important of these is the cutch of Bombay, with which the true "khaki" cloth is dyed and shrunk. This is the wood of *Acacia Catechu* and other species, cut up and boiled down to give a strong extract. Myrobalans, the fruit of species of Terminalia, are also largely employed. Gambier, in the Straits Settlements, is also of importance; the twigs and leaves of the shrub (*Uncaria gambir*) are boiled down to give an extract. Mangrove bark gives a cutch of some value, and was formerly exploited in Ceylon by a company which has since given up operations. The bark of *Acacia decurrens*, cultivated in Ceylon, India, Brazil, etc., yields large quantities of tan. The pods of the divi-divi (*Caesalpinia coriaria*) are exported from the West Indies and Colombia, and a good many other plants also yield tannin in sufficient quantity to be worth collecting, at least upon a small scale, for local use. There seems some prospect of a great scarcity of tanning stuffs, and the industry shows more probability of success.

CHAPTER XII

OIL YIELDING PLANTS

OILS may in general be divided into two classes, fixed and volatile oils. The former are those contained more especially in seeds, where they form the greater part of the reserve store made by the plant for the growth of the new plant from the seed, and are consequently present in large quantity. The latter are usually those oils which give their perfume to flowers, leaves or other parts, and are present only in small quantity. The former are generally obtained by crushing, the latter by some form of distillation.

Fixed Oils. The most important of these in the tropics is probably coconut oil, which has already been sufficiently considered under the head of coconuts. Enormous quantities of this oil are exported from the tropics to Europe and America, where it is mainly used in soap manufacture, but also for hairdressing and many other purposes. Not only is the oil exported, but also vast quantities of copra, from which the oil is extracted in Europe.

The next most important source of oil is probably the oil palm of West Africa, *Elaeis guineensis*. About 125,000 tons of oil and 325,000 tons of kernels are annually exported from the West African coast, and until cacao rose to such importance, this was by far the most important export there.

The palm produces clusters of brown or reddish plum-like fruits, which are gathered and thrown into a pit for a week or so until a little decayed, when they are pounded to get rid of the fibre of the husk, and then boiled in water, or sometimes they are boiled at once. The oil of course floats on the surface of the water, and is then usually boiled to get rid of the excess of water.

Until recently the industry has been entirely in the hands of the natives of West Africa, who do not cultivate the palm, and who waste the oil in preparation. In previous editions of this book it was stated that for real improvement it must pass into European hands, and this is now rapidly happening. The Dutch planters of Sumatra have taken up the cultivation with success, and already have over 20,000 acres under oil-palms, whilst extension is going on rapidly. They obtain a much larger yield, and of better quality, than in West Africa.

Apart from this obvious improvement, much may be looked for in the direction of selection of seed from the palms which bear the most and best oil.

Of late another oil has also been obtained from the seeds of the palm, which are crushed for the purpose.

Another oil which is used in enormous quantities is ground-nut-oil, the oil of the seeds of *Arachis hypogaea*, the ground-, pea- or earth-nut, a native of South America. Being a crop of only a few months' duration, it can be grown also in temperate climates, and is in fact largely cultivated in the United States, where the pea-nut is a favourite delicacy. Within the tropics it is mainly grown by the Tamils of the Madras Presidency, more especially of the French colony of Pondicherry.

The plant is a small herb growing only to a height of about a foot, and bears small flowers which push themselves beneath the ground to ripen, and there form curious fruits, with pitted markings on the outer coat, and containing one, two or three oily seeds, which are in great favour as articles to chew, either plain or roasted.

The plants are put out in rows, and in a few months the crop is ripe, when it is hoed up, the fruits taken off the plants, dried in the sun, and exported. While there is a small demand for the finest quality of nuts for eating, the great demand is for oil for soap (and to adulterate or replace olive oil). The trade in this oil is largely centred in Marseilles.

Gingelly oil, the oil of *Sesamum indicum*, is another oil of considerable importance, though it is but little exported. No less than 2,500,000 acres in India and Ceylon are devoted to this crop, which is a small herbaceous plant. The oil expressed from the seeds is used for culinary, soap-making and perfumery purposes.

Innumerable plants are used as sources of oil by the natives of tropical countries, but the fact need only be mentioned here. Other important sources of oil than those mentioned are cotton-seed, in which oil there is a large and growing trade, especially in the United States, niger-seed (*Guizotia oleifera*), now largely grown in India, Africa, etc., castor-oil (*Ricinus communis*), mustard (*Brassica oleracea*).

Volatile Oils. Perhaps the most important of these is citronella, in which a large trade has been carried on from Ceylon for many years. The extreme south of the island contains about 20,000 acres devoted to the cultivation of citronella grass (*Cymbopogon Nardus*), and the export figures in recent years have been over 1,000,000 lbs. of oil per annum. Of late, Ceylon oil having acquired a bad reputation from the adulteration practised by the Sinhalese in whose hands the cultivation is, Java has begun to take up the cultivation, with properly equipped factories under European management, and is turning out a much better quality of oil which commands a much higher price.

The grass is grown in tussocks on open hill slopes, is cut every three months or so, and distilled by passing steam through it, when the oil passes over with the steam and may be condensed. An acre yields perhaps 30–50 lbs. of oil in a year, and the best varieties of the grass want replanting every second or third year. The oil is mainly used in the preparation of scented soaps, and is also a good preventive of mosquito bites.

Lemon-grass oil, the product of the grass *Cymbopogon citratus* St., is as yet mainly grown in South India, but the cultivation is also being taken up in Ceylon. The treatment is the same as for citronella, but the grass is smaller, and yields a much less amount. The price of the oil, however, is higher.

Other useful scented oils are prepared from the cinnamon (q. v.), the clove (q. v.), the patchouli (*Pogostemon Patchouli*), the sandal-wood (*Santalum album*), the bay (*Pimenta* sp.), and other plants.

CHAPTER XIII

INDIARUBBER, GUTTAPERCHA, AND CAMPHOR

Indiarubber. This is one of the indispensables of modern times, and there is now an enormous trade in it, over 300,000 tons being annually consumed. The supply is almost entirely from the tropics, and the demand is constantly increasing. Until quite recently the supply was all from wild plants, usually of forest origin. By far the most important of these is the so-called Pará rubber, *Hevea brasiliensis*, the source of the finest Brazilian rubber; other species of Hevea are also employed. African rubbers are derived from various species of Landolphia and other genera; Lagos rubber from *Funtumia elastica*; Borneo rubber from *Willughbeia edulis*; Ceará or Maniçoba rubber—a very important kind—from *Manihot Glaziovii*, and to a less extent from *M. piauhyensis*, *M. dichotoma*, and other species; Central American and Mexican rubbers, as well as the caucho of the Amazon, which comes mainly from the upper parts of the valleys, from *Castilloa elastica* and other species; Guayule rubber from *Parthenium argentatum*; India rubber from *Ficus elastica*; Mangabeira rubber from *Hancornia speciosa*; and there are several more. The most important, next to the Pará rubber, are the Africans, Guayule, and Ceará.

The rubber is obtained in various ways, but in general by bleeding the stem with an axe or other coarse tool, and collecting and coagulating the milk or latex which flows from the wounds. In many countries the tree itself is destroyed in this process, and in all cases it is very injurious. The natural result is that the trees are becoming more and more scarce, and the trade in wild rubber from India, from much of Africa, and elsewhere, has very largely decreased. Even in Brazil, whence the

best rubber of all is obtained, the collectors have now to go
further afield to get their supplies.

As it therefore appeared evident that the history of cinchona
(Ch. IX, above) would repeat itself in rubber, an expedition was
sent to tropical America in 1875 by the Indian Government,
assisted by Kew Gardens, and Mr (now Sir Henry) Wickham,
who conducted it, and Mr Cross, who led a second expedition,
brought back many seeds and plants, which were carefully
nursed at Kew and sent out to the tropics, mainly to Ceylon,
it being evident that the climate of the greater part of India
was unsuited to the growth of the trees. Since that time, from
the produce of the Ceylon trees, the Indian Government has
established plantations in Burma and elsewhere.

The first rubber plants to flower in Ceylon and come into
free bearing were the Ceará rubbers, and during the period
from 1879 to 1884 this rubber was largely planted in Ceylon.
In these early days of rubber planting the methods of tapping
to get the rubber were not very well understood, and the yield
was but small, while the price of rubber was then comparatively very low. The result was that the plantations did not
pay, and very many of them were entirely rooted out to make
room for tea, which was just then coming into prominence in
the island, and was proving to be very profitable. The export
of rubber soon sank to a few hundredweights a year, and
remained at that figure till Pará rubber came in.

The Pará rubber-trees introduced into Ceylon flowered in
1881, and from that time onwards every seed has been used.
At first the very small supply was used in other Government
botanic gardens all over the tropics, so that now the tree is
very common everywhere. About 1884 a few began to be
distributed to estates in Ceylon, and many places now have
fine old trees from this seed. But little interest was taken
in the trees for about twenty years, except by the heads of
the botanical departments in Ceylon, Java and Singapore. In
Ceylon the largest single tree was tapped every second year
from 1888 to 1896, in a very crude manner, large V's being
cut in the stem at intervals with a hammer and chisel, and
the milk allowed to run down into coconut shells at the foot

of the tree, where it dried. In this way 13½ lbs. of dry rubber were obtained in nine years, or an average of 1½ lbs. a year; the tree was ten years old when first tapped. At the then price of rubber a yield like this, only obtained after waiting ten years, was hardly sufficient to tempt anyone into the cultivation, and in this condition the question remained until 1897, when further experiments were made, and the important discovery, or rather rediscovery—the facts being well known to the natives of the Amazon valley—of the "wound-response" was made by the writer. In the following two years this was fully worked out by Mr John Parkin, then Scientific Assistant in the Royal Botanic Gardens of Ceylon, and an abstract of some of his results may be of interest. In general it is found that if a small area of the bark be tapped a second time within a short period, the amount of latex that flows from it is larger than at the first tapping, and this increase may even go on for a considerable time. Thus from 40 incisions made on March 25, 1899, only 60 c.c. of latex were obtained; on March 30, from a further 40 close to the old, 105 c.c. flowed; on April 6, 220 c.c., while in the thirteenth tapping on June 1, 328 c.c. were obtained, and on June 6, 449 c.c., or nearly eight times the amount realised by the first tapping. These were no doubt exceptional figures, but in general his work showed that about three times as much milk would be obtained later, as at the first tapping. On the basis of these and other experiments, results were published, showing that there was a possibility of a profit of about 27 °/₀ after the tenth year, and as seed was then beginning to be available in some quantity, people began to take up the planting of rubber, and the area under this cultivation has increased from year to year. In 1907 rubber planting was the main topic of conversation in tropical planting circles, and a great "boom" went on in it. The earlier pioneers of rubber cultivation made much larger profits than the 27 °/₀ anticipated, because the trees proved to give a yield at five to seven years old instead of ten, the yield was larger, and the price of rubber was very high during the last few years. When this was realised in Europe, there was a "boom" in rubber upon the stock exchanges during 1910 that completely overshadowed the eastern boom of 1907. As a result there is now an area of probably 3,250,000 acres or more planted in rubber, chiefly in tropical Asia, and there especially in the Federated Malay States, where a vast area of virgin forest has been removed, and the country has become a rubber country, thanks mainly to the work of Mr Ridley, late director of the Botanic Gardens of Singapore.

Not only did Mr Parkin work out the wound-response, and thus change what appeared to be only a moderately remunerative industry into a very profitable one, but he also worked out the way of coagulating rubber into "biscuits," the form in which the bulk of the cultivated Pará rubber has hitherto appeared on the market (for the sheets of Malaya are simply larger biscuits). Instead of allowing the latex to run down the tree, and thus become dirty, and instead of allowing it to dry into a mass of dingy black rubber in a coconut shell, he showed that it could be collected in little tins, placed one under each cut, and then mixed, heated, and coagulated by the addition of the calculated amount of acetic or other acid. The milk having been filtered before clotting, this resulted in the formation of clean biscuits free of all tangible dirt, which is so largely present in all the wild rubbers of commerce. These biscuits as a matter of fact lose but little in the washing and drying through which crude rubber subsequently goes.

During the last ten years an enormous trade in rubber biscuit, sheet, and other forms has sprung up between the Malay Peninsula, Ceylon, and the other equatorial countries of Asia, and the markets of Europe and North America. The following figures of export are of interest in this connection :

	Ceylon
1901	66 cwt.
1904	676 „
1907	7,093 „
1910	32,000 „
1912	134,000 „
1914	316,000 „
1916	488,000 „
1918	413,000 „
1920	790,000 „

British Malaya

1905	1 ton
1907	885 ,,
1909	2,713 ,,
1913	23,465 ,,
1917	79,831 ,,

Plantation rubber now provides about 320,000 tons out of a total of 360,000. The largest output of wild rubber, that of Brazil, is about 35,000 tons.

In the earlier and highly profitable days of rubber planting, much injury was done to the trees by excessive tapping in spirals, half spirals, and in other ways, but gradually opinion has come round to the view that to tap about one-quarter of the tree in any one year is sufficient, and there seems little reason to anticipate the destruction of the trees by excessive tapping.

With the enormous growth of the plantation industry, combined with the fact that the plantation rubber is of uniform good quality, and perfectly clean, while also produced at a very low cost, it is obvious that a tremendous competition is springing up for the countries which produce the wild rubber, and already Brazil, the most important of these, has had to begin to set her house in order. The cost of placing the wild rubber of Brazil on the market is undoubtedly ahead of that of plantation rubber, and the great problem is how to reduce it. It may be divided into three main heads, export duties, freight and dock charges, and actual cost of collection. The export duties are being gradually reduced from their present figure of 20 % *ad valorem*; freight costs are being reduced by opening up the Amazon valley with railroads and in other ways. To reduce the cost of collection is the most serious problem. Attempts have been made to introduce the rational eastern systems of tapping in place of the destructive machadinho, or hatchet, which is at present employed. The possibility of success in this direction lies in the fact that they appear to give more rubber, and perhaps do less harm[1]; the difficulty lies in the

---

[1] Some tapping of this kind recently carried out has resulted in great injury by disease. It is evident that a careful experimental investigation is first required.

XVIII (a). Rubber Plantation in Ceylon

XVIII (b). Making biscuits on the small scale

adoption of this method on trees that have already been much injured by the machadinho. But there is little doubt that there are great numbers of trees that have hitherto been untouched, because small, which could be tapped remuneratively in the eastern way. And it must not be overlooked that the collectors at present work fairly short hours, and could if pressed obtain more rubber.

Another direction in which improvement is possible is in the methods of preparation, which are rough, and lend themselves to easy adulteration, so that every ball of Amazon rubber has to be examined for enclosures and quality, and valued accordingly. At the same time, the greatest care must be taken not to lose the great value of the present method, which can and does turn out the finest rubber on the market. A very important improvement, which is at the same time cheap, and practical in the sense that it offers no difficulty to a man who is accustomed to existing methods, has been lately introduced by Admiral José Carlos de Carvalho and others, and is stated to be spreading on the Amazon. It turns out the rubber in sheet instead of ball, so that adulteration is rendered very difficult if not impossible, while at the same time the rubber is of the same quality as the fine hard Pará of the present system.

Yet another great problem is the scrap or sernambý, which at present is turned out in large quantity, and is but of poor quality. In some districts, such as the islands at the mouth of the Amazon, where the trees have been tapped for long periods, the collectors have now to climb to great heights to obtain suitable places for tapping, and in such circumstances they cannot be expected to turn out hard fine, and in fact get almost entirely sernambý (Cameta negroheads). In other districts the sernambý is regarded as the private property of the collector, while the balls of hard rubber must be exchanged at the store against supplies ; consequently the collector does nothing to decrease the quantity of sernambý and increase that of hard fine. Sernambý also increases in rainy weather. Attempts are being made to wash the sernambý, and thus improve its quality and reduce the freight, while at the same time the present vicious system of supply of necessaries to the collectors, who get only just what they want in exchange for all their ball rubber, is tending to break down by economic pressure, so that the collectors may find it to their advantage to turn out larger supplies of fine hard.

Another highly important line of work lies in the encouragement of cultivation of food stuffs, etc.; at present the vast basin of the Amazon, 2,000,000 square miles of the richest tropical land, depends for its supplies mainly upon food brought up-river, whereas it might quite well grow enough for itself at once, and later export large quantities. But here comes in the difficulty of getting over the established system of storekeepers on the rubber properties, who exchange food and other goods against the rubber brought in by the collectors, and naturally do not desire to see the latter grow their own food. Cost of production is further increased by the fact that there is no local labour, and all has to be imported from the northeastern states of Brazil, so that attempts at proper colonisation are being made in the Amazon valley.

Manufactories of rubber goods are being opened in Brazil, hospitals are being established in the Amazon valley, and in many other ways the amelioration of the inefficient and at times even vicious system under which rubber is at present collected is being taken up. The reduction of costs of production in Brazil is a large and complicated problem, but it is being taken up with determination, and there seems every prospect of success; incidentally it may be the best thing that has happened to that country, by forcing the Amazon valley to establish itself on a more sound, prosperous, and varied economic basis, giving it a fair chance of developing into what it ought to be, the richest and most prosperous agricultural country of the tropics.

As regards the other countries which supply wild rubber, they are as yet doing little or nothing to meet the new situation which is coming upon them, and there seems very fair likelihood that much wild African rubber, for instance, may disappear from the markets of the world. Since the beginning of 1913 plantation rubber has occupied first place on the market as regards quantity. Ultimately, when the manufacturers have realised that a reliable source of supply of good and uniform[1] rubber is open to them, and have made the necessary alterations in vulcanising machinery, formulas, etc., this rubber, which at the moment of writing is realising much less than Brazilian, will in all probability realise practically the same price, and being present in such enormous quantity will largely determine the market value of rubber.   At present, however, it appears to be true that the finest qualities of Brazilian rubber are finer, stronger and more durable than the plantation rubber[2].   At the same time, there is little doubt that the latter is strong and durable enough for many practical purposes[3].

Until a few years ago the price of rubber, owing to varying, but increasing, demand, and uncertain supply, underwent many and often violent changes, but with the enormous increase due to the opening of so many plantations, the price has fallen very considerably in recent years, and at the moment of writing (1921) is in the neighbourhood of 10d. a pound, a figure which allows of no profit to the cultivators.   Unless therefore the demand increases, many estates may be forced to go out of cultivation.   The first essential for a permanent and steady prosperity of the industry, however, is that there shall be a steady market value with but slight variation, as in the case of other world-staples like tea, coffee, cotton, sugar, etc., and there can be no doubt that like them, rubber will adjust itself to the market, though the process will be accompanied by hardship to many.   A low price will also have the effect of discouraging attempts to find a cheap substitute.   The industry of collection of wild rubbers will also fall to a very low figure, unless perhaps in Brazil, whose rubber is still the best, and is now tending to

[1] At present, the most immediate desideratum in plantation rubber is this quality of uniformity, in which it is sadly lacking.

[2] The writer showed, at the Rubber Exhibition in Rio de Janeiro in October 1918, a borracha or bottle made in Brazil in 1817, or thirty years before vulcanisation, which was still sound, though no longer elastic.

[3] Samples prepared in 1899 from plantation rubber made by Parkin's process are still good. A good deal of plantation rubber, however, has been but carelessly prepared, and has very poor keeping qualities.   One of the crying necessities for this rubber is for plantations to adopt standard methods of preparation, and turn out the rubber in a few standard qualities that can be relied on, as Brazilian rubber is relied on.

be consumed in factories in Brazil itself, for the supply of local demands for tyres, etc.

Another important influence in determining the market price of rubber is the fact that old rubbers can now be devulcanised, and used again, and a vast quantity of this "reclaimed" rubber is now being used for the cheaper qualities of rubber goods. There have also been several scares about synthetic rubber, which will doubtless come in time. Hitherto, however, the cost of production of such rubber is much too great, and the reduction in price of the natural rubbers will stave off its arrival upon the markets.

Pará rubber, which is the only one whose cultivation has assumed any importance, is strictly equatorial, growing within about 10° of the equator, though it will also grow in southern Brazil, which, while on the edge of the tropics, has a very equable climate. It will grow up to about 2500 feet above sea level, though only slowly above 1000 feet. It is usually planted out from nurseries at about 15—25 feet apart, and needs plentiful rainfall and good drainage. In suitable places the trees increase in girth at the rate of about 4 inches a year, and when they measure about 24 inches at a yard from the ground, tapping usually commences, i.e. at about 6—7 years. During the last few years it has been realised that excessive tapping is a mistake, and that time must be allowed for the new bark to form properly over the tapped places. The usual method has hitherto been the herringbone, or more commonly the half herringbone (vertical channel with lateral gently sloping cuts on one side), but of late a single large V, cut on about a third of the circumference, is coming into use. The wound is renewed, and the full effect of the wound-response obtained, by shaving off a thin layer on the lower side of each of these lateral cuts every day, or at less frequent intervals. Recent work done in Ceylon by Dr R. H. Lock seems to indicate that in the long run as much rubber is obtained by the use of longer intervals, while the bark of course is used up at a much less rapid rate, and labour is saved.

The milk runs down the central groove into a tin placed at the base, and being collected and taken into the factory is there

XIX. Rubber tapping on the Amazon by aid of a scaffolding

*(Original in possession of the Kolonial Wirthschaftliche
Komitee, Berlin)*

coagulated, usually by the method introduced by Mr Parkin, by the addition of a small amount of acetic acid, sufficient to render the solution slightly acid. This brings about the coagulation of the proteid in the fluid, which entangles the caoutchouc and produces a clot. The rubber exists in the milk as an emulsion of fine globules, which quite possibly are not pure caoutchouc, but polymerise at the instant of coagulation to form it. The clot is left till it has firmed somewhat, and may then be prepared in various ways, the two most popular being biscuit or sheet, made by pressing and drying, and crepe, made by passing the clot between rollers that move at different speeds and turn it out in a kind of crinkled sheet. Either of these forms may be made into block. The great difference between this rubber and the Brazilian is that it is quite dry, instead of containing over 15 °/₀ of included water.

Other species of rubber than *Hevea brasiliensis* are but rarely cultivated. The most important cultivation is that of *Castilloa elastica* in Mexico; this tree, however, is very uncertain in its yield, very delicate to grow, and very liable to serious injury by overtapping. The various Manihots, and especially *M. Glaziovii* and *piauhyensis*, are largely cultivated in German East Africa and Brazil, and to a smaller extent in other places, and *Funtumia elastica* is a little planted in West Africa. But Hevea certainly forms 95 °/₀ of all cultivated rubber.

Guttapercha. This substance, allied to indiarubber, and obtained from trees of the family Sapotaceae, especially species of *Palaquium*, has as yet been mainly collected from the wild trees in the islands of the Malay and Philippine Archipelagoes, but of late attempts to cultivate it have been made in Java and elsewhere, the gutta being obtained from the leaves by a process of maceration. Recent work in this direction has been very successful, and the plantation is being extended. The pure gutta obtained is used to mix with the inferior stuff procured by the ordinary methods, and obtains a much higher price. The demand for gutta, however, is at present but small, and rubber has taken its place for certain purposes, though not for cables.

Camphor. This product also requires mention, and being a deposit in wood and leaves, will perhaps come best along with rubber. The tree (*Cinnamomum Camphora*) is a native of Japan and Formosa, and until lately has not been much cultivated outside of those countries. There the camphor is usually obtained by felling old trees, cutting up the wood and distilling it with steam. In recent years the Japanese Government has endeavoured to establish a monopoly, an attempt which of course has stimulated the wish to grow it in other countries. The botanical department in Ceylon, for instance, has been carefully fostering this cultivation for a good many years, until now there are probably about 700 acres planted in camphor in Ceylon. There are also appreciable areas of camphor in Florida, California, and several other countries, though the export as yet is small.

The plant is grown in rows, and rapidly expands into a small tree, which is kept more or less coppiced. At about three years old it can be used for obtaining camphor; the young twigs are cut off, and are then distilled with steam, the vapour being passed into a large wooden receptacle, when the camphor condenses around it. About $1\frac{1}{2}$ % of the weight of the green twigs is obtained as camphor.

XX. Plantation of camphor in Ceylon

CHAPTER XIV

MIXED GARDEN CULTIVATION BY TROPICAL NATIVES

As already mentioned, this is perhaps the most common form of "cultivation" among the poorer villagers in the tropics. Though the yield in general is extremely poor, the mixture of plants gives one at least of the advantages of rotation of crops, the comparatively slow exhaustion of the soil, owing to the fact that the various crops take different proportions of the different elements of the food supply from the soil, and consequently the latter tends to become exhausted at a much slower rate, if at all. In this way, therefore, the villager can grow the old familiar crops on the same land for an almost indefinite period, and this alone makes a great appeal to the man without any capital, for if his crops were to give out, he could not afford to bring a new piece of land (even supposing that he had such a piece) into cultivation, and wait several years for any return. The majority of tropical crops are not annuals.

No cultivation, in the proper sense of the word, is carried on in these mixed gardens, but trees, shrubs, and herbs of many kinds are simply allowed to grow together in the most casual intermixture, and the ground between them is never turned over, but is allowed to grow up in turf, upon which a few miserable cattle are put out to graze. The typical mixed garden of Ceylon may be seen in Plates I, IIIa, and Xa.

In the wetter southern parts of Ceylon, in Java, in much of India, and in the West Indies, this system—or want of system—may be seen in full development. The principal trees in southern Ceylon are the jak, the mango, the areca, the kitul, the coconut, the candlenut, the shrubs oranges, limes, papaws, pomegranates, plantains, etc., the herbs, yams, pepper, brinjal or egg-fruit, bandakai or okra, pulses and other things. In Malaya the durian takes the place of the jak, in the West Indies the areca is little grown, and so on, but the general look of these jungly gardens is much the same. Nothing is pruned or properly taken care of, with the result of a miserably poor yield, but the villager does not realise this, nor if he did would he be likely to change to any system which would involve more work, or more expenditure of capital. Until the provision of cheap capital has been thoroughly well attended to, there is but little chance of any alteration in this system. Could the villager even afford to manure his ground or to till it, it is probable that his yields would be increased, but want of capital and dislike to more work prevents this.

No system is adhered to in planting out such gardens, but in actual fact it is found that their composition is not unlike, in any one district, in the kinds and numbers of plants upon any one acre. As we cannot suppose that the villagers copy one another in the numbers of plants, though they probably do in regard to the kinds, we must look upon this wild jungly garden as representing what is now usually termed a "plant-society," suited to the soil upon which it is growing, and to the general conditions of life in the place.

The great area devoted to this form of cultivation—if indeed it can be called cultivation at all—indicates the kind of thing that is likely to happen with a purely peasant population, unstimulated by the presence of more enterprising agriculturists who have some capital at their disposal, who can give work upon their estates, and who can create a trade that will absorb anything in the nature of "export" products that the villagers may have to sell. A country in which there are none but peasant cultivators must be extremely poor in everything that means money, though there may be no actual lack of the necessaries of life. The chief taxable value in most tropical countries being the exportable goods, the revenue of such a country must be exceedingly small, there will be no money for public works, the country will go back instead of forward, and practically drop out of the progress of the race. We shall return to this subject in Part III.

CHAPTER XV

THE DISEASES OF PLANTS IN THE TROPICS, AND THEIR TREATMENT

INSECT and fungus enemies to plants are very numerous in the tropics, and seem, probably owing to the fact that so many crops are perennial, and to the fact that there is no winter to check them, on the whole more injurious, and more to be feared, than in Europe. The great classical example of injury is of course the terrible attack of the *Hemileia vastatrix*, or coffee-leaf fungus, upon coffee cultivation in Ceylon from about 1875 to 1885, during which period a once very large and prosperous industry was reduced to abject ruin.

Nowadays, there seems much less likelihood of such an event occurring again, since the rapidly extending agricultural departments in the various tropical countries are in most cases provided with the help of a Mycologist for the study of fungus, and of an Entomologist for that of insect pests, and, still more important than this, the agriculturists themselves are now realising that it is much more to their advantage to give timely notice of any attack of disease upon their cultivations and to get suggestions early as to the best mode of treatment, than to conceal it until perhaps it has got such a hold that it is no longer possible to eradicate it. True it is that in this way many diseases are treated which would not absolutely require such treatment, i.e. diseases which are merely sporadic and would not spread, but this does not affect the general position that all diseases are in general treated early, and that disease is thus usually kept under control. It must also be admitted that it is in general only by white planters in the tropics that measures

of this kind are taken with any precision or regularity, but it
so happens that it is upon their cultivations that disease stands
the greatest chance of getting out of control, for the natives
have usually either the mixed cultivations in which disease
does not so readily spread, or rice or grain fields, which are
annually left fallow or rotated with other crops for considerable
periods. Thanks to the efforts of many students, especially in
the United States, the methods employed in combating disease
are becoming more and more systematised. It would lead too
far to go into details here, but the chief methods in use may
be summed up under the following heads:—

(1) The destruction, in general by fire, of diseased trees,
plants, or parts of plants. In this very simple way the spores
which carry the infection of the disease are absolutely destroyed,
and if this method be steadily practised, the disease may be
prevented from spreading, and may even in time become almost
eradicated. One great difficulty in the way of such treatment
upon many estates, is the lack of any vacant areas upon which
the fires may be lighted.

(2) The collection and killing of parasitic insects and their
eggs. This is obviously the corresponding remedy to the last-
mentioned.

(3) Spraying. This in general means the wetting of the
diseased, or in preventive cases the healthy, areas of the
infected plants (or in some preventive cases, the healthy plants)
with a stream of some fluid in which, so long as it remains
upon the leaf, stem or fruit, the spores of the fungus cannot
germinate, or the eggs of the insect cannot live, or which makes
the plant distasteful to the fungus or the insect, or which kills
the insect or fungus upon the plant. There are almost innumerable forms of spraying compounds, but in general they
contain, if for attack upon fungi some salt of copper (as for
instance copper hydrate in the commonest spray of all, Bordeaux mixture), if for attack upon sucking insects an emulsion
of kerosene oil, and if for attack upon biting insects some
compound of arsenic. For attacks upon mites, sulphur is the
usual foundation of any insecticide. The forms of instrument
through which they are sprayed on to the plants are equally

numerous, but in general they consist of small receptacles which can be carried by one man, from a compressed-air chamber in which a stream of air drives a fine jet of the compound through a nozzle which breaks it up into a fine spray. The large horse and steam sprayers employed in California and elsewhere have not yet come into use in the tropics.

(4) Isolation of the diseased plants by digging trenches. This is in general adopted for the purpose of checking the spread of root-attacking fungi, and is usually very effective, provided the trench be made outside of the outermost range as yet covered by the fungus. Jungle stumps left in the ground when clearing are the great hotbed for such root fungi.

(5) Prohibition of the removal of plants, seeds, or parts of plants, from districts already infected by disease, into districts not already infected. This is more a precautionary measure, and simply checks the transfer of infection into new districts.

(6) Isolation of small areas of the cultivated crops by the planting of "shelter belts" of trees through them, as is so common in Ceylon, where the tea estates are divided into "fields" by such belts. In this way, a pest is checked from spreading to another field, when it has devastated the first one attacked.

The mention of method (5) above leads on naturally to the subject of quarantine regulations against diseases, which are in force in a few countries. These regulations may take various forms, as for instance the prevention of the importation of plants of a particular kind from a country in which plants of that kind are known to be subject to a disease not as yet known in the country in which the law is put into force. Thus the importation of pepper plants into Ceylon is prohibited, so far as South India is concerned, there being a very bad disease widely spread among pepper plants in that country; so also the importation of cacao from the Dutch East Indies is prohibited, on account of the disease known as "krulloten-ziekte."

A very common phase of the quarantine regulations is the compulsory "fumigation" at the port of entry of the plants or fruits or seeds. The skins of oranges or other fruits very commonly carry living scale insects, often of dangerous kinds, and such consignments are often compulsorily fumigated with the vapour of hydrocyanic acid gas or other destructive agent to kill any scale or other insects that may be adhering to them. Against fungus pests this method is not successful.

Ceylon has lately established a "Pests Ordinance," under which any dangerous pest may be proclaimed, with the methods recommended for treatment. The employment of these is then compulsory, and recalcitrants may be fined in the police courts. Inspectors are appointed for every district in which the disease occurs. They instruct the headmen in methods of recognising and treating it, and with them make lists of all infected places. Notices are then served on the occupiers to take the necessary measures, and the headmen have to see that this is done, and prosecute where necessary.

Our experience of some years with the treatment of diseases in Ceylon leads us to suppose that the propagation of disease in a district follows to some considerable extent the ordinary laws of diffusion, and may, like diffusion, be altered by the interposition of obstacles. Suppose a district in which there exists a disease that has long been known in that locality, and in which no measures for its extirpation are being taken; then it will exist there at a certain average density which will only be varied, like the average density of any other plant or animal, by the immediate local conditions, such as supply of food, suitability of the substratum on which it grows, etc. Suppose an estate in this district to extirpate it; the estate will soon be reinfected to the same average density as before from its surrounding infected neighbours. If all the estates in the district take measures simultaneously against the disease, its average density will be greatly reduced, and by the continuance of those measures may be kept at a low figure; but if they be given up, the disease will again multiply to the average density allowed by the local conditions.

When on the other hand a new disease, or one which until then has been very rare in the country, commences to spread, it seems usually to diverge from some one locality, and impinge upon the surrounding neighbourhood, hitherto practically free from it, with considerable virulence. In the case, which some-times occurs, of a disease absolutely new to the neighbourhood, this may be due simply to the fact that no natural enemies have as yet appeared, but in the case of a disease already known, though rare, in the district, there must presumably be some alteration of the conditions that hinder its growth, or it may be, as in the case of most of the weeds that have at different times spread over Ceylon, that a longer or shorter period of acclimatisation, or of accumulation of energy, is required before a rapid spread can take place. Be this as it may, however, this case of the rapid spread of a "new" disease is the one that most often comes to the notice of the officers concerned with diseases. Here the density is greatest nearer to the edge of the affected area, and is decreasing in the middle. The attack therefore, should be chiefly at the points of maximum density, and outside of these, whereas in the middle, where the density is decreasing in any case, attack will do very little good in comparison. If the disease be left to run its course, it will spread over a greater or less area, reach a maximum density at each point in succession, and then fall off to an average density which may often be so low that most people think that it has entirely disappeared. All these various phenomena, the ap-pearance of a new weed, like the Mexican sunflower in Ceylon, the appearance of a new disease, or the springing up of a new industry, like that of rubber cultivation, behave in the same way, and a recognition of this fact would simplify measures for dealing with them for repression, encouragement, or whatever else was required.

Just as diffusion may be hindered by the interposition of obstacles, so also may the spread of disease. Shelter belts of forest may be left in the country, or shelter belts may be planted by agriculturists between their fields; trenches may be dug round infected areas, and so on.

CHAPTER XVI

STOCK

As this book is not intended as a handbook for the practical field agriculturist, there is no need to go in any way into the question of the different kinds of stock of all sorts that are to be found in the tropics, nor the ways of feeding them. There is a very great variety of different breeds of cattle, sheep, pigs, horses, goats, and poultry in the tropics, more especially in India, and it would lead too far to describe them.

Cattle are used in the tropics mainly for draught, drawing carts, ploughs, trotting carriages, etc., and the great majority of the breeds have been evolved for this purpose, most of them being of the zebu type, with a large hump behind the neck, upon which the yoke pulls. Milk cattle are comparatively rare, the bulk of the milk used coming from the draught cattle, which will not as a rule yield milk unless the calf be allowed to remain with them, a fact which still further reduces the already small amount of milk.

Speaking generally, the best breeds, whether of cattle or of sheep, have been produced in those districts where there is plenty of grazing land, as for instance in Gujarat and other parts of the north of India. As we pass south, into the Dekkan, where there is little grazing land, and a somewhat precarious rainfall, or into Travancore and Ceylon, where there is hardly any proper grazing land at all, and too much rain, the breeds generally deteriorate. In Brazil, the best breeds of cattle, and the chief dairying industry, are in the highlands of the south, while in the north they are but poor.

The best breeds, also, are in the districts where large herds or flocks are found under the care of men who are practically professional herdsmen, whereas in districts where the breeding is casual, and in the hands simply of villagers, the breeds are poor.

Again, a decided cold in the winter season seems to give better results, and consequently, other things being equal, the breeds deteriorate from north to south.

Buffaloes, which must not be confused with the American bison, are mainly used in ploughing in wet rice fields and are extremely useful animals for this purpose, being practically water beasts.

Sheep in the equatorial regions of the tropics are very slim and leggy animals, but as we go farther north, as with cattle, the breeds improve. Of horses much the same is true; the best animals in use in the tropics for drawing carriages or for riding are in general what are locally known in the east as " walers," the imported Australian horses, which do not generally breed in the tropics.

One great point for consideration here being what can be done to improve the breeds of cattle, sheep, horses, etc., we must consider the general conditions of such work. Many people, who have not properly thought out the question, say, import European stock, and cross the native with it. This however is really one of the worst things that can be done, speaking in a general way, and leaving out of account any special requirements of the small European community in the tropics. As a rule, the animals imported from cold countries rapidly deteriorate, and native stock crossed with large imported breeds produces leggy weedy animals inferior in power and stamina to the pure native stock.

In each district the type of beast has come to what we may call an equilibrium with the food supply, and we must not change the former without first changing the latter. The general type of the beasts may strike a European visitor as small and inferior, yet it may be the best that the district can do, with its present conditions of food supply. In Ceylon, for example, there is but little pasture land, and the beasts are simply turned out to graze where they can in the majority of cases, and get but poor quantity or quality of food. Were the breed suddenly "improved" and larger or more powerful or energetic beasts produced, the villager would be utterly unable to feed them properly. This is a very important consideration which is generally lost sight of.

Again, the present size and habit of the beasts is suitable to the present size and build of the various agricultural tools in use in any locality, and were the former altered in any serious degree, the latter must be altered likewise, or there would be simply a waste of power. The alteration of the beasts employed for draught purposes must go on hand in hand with that of the tools or implements they are to use, and we shall see that any alteration in the latter must be very slow and gradual.

In breeding in the tropics, we must not be in too great a hurry to make what we may imagine to be improvements in the breed. There may, for instance, be certain characters in a given breed which we may think to be objectionable, and yet which may in reality be due to the climate or other local conditions, and which if removed would spoil or seriously deteriorate the breed.

Strictly speaking, we want to know the history of the steps by which each breed has come into its present condition, and the forms from which it was originally evolved. But in practice this is quite beyond the skill of the average breeder, and we must be content to go slowly, and to improve the breeds by the selection of the best only for parents, by prevention of indiscriminate crossing, and by an occasional cross with another nearly related breed. At the same time that the breed is thus gradually improved, the improvement of the implements that are to be used by the cattle can be taken in hand, and for this among many other reasons, the veterinary department should in all cases form a branch of the department of agriculture, so that the work may be properly coordinated.

Proper selection and mating of the male and female wants careful attention; it is very little use giving good males to cross inferior females. Attention must be directed to the improvement of the females also, and to the liberal feeding of the young, which will let them grow up into better beasts.

The provision of the best possible food supply is another

matter that requires very careful attention; there is too much casual or insufficient feeding going on among village cattle. It is far better to keep only a few cattle and to feed them well, than to keep more and feed them badly. In particular the proper feeding and rearing of the young stock wants careful attention. Even if the villager has plenty of food, he rarely knows how to feed the beasts to the best advantage with it.

There are many directions in which, on the other hand, improvement can be at once put in hand, for instance in the castration of cattle, which in many tropical countries is very clumsily and cruelly performed, and in the treatment of epidemic diseases, such as rinderpest, by prompt and careful sanitation.

One direction which the breeding of improved races of cattle might take, for example, is the production of a race of good milkers. Almost all the breeds hitherto existing are for draught, and the few milkers are not very well suited to other climates than their own.

Pig rearing is practised to some extent in the Malay Peninsula, and in other countries frequented by the Chinese, who regard pork, etc., as great necessities of life, and also in southern Brazil, but the animals are but poor in quality, and there is little doubt that the breeds could be further improved in many ways.

Poultry in the tropics are as a rule of very mixed breeds, and could, having careful regard to the limitations of the food supply, be very considerably improved.

[Brazil has in recent years gone so far ahead of all other countries in the tropics, that cattle-breeding, and the employment of the produce, has reached the higher stages of perfection, comparable to those of Argentina or of North America. Brazil is now fifth in the world with 28,962,180 cattle, second with 17½ million pigs, third with 7 million goats, second with 3¾ million asses and mules, besides having 6 million horses, and 7 million sheep. A large portion of all these are in the southern subtropical parts, but many cattle and other animals are in the tropics. Zootechnic stations are kept up in many places, with the best stocks from which to breed.]

PART III

AGRICULTURE IN THE TROPICS
(GENERAL)

CHAPTER I

VILLAGE OR PEASANT AGRICULTURE

AGRICULTURE in the tropics may be fairly well divided into capitalist or "planting" enterprises, and "village" or peasant cultivations of rice-field, grain-field, or yam-garden, and fruit-garden, worked upon the very small scale, without hired labour.

The ideal of some administrators in the tropics has apparently been, and of a sprinkling of people in Europe and America who have no acquaintance with actual tropical conditions still is, a kind of "old-fashioned socialist" one—a dense population of small cultivators, each tilling his own little piece of land, and growing or making practically everything that he requires. The nearest approach to this is probably to be seen in outlying districts of many tropical countries, remote from the influence of Europeans or Chinese. In the most extreme cases there may be practically no capitalist enterprise in the country at all, and the corollary is of course the absence of any appreciable export trade, or in other words, so far as the remainder of mankind are concerned, the country might almost as well be non-existent. This is agriculture reduced to its greatest simplicity, and the agriculturist must not have any but the very simplest wants, as he must himself supply them.

The following description of village agriculture in Ceylon may therefore serve as general, since the differences are mainly in detail; in much of India, for instance, other grains take the place of rice, and in the West Indies yams and other vegetables do the same.

The ordinary Ceylon villager, living on his ancestral lands, cultivates, as his fathers cultivated, with cheap and primitive tools, the few products necessary for his simple mode of life. On the irrigated land, or fields, as distinguished from the un-irrigated or high land, he grows the rice which forms the staple of his food. His little hut stands on the high land, and is usually surrounded by a wilderness of trees, shrubs, and herbs of many kinds, as described in Chapter XIV of Part II. The composition of the wilderness varies in different districts, but the general look is much the same. In it he grazes one or two poor specimens of cattle, or turns them into the rice field after the harvest, or out upon the road.

The greater part of the high land, except in thickly populated districts, is occupied by chena cultivation, or is land recovering from chena, which is a favourite method of cultivation with the villager, as already described in Chapter I of Part I. After two or three crops he abandons the land, which grows up in scrub for ten or more years before it can be again "chenaed."

The villager, especially in the more outlying districts, has but few wants that cannot be supplied by his own fields, or by the labour of himself or his women folk. Cotton fabrics for his scanty clothing, kerosene oil for his lamp where he has become too advanced for coconut oil, a few simple curry stuffs, such as dried Maldivian fish, a few brass and earthenware utensils, simple furniture made by the village carpenter, chunam or lime for his chew of betel, and perhaps a little arrack at times, sum up most of his requirements.

The sale of a little rice, a few coconuts, some betel nuts or leaves, or (if he live near a town and has become enterprising) of some vegetables or fruit, will provide him with these. He is usually in debt for advances on his crops, if not actually for loans on his land itself, to the money lender or the village shop-keeper—often the same individual. Only too frequently the latter becomes at last the possessor of the land, while the former owner works on it as tenant or even as coolie, or drifts away into the town or into the less settled parts of the country.

To live a strenuous life for the sake of gain or social advancement is foreign to the habits of mind and body of the village farmer. Let him but make sufficient for his wants, to bring up his children, and to pay the interest or renewals on his debts, and he is generally content. He does not aim at creating trade ; his caste, unalterable by riches or poverty, is commonly high, he likes to take his ease and pleasure with his family and friends. Further, he has not the capital nor the land necessary for such a speculative occupation as growing crops upon which he cannot actually live, but which he has to sell in a market whose fluctuation is beyond his knowledge or control, and in which therefore he is largely at the mercy of the middlemen or combinations of middlemen who buy his crops. Not that he is averse to making money, but he cannot afford to risk even a small sum, most often, probably, has not the sum to risk. This is the true explanation of much of his obstinate conservatism— a conservatism by the side of which that of the small European or American farmer is change and progress of the swiftest.

It is hard to see upon what grounds the "socialist" position, described above, can be justified, or logically defended, though at the same time it is that to which nearly all tropical countries would come were it not for the presence in them of Europeans or Chinese. Leaving out of consideration the fact that there is usually *some* capitalist enterprise among all but the most backward races, the white powers are in actual possession of most tropical countries, and must so settle their agricultural conditions that there shall be an export from them of those products which are unattainable in the colder climates. The present native of most tropical countries having come there by ousting someone else, there is no ground on which to object to an invasion of the more efficient races who will produce such a trade, if the natives do not.

Furthermore, for such a simple ideal, it is very great waste to provide the tropical countries with roads and railways, as is rapidly being done, for they are almost fatal to, and quite unnecessary for, such agriculture.

There is further the ethical objection, that no country has a right to exclude itself from the general progress of mankind, as must under these conditions almost necessarily be the case.

A country in which a peasant proprietary has largely come into existence in recent years is the island of Montserrat in the West Indies, and from an interesting report upon that island by the Hon. Sir Francis Watts we may quote as follows:

"It may be interesting to draw attention to the circumstances of the people living in the northern district of Montserrat.... Lying beyond...Church Hill there exists a somewhat isolated and self-contained community, largely consisting of peasant proprietors, or of peasants cultivating land upon a share system. These people suffered severely in the hurricane; all their houses and practically all their belongings were destroyed. They have now built up the elements of a small peasant community, which has no means of wage earning, but which grows its own food and obtains the small amount of money necessary for the purchase of clothing, tools, and the like, from its small exports from the district. These exports consist of sugar, grown and manufactured on a share system; of vegetables taken to the village markets in other parts of the island; of small numbers of cattle, horses, and small stock: and of vegetables and fruit, chiefly bananas, shipped to Antigua. All these exports are small, but they suffice for the modest requirements of the district. This district will probably feel somewhat acutely the loss of the papain industry[1]. The conditions of life here are on a comparatively low plane, but they are interesting as illustrating what results from a peasant proprietary, cut off from the power of wage earning by the absence of regular estates employing labourers. The habit of wage earning has been weakened or lost. This is seen by the fact that, when a short time ago the Montserrat Company planted a small area in cotton in this district, difficulty was found in obtaining labour, and comparatively high rates had to be paid. The resources of such a district are few, civilising influences are apt to weaken, roads are likely to be poorly kept, public works, in the way of

---

[1] Which by the way, was mainly destroyed by the competition of Ceylon, showing that even the poorest peasant community cannot altogether escape from the world-wide competition that now goes on.

bridges, buildings or improvements, will be difficult to secure, and the governmental administration will have to come down to a similarly low level. Such conditions remind me of those prevailing at Tortola, where, while there is practically no poverty, life is on a low level, and progress is slow or absent.

"A district so constituted is liable to rapid fluctuation in its prosperity. A drought means starvation and distress from want of resources; propitious seasons as quickly restore the small measure of prosperity.

"With a peasant proprietary body, the exports of a community will be small; the individuals will be chiefly engaged in raising food, and in producing a limited quantity of articles for export, in order to supply the small amount of clothing, and the tools and implements which must be imported. Should the tendency be towards extensive exports, the peasant-proprietary system, by acquisition of property, will pass into the estate system."

The white races of Europe and America at present control the tropics, and they must and will have the products of the latter in large quantities. This is evident from a glance at the list of tropical cultivations described in this book. They include rice, tea, cocoa, coffee, coconuts, sugar, pepper, cinnamon, tapioca, many fruits, sago, tobacco, quinine, indiarubber, and many products of less importance. The white powers cannot and will not allow the largest and perhaps the richest areas of the world to be wasted by being entirely devoted to the supply of their own native population, when they are capable of both feeding a large population of their own, and supplying the wants of the colder zones in many foodstuffs, fibres, oils, timbers, and other useful products, otherwise unattainable.

The white races govern the tropics on the ground that the native is unfitted to govern himself in a way suitable to the general political state of the world, and the same consideration applies with equal force to agriculture. Native agriculture, far from being efficient or perfect, is on the contrary very backward in many respects, and must be improved. Even in the industry which of all others should be best understood and practised by the races of tropical mankind, that of rice-growing, the white man is able to produce a larger crop at less cost; while his labour is ten times as costly, he produces, man for man, about twelve or more times the crop. Similar phenomena are seen in the results in the tropics themselves of European enterprises worked with native labour. The Ceylon tea planters, by the use of large machinery, and by good methods, have been able almost completely to undersell on the markets the produce of China, made by the most cheap and industrious native labour in the world, and similar results have followed other similar enterprises. The same phenomenon is apparently about to occur in a competition between the rubber grown in Ceylon and the Malay peninsula, and that collected in the forests of Africa, etc. It is not *easy* to improve upon native methods in agriculture, and the improvement must be gradual and cautious, but of its possibility there can be no doubt.

Though this ideal of a vast population of small cultivators, growing all that they require and consuming all that they grow, has long held a more or less acknowledged sway, it is now rapidly disappearing, and it is being recognised that native agriculture is just as susceptible of improvement as European. Furthermore, as already pointed out, the directly contradictory course of opening up roads and even railways has already been embarked upon beyond the possibility of drawing back, and this course is necessarily more or less fatal to such simplicity in agriculture. Such extreme simplicity may yet be found in villages in India and elsewhere far removed from the stream of traffic. But with the opening up of the country, it almost necessarily becomes gradually obsolete. The villager learns new wants and needs money to satisfy them, and at the same time markets for his produce become available to him.

The wants of the poor villager, other than those that can be satisfied by his own labour or that of his women folk, are even yet of the simplest, but the essentially important point is that they now exist, and in all reasonable probability will grow. This then, being a natural tendency, is one of the features of agricultural progress to be encouraged, and we must consider what are the chief difficulties in the way of such progress, and what may be done to remove or lessen them.

It is a main thesis of this book to point out how complex such improvement or progress really is. The scientific improvement of crops or methods is only one factor, and by no means, in the present comparatively poor condition of most tropical countries, the most important. One may easily conceive of an improvement, which, though an *absolute* improvement, yet would bring distress instead of benefit to the cultivators by lowering the price obtained for the increased yield.

Or imagine the case of a man who has two crops A and B for sale. A is all produced, and all used, in the country. An improvement is introduced: the first to employ it make better profit but soon everyone else is forced to adopt it in self-defence, and the net result is consequently nil, except a gain in efficiency, and an improvement in the financial position of those who were enterprising enough to adopt it promptly. B is produced in many countries, and has a world market, like wheat, rubber, or tea. Again an improvement will benefit first those who first try it, but even if all in the country take it up, they may all benefit, till this or another as good is adopted elsewhere. Of course there are many other possibilities besides A and B; these are only brought forward to show the complicated nature of the problem. Agriculture is an art, not a science, though it has a science[1].

[1] An interesting analysis of the present condition of peasant agriculture in Grenada, showing the proper scientific way of setting about agricultural improvement, is to be found in a paper by G. Auchinleck, in the *West Indian Bulletin*, vol. xiii, 1912, p. 83.

CHAPTER II

THE RELATIONS OF THE PEASANT TO THE LAND AND CROPS; CULTURE SYSTEMS, ETC.

In a general way it is not untrue to say that the villager is the owner of his own land, or is a peasant proprietor, but there is much variation in different countries, and not infrequently he is only the tenant of a large landowner. Except in crowded countries, he can usually obtain by purchase what land he wants.

If he is not to settle down to the very simple and primitive type of agriculture described in the last chapter, proper transport facilities must be provided, and his land made accessible by roads, canals, or in other ways. Next to the financing of his cultivations, this is the most important thing to be attended to if he is to make any progress, and we may again draw attention to the remarks under this head in Chapter IV of Part I. In a country already thickly peopled, it is evident that the system there suggested, of laying out road reservations in two directions at right angles, and at distances of a mile apart, would be impracticable, or too expensive, and in eastern countries would not divide one village[1] from another. In such a case the country should be carefully surveyed, and the existing lines of transport and foot traffic followed as much as possible, being widened where necessary. So far as practicable the roads should be made to divide the villages, the boundaries

[1] The term village in India and the east corresponds more to that of parish in England, the whole country being broke up into villages, which meet by irregular boundaries. Each village is under a headman who is responsible to higher Government officials.

of the latter being re-defined, if necessary, in places. In this way the country will be broken up into villages bounded on all sides by roads, and with the opening up of the country that would thus be brought about, there would be some chance of the villager growing "commercial" products, and taking some part in the trade of the country.

Not only should roads be made, or demarcated, on these lines, but also, when the natural drainage is not good, drains, which may also become very useful, if large enough, as canals for the cheap transport of produce. Every buyer of land, however small a piece he may purchase, should be able to secure that he will somewhere have a frontage upon a road, and that he will be able to drain it.

It is almost needless to remark that the roads and drainage-canals must give access to markets where the produce can be disposed of. The provision of local markets is a very important consideration in the development of agriculture, and peasant agriculture should, at first at any rate, be encouraged to grow produce for local markets. Should the villager grow good fruit or vegetables, of kinds not too novel in the neighbourhood, he can usually dispose of them locally, especially if he be near a town, or near a population say of fishermen, who do not grow for their own consumption. If on the other hand he grow "export" products, he should be provided with a local market, say by the agency of planters growing the same products and purchasing his. If there be no local market of any kind in a district, it is practically idle to expect that district to progress in agriculture, unless a market can be provided, e.g. by coopera-tion among the growers to send their produce to a distant market.

As already mentioned, differences of race are often to be found among the agricultural population in any given country in the tropics. Thus in Ceylon, there are English, Sinhalese, Tamils, and Mohammedans, in Jamaica English, Negroes, East Indians, and so on. Where there is this mixture, the proper use of it becomes a matter of considerable importance in settling new districts, or in increasing the density of population in the districts already settled. If we accept the principle

XXI (a). Mule Plough in Mexico

(Original in possession of the Kolonial Wirthschaftliche Komitee, Berlin)

XXI (b). River transport in Ceylon

above indicated, that progress in cultivation of crops for market is desirable of encouragement among the villagers, then it is important that they be broken into groups, each more or less of one race, having among them larger agricultural enterprises, better educated agriculturists, and the traders whose presence is involved by that of the larger enterprises. The small peasant cultivator, unstimulated by the presence of any other type of worker, and without the example offered by a larger and better managed agricultural enterprise, will progress, if at all, with the utmost slowness. But though very conservative, he is not quite blind to his own interests, nor unwilling to improve his methods to make more profit or to save labour, but he will not do this on mere hearsay; he wants concrete examples near his own door.

Mixing, such as is here suggested, of races of men and types of agriculture will also have a tendency to raise the general standard of living in the country, and thus to create a larger local market for produce. It is practically idle to expect the poor villager to grow crops for which he cannot obtain an immediate market in his own district (as will be more fully dealt with below). If he is to progress in agricultural enterprise, he must be tempted into it by finding that it is profitable, with immediate returns, or else he will (if progressive) go to other occupations which hold out greater attractions in pay or in type of work, and abandon his fields. The only alternative is force, which was formerly fairly commonly employed in dealing with "native" agriculturists, but which is now nearly obsolete, surviving only in the treatment of dangerous diseases. Even in Java the old "culture system" is extinct. No experiment in the promotion of agriculture among Asiatic natives has attracted so much attention as this famous system, introduced in 1830 by Van den Bosch, then Governor-General of the Netherlands Indies. Though in many ways it was or became harsh and oppressive, it seems certain that it has had a considerable share in rendering Java such a nation of industrious and comparatively skilled cultivators as it now is. But the effects of dense and rapidly increasing population, of the opening up of the country by a splendid system of communications, and of the absence of mines or other competing attractions, must not be forgotten. Java is now so densely populated that her people must work hard to make a living, and they have no other large industry but agriculture, while at the same time they have easy local communication and good local markets. A similar state of affairs may be seen in the extreme north of Ceylon, and in much of Bengal or Madras and the more densely populated West Indian islands.

To quote Prof. Clive Day, the plan of the culture system was in brief as follows: instead of paying to the Government a certain proportion of their crops, the natives were to put at its disposal a certain proportion of their land and labour-time. The revenue would then consist, not in rice, which was almost universally cultivated and which was of comparatively little value to the Government, but in export products grown under the direction of the Government contractors on the land set free by the remission of the former tax (for of course less rice would have to be grown). According to the estimate, the natives would give up only one-fifth of their land and one-fifth of their time in place of two-fifths of their main crop. The Government promised to bear the loss from failure of crops if this was not directly due to the fault of the cultivators, and moreover promised to pay the natives a certain price for such amounts as they furnished. The Government proposed in this way to secure products suited for export to the European market, on which it expected to realise profits largely in excess of the prices paid to natives and contractors and of the costs of administration. To the natives it promised increased prosperity and a lighter burden of taxation, as a result of the fuller utilisation of their chances under the far-sighted management of Europeans. The labour that before, through carelessness and ignorance, would have been wasted in idleness or in the cultivation of some cheap and superfluous crop, was to supply a product of great value in the world-market, and the natives were to share in the resulting profits.

"The plan of the culture system is on its face attractive, and the system has been judged so often by the plan and professions of its founder rather than by its actual working that it has been the object of pretty general and sometimes extravagant praise.

"During the period of its working the culture system was applied to the cultivation of a long list of products. The Government experimented with coffee, sugar, indigo, tea, tobacco, cinnamon, cochineal, pepper, silk, cotton, etc., and dropped from the list the products which after an extended trial gave no promise of returning a profit to itself. From the fiscal standpoint, coffee, sugar, and indigo were the only products that ever attained importance."

In actual fact the system soon developed into one of forced labour, and as it returned enormous profits to the Dutch exchequer, the whole system of Government in Java became organised to suit it. From 1840 to 1874 the profits returned to Holland[1] are supposed to have amounted to no less than 781,000,000 florins, but there is little doubt that had the natives been fairly paid and treated this profit, nor anything approaching it, could never have been realised. One great benefit it conferred upon Java was forcing the Government to make a splendid system of roads which in themselves opened up the country and made markets accessible.

That it is not impossible to apply compulsory measures in agriculture, even at the present time, is of course obvious. The rules in force in several tropical countries, fixing dates of sowing, planting, harvest, etc., are an instance. These rules, however, are, like those in force in America and other advanced countries, mainly to protect those engaged in agriculture from the dangers to which they might be exposed by the carelessness, neglect or delay of their neighbours.

It seems hardly feasible, however, at this period of time, to force an unwilling population to engage in agriculture, or to alter their methods. What must be done is to make it attractive, and to pass such measures as may be necessary to prevent waste, injury and neglect.

Though naturally indolent, the villager is by no means blind to his own interests, and knows fairly well what will pay

---

[1] For the Dutch colonies are worked on a different plan to the English, and do not get their own revenue for their own expenditure.

him best with the least labour. He would like, in many countries, to engage in chena or ladang cultivations, or failing this to cultivate coconuts or other easily marketable crop. Even this easy cultivation, however, he is liable to abandon if he finds that he can make money more easily in other ways. All this is perfectly natural, and a sound agricultural policy must take account of it and utilise it to further the end in view.

Let the native be once convinced that there is a profit to be made by the cultivation of any particular crop, if not too troublesome or costly, and he will soon take it up; witness the large extent of land formerly occupied by coffee in the Malay States and Ceylon, and that now in rubber in the same colonies.

We may therefore say, let the native grow what he prefers, and encourage him in this cultivation. He will in general pick out coconuts, vegetables, and crops for which he has a ready local market, and such crops as he sees the planting enterprises near him engaged with, and for which he can obtain a market upon the planting estates.

A word in conclusion about chena. This is a vicious mode of cultivation, and both wasteful and destructive. It should be put a stop to as soon as possible, at any rate on lands owned by the Government, and experiments to determine the best rotation of crops to practice upon the chena in private hands should early be put into practice. There is little doubt that the common contention of the natives, that the land is too poor to stand continuous cropping, is untrue. The real reason, in many cases, at any rate, is that in two years it gets too weedy, and that it pays them better to chena a new piece of land. In fact, like most things in agriculture, it hinges on finance. It is possible for a poor man to chena, when he cannot afford real "cultivation."

CHAPTER III

THE FINANCING OF VILLAGE AGRICULTURE, AND THE PROVISION OF LOCAL MARKETS

WE now come to the next point, that of finance, upon which all the rest really depends. Agricultural enterprises, other than the very smallest villagers' gardens, require some capital, however small, to carry out clearing of land, waiting for harvest, etc., and such cultivations as are chiefly taken up by European planters, such as tea, rubber, sugar, or coconuts, often require very large amounts. The smaller the scale upon which the agriculturist works, the more does he live from hand to mouth, and the more likely is he to need a loan to carry him over the unproductive period, or to help him in a season of bad crops. The lower the stage in this scale, too, the higher the rate of interest, the security being so much the poorer. The general result therefore is that in most tropical countries, the villager is largely in the hands of the local money-lender, who charges a rate of interest that is rarely below 50 %.

This being the state of his financial affairs, it is of course idle to expect the villager to adopt agricultural improvements which cost anything, to try new products, or in fact to take any risks, even though he may know in a general way that the expenditure of a penny may bring in a shilling.

Probably the most generally feasible scheme that has yet been put forward for freeing the villager from the money-lender's exactions is the institution of Cooperative Credit Societies, now so common in Europe and North America, and first instituted by Raiffeisen in Würtemberg. Such societies are now in extensive operation in India, where they have expanded in a wonderful manner, and in Ceylon.

The essential principles of the scheme are that each society is confined to a village or other community, all of whose members are of course acquainted with one another, that the funds are collected from the members of the society, each of whom pays as a rule a commencing subscription, and that the liability is unlimited. The societies, in India at any rate, being officially audited and inspected, their credit is good, and they are able to lend to their members (for outside loans are not allowed) at low rates of interest, with easy repayment in instalments at crop times.

The society is usually managed by a committee (unpaid) of its own members, who have control of its funds, and lend small sums to local cultivators for various purposes, when they are convinced that the said cultivators have the ability and the intention to repay. As the committee will of course be well acquainted with the would-be borrowers, and as, owing to the unlimited liability, all losses fall on all the members of the society, great care will naturally be taken to lend only in fairly safe cases. This, incidentally, has worked for good in the thousands of European villages in which such societies are now at work, by making the villagers careful of their ways in regard to drunkenness and other offences. All profits which are made by the society, after repayment of any money it may have borrowed at the start, are returned to the members in the form of dividends, so that the rate of interest charged, provided only that it is a good deal lower than that charged by the local money-lenders, does not much matter. $12\frac{1}{2}$ % is the usual rate in India.

In this way the respectable peasant agriculturist is able to get money at lower rates of interest and on easier terms of repayment than from the money-lenders, while all profits made by the society, after the commencing loans have been paid off, come to him in the form of dividends.

It is obvious that in most cases such a society, starting in a tropical village, would have to borrow some capital to begin upon, otherwise its members would be like the inhabitants of the famous island who eked out a precarious living by taking in one another's washing. This small amount of capital, if it cannot be got from local capitalists, might very well be advanced by the Government at a low rate of interest. The successful working of any such schemes in tropical countries of course largely depends in any case upon the warm support and countenance of the Government and its local officers.

An organisation perhaps even better for the majority of tropical villagers than the Cooperative Credit Society, at least for a start, is the Cooperative Seed Supply Store, which is already in operation in several places in Ceylon. A small store of good rice or other seed is opened at headquarters, by the assistance of local capitalists, or of the Government, and from this store the villagers can get their seed rice at an interest of say $12\frac{1}{2}$ %, paid in kind at harvest time. There is no need in such a case for the villagers at first to be actual shareholders in the concern, and by the time that it has repaid its commencing loans, they will have come to trust it, and to join in it definitely. Such a store should at first confine its operations to rice, or whatever may be the staple crop of the district, but as time goes on, and the villagers come to support it, it may go in for other crops also, and instead of issuing the local rice again in the following year, may take to getting better qualities of rice and other things from elsewhere.

Following the Credit Societies, or the Seed Supply Stores, some more ambitious scheme of Agricultural Banks, say on the lines of the Crédit Foncier of France, may be put into operation, and will benefit the small village capitalist, but as yet it would seem too early for any such scheme to be tried with much chance of success in a tropical village.

Similarly, organisations for the purchase of the manure or other things required in a village may be commenced. The local agricultural society at Baddegama in Ceylon, for instance, has organised the purchase of manure from one of the large Colombo firms, first of all finding out how much each villager will require, and then ordering the whole amount in bulk and distributing it to the villagers at the actual cost of purchase and transport. In this way the villagers have got a very much better quality of manure. An unexpected difficulty has cropped up in connection with this scheme, the local vendors of manure adulterating theirs so much that they can sell it a good deal cheaper than the pure stuff supplied by the society. In a case like this the only thing to be done is to show that the good manure gives much better results, or to adulterate it to such an extent with sand or something harmless that it can be sold at the same rate as the worse adulterated stuff sold by the local people.

Having got over the difficulty of the want of cash for the commencement of agricultural operations, we must now work at the other end of the problem, and consider the question of supply of a market to the villager for his produce. In the case of rice or other staples of long standing there is as a rule a good enough local market, through travelling middlemen or otherwise, for any that the peasant may have to sell after supplying his own wants, but in the case of other things, more especially anything that may be new in the district, a market must be supplied, or the villager will not have gained anything. He should if possible be kept out of the hands of the travelling middlemen, for of course, being entirely ignorant of market fluctuations, he is to a large extent helpless in their hands. One of the first matters to be attended to, therefore, if the cultivation of vegetables or other things of local consumption is to be encouraged, is the provision of local markets within easy reach of the villagers. Along the coast of Ceylon, for instance, there are such markets at every few miles, in the larger villages near the seaboard, where the fishing community, who do not grow vegetables, etc., for themselves, can purchase the productions of the interior villages. If the population in a district is too small, or too entirely engaged in agriculture for the establishment of such a market to have much likelihood of success, then the encouragement of the cultivation of produce for which the demand must be local will be of little use unless some scheme of the nature of a cooperative selling association can be also established. Such an association for instance is in operation at Vavuniya, in the north of Ceylon, where there is also no local market at all among the very small population. It collects produce from the villagers, and forwards it fortnightly to Colombo, where it is sold by auction in the local market, and realises better prices, even after the payment of all costs of collection and transport, than it could have realised in Vavuniya.

The next question to be dealt with is the provision of a market for any "export" produce that may be grown by the villager, for it is obvious that he cannot export it himself, being unable to wait so long for his monetary return, even if he could export enough to be worth while. In the case of such products as coconuts, he can sell them readily enough to the local travelling middlemen, but in this way he gets a very small return, and some more profitable system seems desirable, while in the case of such a product as tea or rubber, there are no middlemen who purchase such things.

It has been suggested that the Government should subsidise capitalists to open factories for the produce of the country, and buy up at fixed prices, paid in cash, all produce grown in the district by the villagers. This scheme is practically the Java culture system over again, with the compulsion left out, and would be liable to failure at starting, for the native would not grow till he saw a certain market, while the factory owner would not start till he saw a certainty of grist for the mill. If such a scheme is put into operation, therefore, it should be in a district where there are already planters growing the particular crop to be dealt with, and their factories might then be subsidised, if necessary, to buy the produce of the villagers.

The villager in general turns out a poor grade of article, as well as a poor yield, and the markets of the north do not want poor grades. It follows therefore that the villager should be encouraged chiefly in the cultivation of the products in which he is able to turn out a good grade, such for instance as coconuts, while other products should only be introduced as he learns to handle them, unless they be such as rubber, in which he can sell the milk to the factory, which can then work it up into as good a grade of rubber as it prepares from its own milk. He should not, so to speak, be turned loose on such a product as cotton, which requires careful selection of the seed in every generation to keep up the quality, unless at the same time an officer of the Government be appointed to attend to seed selection, as is done in Egypt and the West Indies.

To put it in other words, the cultivator must grow for a market, and the larger the market, the steadier the price, and the less the risk of over-production. He should be educated through the stages of local market, market in the country, and world-market. But of course with this must go the better provision of capital, for the more distant the market the more capital is required. Cooperation will turn an association of peasants into a power corresponding to a capitalist, and give them as strong a place in the general organisation of agriculture, when without it they cannot hope to rise. By the proper and gradual introduction of cooperation, the villager may be taught to help himself, whereas by the sudden provision of the necessary capital he would simply be encouraged in extravagance.

Capitalist planters are often strenuously opposed to the encouragement of villagers in growing "export" products, for they steal from the large plantations, and use their own few trees as a blind. But this difficulty can be got over by more stringent legislation, especially by licensing all dealers.

CHAPTER IV

THE CROPS AND METHODS OF PEASANT AGRICUL TURE, AND THEIR POSSIBILITIES OF IMPROVEMENT

WE must now pass on to consider village agriculture proper, its crops and methods, and their possibilities of improvement. Without the provision of capital there is little possibility in this direction; the villager cannot afford to try experiments, nor even to adopt an improved crop or method, if any monetary outlay is required. Though he may know that an expenditure of a penny will bring a shilling, he must first have the penny. Experimental Gardens and other similar methods of work for improvement of agriculture and horticulture can do little or nothing for the poorer villager until this primary difficulty is got over. They may introduce or breed much better varieties of plants than those the local people use, but the latter cannot afford to buy them. If the Government give them freely they seem to be undervalued. A common experience in the East is to give good seed to a villager and then to find that he has eaten it in his curry or sown it somewhere that it has no chance of success.

One great mistake that is often made in endeavouring to introduce improvement in agricultural crops or methods is trying to go too fast. Evolution works by almost indefinitely small steps. Agriculturists, especially natives of the tropics, are about the most conservative of mankind. Great harm has been done to the cause of true scientific progress by enthusiasts anxious to go rapidly, forgetting that the gap between the native and the European is to be measured in centuries. Similar unsound ideas have been at the root of the ruin of many well-considered schemes for agricultural improvement also. Instead of fixing upon a definite system, and adhering to it steadfastly for long periods till it has had a chance of showing results, we treat it only too often like children treat the plants in their gardens, digging them up at frequent intervals to see how they are getting on, and soon throwing them away because they have not grown unnaturally quickly to suit their wishes.

When we take a survey of native agriculture as a whole, it is easy to see that there are many points in which improvement is possible. Such are (1) the variety of products cultivated; (2) the kinds or varieties of particular crops cultivated; (3) the methods of cultivation ; (4) the cleanliness of cultivation and freedom from weeds and disease; (5) the preparation of the produce for sale ; (6) the breed and quality of the stock ; and so on.   There cannot be the least doubt that all these are capable of vast improvement, though one still at times hears the contrary stated with regard to at least (3).   Speaking broadly, native agriculture is wasteful and inefficient, and urgently needs improvement.   But, and this is a point of the most vital and essential nature, we must go slowly, and be quite sure what we are doing, or we shall do more harm than good.   The proper course is to find out first of all the actual facts of native knowledge in all agricultural matters, and then to work from these—or, in other words, to apply the methods of pure scientific research and induction.   The science of agriculture is yet largely in an embryonic condition, and its generalisations are almost entirely based (as in the case of other biological sciences) upon work done in the totally different climates of Europe and North America.   To apply these directly to tropical conditions is often to court failure.   We must begin again, using the results of temperate-zone work as a guide, and collect facts patiently, group them, make inductions from them, and test these again, until we have built up a sound science of tropical agriculture.   Scientific agriculture in the north has now overtaken the empirical knowledge of generations of farmers in many departments, and explained it, using the generalisations thus obtained to deduce further rules of action, but this is by

XXII. Cart Transport in Ceylon

no means yet the case in the tropics. We must first learn all the facts that village agriculturists, planters, and others have learnt, and then use these as a basis for further work. Not merely must we learn the facts, but we must find out the " why " of them. Why, for instance, does the Sinhalese villager manure betel-pepper only with the leaves of *Croton lacciferum*, and refuse to employ another manure apparently as good or better ? He himself does not know, but we must find out, and perhaps in so doing we shall find some valuable knowledge throwing light on other problems as well as on manuring.

To deal in order with the points in which improvement is required, the first is the variety of crops cultivated. There is a want of variety in village cultivations, and " new products " are desirable in many places, to avoid the risk of having too many eggs in one basket, to lessen the risk of epidemic disease, and to increase the variety of products available in the local market, and thus help in raising the general standard of living. But to introduce and establish these new products involves many considerations. They must be shown to grow well in the district, to be easy of cultivation, and to yield greater profit or better food than those things that are already in cultivation there, or at least as much. There must also be a reliable market for them. In effect therefore, each product wants full and careful experiment in each district. To have an Experimental Garden in each district is almost beyond possibility ; the cost would be too large in comparison with the result to be hoped for. But an Experimental Garden on a scale suited to each village can easily be provided in the schools, and the school garden scheme outlined in another chapter is recommended on this ground alone, apart from other advantages. A preliminary investigation is required to find out exactly what products are already cultivated in the district, and then the garden should be supplied with others not yet familiar to the local villagers. In this way it can be tested whether the particular plants will grow well in that district, and what kind of market or domestic use there is ' for the produce. The villagers will see the plants for themselves, and be able to get a few for trial, and gradually those that prove desirable will

11—2

come into local use. In Ceylon the school gardens have already introduced a considerable number of new products into the villages at a minimum of cost. The products thus introduced are those likely to prove really suitable, and will not be thrown away again or neglected, as so often happens when a plant is distributed by Government officers, perhaps without any previous tests as to its suitability.

It would therefore seem that by the intermingling of village and estate agriculture, whereby the villagers will have large practical object lessons at their door, and by the institution of school gardens on the lines indicated, the introduction of new products will be sufficiently furthered, provided that the provision of cheap capital has been attended to. Without this the only result will be to add a few more ill-kept plants to the wilderness of the average village garden. Even this, however, is something to have gained.

The next point for improvement is the varieties of the particular crops grown. Most of the native fruits, for example, are capable of improvement, and the same is true of the vegetables, and even of crops like rice or coconuts. This subject is elsewhere dealt with from another point of view. The question here is how to introduce the better kinds when we have got them and when we have also—and this is very important—assured ourselves that they still remain better when grown in the villagers' gardens or fields by their local methods.

The majority of improved strains of field crops, such as rice or cotton, have been obtained by continual selection of seed from the best parents, and they can only be kept up to their high standard by continual repetition of this process in every generation. Treated as they are sure to be treated in village agriculture, they will rapidly deteriorate, and in two or three generations at most be as poor as any village crop, or as the original strain from which they started. Non-recognition of this fact is at the bottom of a great number of failures of well-meant endeavours to improve the village crops in eastern countries. " Good seed " is introduced at considerable expense from Europe, but in a short time all trace of it has gone for want of selection. If even educated Europeans with special taste for gardening cannot be induced to select seed from the best parents, we cannot expect that the villager will do so. If improvement of the quality of local strains is to be made by selection, then some such method as that which is, we believe, in force in some places must be used. Seed-parent plants are marked by Government inspectors, and their seed separately collected by the Government, and paid for. The cultivators have to save their own seed and exchange it against the Government supply. In this way only good seed is used.

Another way of attaining the same end would be the establishment of definite seed gardens at suitable places, where the breeding of improved varieties could be carried on, and seed produced in large quantities. These seeds, whose value would then be accurately known, could be exchanged against the villagers' seed, and the latter sold in the ordinary market in partial repayment of the expense incurred. Without some such system as this, carried out over long periods upon a definite plan, it is idle to expect any improvement in village crops so far as varieties grown are concerned, except in cases where one can introduce a "fixed" strain, such as many "gardeners' varieties" represent, which will not seriously deteriorate under village methods of cultivation, being independent of selection for the retention of its peculiar excellences, though selection will always improve these. It is well, however, to point out that such varieties are rare in field crops.

In the last few years enormous advances have been made in the science of plant breeding, and by the careful application of the principles first enunciated by Mendel we are able to produce more certain results in much less time.

Breeding has been but little practised in the tropics. While the cultivated plants of the colder zones are often incapable of surviving if left to themselves in competition with the wild vegetation, this is but rarely the case in the tropics.

There is every reason to hope that by skilled scientific work great progress may be made in the improvement of tropical crops, and that within a reasonable time. But there are many difficulties in the way. One, for instance, is that so many crops are perennials, and do not generally flower for some years. Not only, therefore, is there a long time between each two generations, but the cultivator will not root out established plants to make room for better ones.

If this line of work is to become, as all present indications point to its becoming, one of the most important duties of a tropical agricultural department, it will obviously be necessary to have proper seed-producing gardens, fully equipped with trained breeders and all necessary fittings, from which seed can be supplied to the cultivators. And this the more especially at first, because the improved kinds will cross with the inferior kinds cultivated round about, and the resulting seed be consequently inferior.

In many cases, of course, it is possible that varieties better suited to local conditions may be obtained from other countries, and this is especially probable in a country where local agriculture is backward. This sort of work is of course one which should be attended to in Experimental Gardens, but the trials should be on a commercial scale, should be thoroughly thought out in advance, and should deal only with one or two things at a time. Local varieties should of course be tested against the introduced ones, under as many conditions as possible. Once the Experimental Garden has shown the probability that a certain variety, whether introduced from abroad or bred in the garden, is apparently an improvement upon the local ones, further tests as to its suitability may be made through the school gardens, and if it pass successfully through these, it may then be safely recommended to the villagers.

It is of very great importance in dealing with eastern natives to be quite sure of the result before recommending any action to them, especially in matters of agriculture. Even when we have shown that a particular variety of some locally cultivated crop is superior in quality and yield to the native forms, it may not be easy to get the villager to adopt it, prejudices or customs standing in the way. An amusing illustration has lately been afforded in Ceylon. The variety of Indian corn locally grown is what is technically known as a "flint" corn, with rounded ends to the grains. This was crossed at Peradeniya with imported American corns of fine kinds, most of which belong to the "dent" type, with dimples in the outer ends of the grains as seen upon the cob. The hybrids are superior to the native corn in quality and yield, but are objected to by the villagers on account of the dent, which they say indicates unripeness. A still more remarkable case is furnished by the history of the West Indian vegetable, the chocho, in Ceylon. Introduced years ago by the Botanic Gardens, this most useful vegetable spread widely in the villages, and was much appreciated. A few years later, a rumour was started among the natives (probably owing to some coincidence of serious illness with the fact that the patient was a great consumer of chochos) that chochos produced rheumatism. This was sufficient, and the cultivation of this vegetable is now extinct.

For products that are already well established in the villages, one of the best ways of ensuring the use of good seed is by means of a cooperative seed supply (already mentioned above in discussing provision of capital). Cooperation is excellent in agriculture, and the reason that the continental agriculturists of Europe are probably more prosperous than their British colleagues is mainly that they have gone in largely for cooperation. A Cooperative Seed Supply is in many ways better for a tropical village than a Cooperative Credit Society. In the east it will of course be mainly concerned with rice. Let the villagers join such a society, they will then be able to get their seed rice from it at an interest of say 12½ to 25 per cent. (the extra rate does not matter, as already explained, for the profits go to the members, and in any case it is far cheaper than the money-lender) to be repaid in crop time. This alone is a very great step in advance, but let the society also get the very best seed, and it may effect a gradual improvement of the crops grown in the district. Let it be first determined what *is* the best seed for that particular district, and then let the society sell the rice brought in to it in repayment of advances, and with the proceeds buy enough of the better seed to sow in the district next season. It is true that in this way the society will have less of profit to divide among its members, but they will get increased profit from the better crops.

A society starting upon these lines should of course attend at first to rice, or coconuts, or whatever may be the principal crops of the district, but once the society is well upon its legs, and the villagers have come to believe in it, and not to think it some ingenious mechanism for defrauding them, it may begin to get seed of the less familiar crops—perhaps from the larger Experimental Gardens kept up by the Government—and to distribute these.   There are also special cases in which it might, in cooperation with other societies, obtain seeds from Europe or from other countries.

The next point to be considered is the possibility of improving native methods in agriculture.   There can be no doubt that such improvement is possible, but it is above all important to know exactly what we are doing, and to recommend no method without being certain of its superiority.   Agriculture is a complex art, and a change in any one item of a process of cultivation may bring entirely unforeseen and possibly disastrous changes in other items in its train, as was instanced on p. 47.

Another formidable obstacle to any change in methods is custom.   The tropical native is usually conservative, and objects to any interference with his time-honoured ways.   Thus, for example, among the Javanese and the Malays, one may see side by side the advanced methods of transplanting the rice, and rotating the crop with others, and the inefficient method of harvesting it by cutting each ear separately.   Yet this is tenaciously adhered to, because the harvest time is the great festive season, when all the young folk turn out into the fields, and engagements are mainly contracted.   In some parts of Southern India the ryots plant their cotton with a drill, in rows; in others they plant it by broadcast sowing, getting a less return from more seed and labour.   If a ryot in the latter districts be questioned, he will often admit that the former method is the better, but "it is not the custom" is his reply to the natural enquiry why he does not adopt it.

Another great obstacle is the indolence of the peasant.   He may know quite well that a particular method is better than his own, and that it will cost him nothing to adopt it, but if it involve more labour than the one in use, or an unaccustomed form of labour, then he will often have none of it. This has been the great stumbling-block in the introduction of transplanting of rice in Ceylon.

Other great obstacles are poverty and ignorance, both of which are dealt with in special chapters.

There are innumerable directions in which native methods can be improved, but very careful study is required, as explained above. To take a few illustrations and suggestions.

The tillage of the ground is by rude implements and by a great expenditure of physical labour in proportion to the result achieved. A great improvement is probably possible by the aid of labour-saving methods and implements. This is evident enough, and many well-meant endeavours have been made to introduce such tools. The mistake has been to try to make too large a step at once. The most modern machinery has been introduced directly. Of course the villager does not understand it properly, he cannot repair it if anything goes wrong, he cannot afford to buy it, and in many other ways it is unsuited to local conditions. The proper way of progress is the scientific one. The local tool should be carefully studied and compared with other tools of similar nature or used for similar purposes, and then, when the principle of the whole subject is understood, the local tool should be modified slightly in the desired direction, so slightly that the villager need not have his prejudices offended, nor find anything that he cannot understand or repair in the new instrument. Further, the cost should not be appreciably increased. Each improvement in the tool should be most carefully tested by comparative trials against the old tool, before it is publicly introduced or recommended. The very best tools and machinery for each purpose should of course be imported from America and elsewhere for local trial, in order to find out the principles on which advance has been made, and what are the difficulties attending the use of such tools or machinery in the country.

Weeding is another direction in which native agriculture appears capable of improvement. The native usually knows well enough that weeding gives a better crop, but he does not always consider the result worth the labour. If some simpler and easier method of weeding could be introduced, say by the use of a tool like the American roller hoe, or like the "cultivator," it might be possible to encourage weeding, and thus get an increased crop in many cultivations. It is idle to tell the native to weed, or to teach him theoretically that weeding is good; he must be shown that it pays, without costing more money or labour than he can afford, or than he is willing to give.

A conspicuous feature in native agriculture throughout southern Asia, which often offends the eye of those who have a superficial acquaintance with European agriculture, is the wild jungle-like mixture of fruit trees, bamboos, vegetables, etc., which forms the average native garden. As pointed out above, it is highly probable that this arrangement gives many of the advantages which have elsewhere to be attained by rotation of crops, and the villager is thus able to grow his familiar foods, etc., on the same ground for an indefinite number of years. Mixture of crops, as well as rotation, require very careful study in detail before any hasty attempt is made to change immemorial custom.

The treatment of the individual trees, or of the crop plants, on the other hand, is probably capable of a good deal of improvement without such great difficulty. If the villager knew how to graft and bud, he might have his fruit trees improved by introducing new varieties. His methods of sowing broadcast are probably often capable of being improved to the saving of seed. He might very well learn the advantages of regular pruning of fruit trees on definite principles, of selection of good parents for seed, of better methods of propagation, of sound systems of manuring, and many other such things. But the motto must always be *festina lente*, and every step proposed must first be very carefully tested.

The next point to be considered is improvement in cleanliness of cultivation and freedom from disease. The mixed cultivation above described is of course a considerable safeguard against disease spreading rapidly over a large area, but on the

other hand is accompanied by a very small return. The peasant
who cultivates such a product as tobacco is often very careful
to keep his plants free of any sign of disease or weeds, but the
average tropical native has much to learn in this respect. A
little compulsion, as is for instance employed in Ceylon under
the Pests Ordinance, is a very good thing.

The fifth point mentioned above for consideration was the
possibility of improving native methods of preparing produce
for market. As a rule, native produce is of inferior grade to
that prepared by European planters. This is partly, of course,
the result of bad cultivation, especially of want of proper feeding
of the plants, but it is also due to ignorance, indolence, or carelessness in treating the product after it is harvested. The
question of improvement is thus on all fours with that of
improvement of methods of cultivation dealt with above. The
fact that even with the object lessons of European estates
before them, and with the practical lesson of lower market
prices obtained, natives do not improve their methods, shows
how difficult it is to do much in this direction. Fortunately,
the natives of any one country are often willing enough to
use the inferior articles grown there, and it thus comes about
that the encouragement of export trade among peasants should
at first be directed mainly towards export from the village. As
they improve in their methods, and as cooperation comes in,
the villagers may export further, but at first the export trade
to the countries of the north is best left in the hands of
capitalists, except in the case of those products, such as rice,
that the peasant properly understands.

The sixth point mentioned was the improvement of the
breed and quality of the cattle and other stock kept by the
peasant. This has already been fully considered in the chapter
on stock in Part II, and only needs mention here. The villager
needs to be taught to avoid indiscriminate crossing, to select
the best stock for parents, to castrate on better and more
humane principles, and so on. At the same time crosses with
other breeds may at times be provided for him, when it has
been quite settled what are the best, by establishing bulls,
stallions, cocks, etc., in the villages for short periods. One

great point to remember is, as already pointed out, to let the improvement of the stock keep pace with that of the food.

To sum up, then, it would appear that the first requisite is to avoid hasty action, and to make a careful study of that which we want to improve, of tools, crops, methods, etc., and to find out all that the villager already knows from accumulated experience. All this knowledge should then be treated comparatively in the usual scientific manner; comparisons should be made with other countries, other crops, other methods, etc., and sound general principles of improvement thus deduced, the experience and agricultural history of the most advanced countries being used as a guide to suggest directions of work and improvement. New products, new varieties, improved varieties, new methods, better tools, and the rest, should be very fully and carefully tested before trying to introduce them into peasant agriculture, remembering that poverty, prejudice, custom, ignorance, and indolence are all formidable obstacles in the path, which must be removed or avoided. Or, to make more concrete suggestions, there should be Experimental Gardens to try experiments with the native crops and tools, and parallel experiments with introduced varieties, improved races, better tools, better methods, and so on. Seed of kinds decided upon as safe to recommend should be distributed among the peasantry from the gardens. Estate and village agriculture should be intermingled, to provide object lessons to the latter in good methods of cultivation and treatment. Legislation for the compulsory treatment of disease should be introduced, to deal with any important crop that may be in any danger from bad or uncleanly methods. School Gardens should be established on the system already indicated, to help in introducing new products, and to inculcate new ideas while the minds are still plastic. Later, peripatetic teaching might be introduced, perhaps in connection with some system of inspecting and teaching in the school gardens, where the necessary concrete object lessons are to hand, or in connection with peripatetic Experimental Gardens, land being temporarily rented in a village, and the local crops cultivated upon it according to the best methods. It is possible also that some system of prizes for well-kept gardens, or for cultivation of new products, might prove of value. Lastly, some system of *village* shows might prove of advantage, with small prizes to the real cultivators and preparers of the produce; in the large shows these prizes usually go to the headmen or to rich natives who have lessees under them, or who have purchased the exhibits from the makers or growers.

CHAPTER V

EDUCATION OF THE PEASANT, AND ITS BEARING UPON AGRICULTURAL PROGRESS

THE thorny subject of education must be lightly touched upon, on account of its very important bearing upon agriculture. Education of the native produces in him new wants, to gratify which he must in some way earn more money. In this way, consequently, education may do much to break up the simplicity of the old self-sufficient villagers' garden type of agriculture, the defects of which were considered in the last chapters. It must, however, be of a nature to guide the peasant towards agricultural pursuits, and encourage him in them.

As yet, in the East, at any rate, the general effect of educating the native seems to be to encourage his tendency to despise agricultural pursuits, and more especially personal hand-labour. If he receive more than a mere elementary vernacular education, he wants to go off to the towns, and become a clerk, a house servant, anything rather than an agriculturist. It is not difficult to understand this attraction of the towns and town life; the same thing is equally common in Europe and even in the newer countries like Canada and Australia.

The main question to be considered here is whether anything can be done in the education of the children or adults to help forward the attainment of the agricultural ideals which were indicated in a previous chapter.

All experience in the tropics seems to point to the fact that but little can be done in the way of direct " education" of the adult native, though much may often be effected by example or demonstration. The question of giving direct agricultural instruction to adults, otherwise than by demonstration, seems

XXIII. A School Garden

almost outside the region of practical politics, and until at least a generation of children has grown up under agricultural teaching influence.

The children, generally speaking, are sharp, and can be more readily influenced than the adults, and perhaps the best way of affecting the agricultural practice of the country as a whole may in the long run prove to be through the children. Deliberate and well-organised attempts in this direction are now being carried on in Ceylon and the West Indies. The establishment of a system of School Gardens and Nature-study lessons should be productive of good results, and is well worthy of consideration.

The scheme of School Gardens, as adopted in Ceylon, has two objects in view, the diversification of agriculture in the village by the introduction of "new products" hitherto unknown to the villagers, and the training up of the younger generation in habits of thought and work favourable to agricultural improvement, making them receptive but also critical towards improved methods, etc. It provides in the villages what are practically small experimental gardens which any villager may see for himself, stocked with the best available kinds of useful and ornamental plants, laid out in as tasteful a manner as possible. Its organisation is simple and inexpensive.

The teaching of agriculture, as such, in village schools is impracticable and inadvisable, except perhaps in large schools, and to boys of at least twelve years old, and then probably best by aid of peripatetic teachers. The school-master is untrained in this most difficult art, and can hardly hope to do as well as the villagers around him. He thus lays himself open to hostile criticism and ridicule, and the end in view is defeated.

What can be done, however, is that master and pupils may learn by personal experience, and by personal labour in the garden attached to the school, under the superintendence of a trained Inspector who shall periodically visit the school, how to grow and treat a selection of useful and ornamental plants not yet known or common in the neighbourhood. They do not thus lay themselves open to criticism to such an extent, they learn the general principles of all agricultural work just as well, and they help to introduce into the district products which are new to it.

The produce of the garden may be divided among the masters and pupils, reserving a small portion for seed. Prizes should be offered for the best gardens, attention being paid to ornamental laying out and gardening as well as to the practical side of the work, for it is important to develop a love of flowers and of the country and its beauty, to help to check the tendency to desert the country for the towns.

Object lessons, or Nature-study lessons upon the work of the garden and the plants contained in it, and upon the various natural objects of interest in the neighbourhood, should be given by the school-masters when competent to do so, at first under the immediate eye of the Inspector. All work and instruction should of course be conducted in the vernacular.

The expense of the scheme is and should remain small. The actual work being carried out by masters and pupils, there is only the cost of tools, of the Inspector and his travelling, of a stock garden for supplies at head-quarters, and a few small prizes.

By some such method as this it may be hoped that the younger generation may be induced to take more intelligent interest in, and have more respect for, agricultural pursuits and country life. If adopted, the scheme should be first put into practice in selected schools whose masters are keen upon doing such work; the work should be made an alternative subject in the school curriculum, and in Government examinations, etc., in order to increase its prestige—a most important point in getting natives of the tropics to interest themselves in anything of the kind.

The more definite teaching of agriculture and allied subjects in the higher schools and colleges under the Department of Public Instruction is a subject for later consideration, when the elementary schools have paved the way. Practical outdoor work and direct technical instruction in agriculture should accompany any such scheme; the high school boys, in the tropics particularly, tend to despise such work, and acquire a smattering of book knowledge of agriculture which is of little or no use, but may lead to disaster if put into practice by natives of the tropics, who are not good at adapting principles to actual practical use in the field or elsewhere.

There are many and great difficulties in the way of organising such instruction. In the first place, as indicated above in connection with nature study and school gardens, there is the difficulty of getting good teachers. The ordinary teacher cannot know about agricultural practice anything like so much as the ordinary villager, and consequently, if he sets to work to teach boys, will render himself liable to ridicule. It is better, as pointed out above, that he should confine his teaching to cultivations not yet understood or practised in the village where he has to teach.

In the second place, practical outdoor teaching is required, and this, apart from any difficulty in getting land, must often present great obstacles. Unless the boys have been accustomed to practical work out of doors by school garden work at the elementary school, it will often be found very difficult to get them to take part in it, especially in the more severe physical labour, and yet, if they do not, they can never acquire a real working knowledge of agricultural practice.

In Indian countries, the caste difficulty sometimes stands more or less in the way of successful practical work, especially if the student who has been trained in agriculture is to be sent to teach among the villagers. The higher the caste, the less inclined, very often, is the man (if he has received an ordinary "good" education) to do hard physical labour, and yet no man but a high caste man can do much among the agricultural villagers, who are very commonly of high caste themselves.

On the whole, therefore, agricultural teaching in the high schools should only be attempted in very favourable cases, and attention should rather be directed to the working of school gardens, which are to a large extent free from the great drawbacks which have been pointed out. The instruction given in these may become more and more directed to agricultural practice as the boys get older. A boy is best kept clear of direct technical instruction in agriculture, in the majority of cases, until he is getting well up in the schools.

Direct technical instruction in agriculture should be the aim of special agricultural colleges, perhaps best kept up in connection with the Experiment Stations maintained by the Agricultural Department. To these colleges should be drafted the boys who show signs of wishing to take up agriculture as a profession, and who have shown promise in the school garden work, etc.

So far, at any rate, as the natives of southern Asia are concerned, it would appear best that the teaching should not be too much bookwork, but should as much as possible be practical, out of door teaching. A few lessons should for instance be given upon insect pests, how to recognise them, how to collect and send in specimens to the official entomologist, and how to deal with the attack. The same with regard to fungus pests, and other things. But in regard to agriculture proper the fewer indoor lessons, and the more outdoor work, the better. A few indoor lessons on the particular cultivation it is intended to teach, and the rest should be outdoor practical work, with field demonstrations.

CHAPTER VI

CAPITALIST OR ESTATE AGRICULTURE

THERE can be but little doubt that, just as in the countries of the colder zones, the continual improvement of agricultural methods, the opening up of roads, railways, and other means of communication, and similar progress, favour the large as against the small cultivator of land, and that the latter will have to take to cooperation, sooner or later, to survive in the competition, or become a labourer on the large estate. Even in the oldest agricultural enterprises of the tropics, as for example rice cultivation, the land is tending steadily to fall into the hands of large proprietors, and on it the small men work upon a system of shares. The most conspicuous form of capitalist agricultural work in the tropics is, however, what is usually known as the "planting industry," which is well represented in Ceylon, India, Java, Sumatra, the Malay States, Hawaii, the West Indies, South America, British West Africa, French and Belgian Africa, and elsewhere, by a considerable number of plantations of tea, coffee, cacao, rubber, sugar, coconuts, tobacco, fruits, cinchona, cotton, and other products. These plantations are perhaps most often, nowadays, owned by companies with head-quarters in the colder countries, and the estates are in charge of superintendents—or planters—resident upon them. A very considerable number of Englishmen are now engaged in this line of work, Ceylon alone, for instance, containing nearly 2000 of them. There are many Dutchmen in Java, etc., Americans in the Philippines and West Indies and Mexico, Belgians in East Africa, the Cameroons, Samoa, etc., Frenchmen in Indo-China and Africa, and so on, while in the eastern countries, Brazil, etc., large numbers of the natives of the

12—2

country are also owners or superintendents of estates, and the number of such men continues to increase.

It is not always easy to draw the line between estate and village agriculture, but the Ceylon definition of an estate—an area of at least 20 acres worked in whole or in part with hired labour—is a convenient criterion.

The great primary essentials for success in agriculture of this type are satisfactory conditions as regards labour, finance, and transport. Next follow such things as irrigation and drainage, and the more strictly agricultural matters of continual improvement of crops, machinery, methods, preparation of produce, etc., the prevention of disease, and so on.

Capitalist agriculture can to a large extent choose its location, and will therefore only come to a given country if it can offer as great attractions as other places, either by its having a monopoly of some particular crop, or by giving good prospects in some crop that can also be cultivated elsewhere. The chief obstacles to a flow of capital into any country are therefore not so much agricultural as in the preliminaries to agriculture, and if these can be satisfactorily settled, it may almost be taken for granted that the flow will begin.

The first country in which these preliminary conditions were sufficiently satisfied to attract European enterprise was the West Indies. Land was available in large enough amount, transport was easy from small islands, roads were easily made, labour—thanks to slavery—was cheap and abundant. Capital was forthcoming from England, and the great sugar industry rapidly sprang up. But, with the abolition of slavery, Ceylon, with similar natural advantages, and with plentiful cheap labour at her very doors, took the place of the West Indies as a field for the investment of capital in planting enterprises, and to this day holds it so far as English capital is concerned, while Java, Mexico, and Hawaii hold similar places in regard to Dutch and American capital. Thanks to the large planting industry, Ceylon has been far more rich and prosperous than it would otherwise have been, and the Government has been able to carry out expensive public works that must, but for planting, have been left untouched.

The history of European planting in Ceylon is a wonderful story of brilliant successes chequered by dismal failures, which again have been retrieved by indomitable pluck and energy. With the conquest of the Kandyan kingdom—the mountainous region of the centre of the island—and the opening of the road to its capital, the country was thrown open to English enterprise. Conspicuous among the first pioneers of planting was Sir Edward Barnes, the then Governor, who in 1825 opened the estate of Gangaruwa near Peradeniya, now the site of a Government Experiment Station. Much money was vainly expended at first in trying sugar, indigo, and other Indian crops, but presently it was discovered that the cleared forest land was eminently suited to the growth of coffee. The time was favourable, the duty on coffee in England had just been reduced, its consumption was increasing in Europe, and the West Indies were hampered by difficulties with the slaves. By 1838 the success of the industry was assured, and in that year 10,401 acres of crown land were sold to planters, while in 1841, when the rush was at its height, no less than 78,685 acres were disposed of. "The coffee mania was at its climax in 1845. The Governor and the Council, the Military, the Judges, the Clergy, and one half the Civil Servants penetrated the hills, and became purchasers of crown lands...capitalists from England arrived by every packet...so dazzling was the prospect that expenditure was unlimited; and its profusion was only equalled by the ignorance and inexperience of those to whom it was entrusted. The rush for land was only paralleled by the movement towards the mines of California and Australia, but with this painful difference, that the enthusiasts in Ceylon, instead of thronging to disinter, were hurrying to bury their gold" (Tennent).

The inevitable collapse soon followed, and for some years the coffee industry was almost paralysed, but by 1855 it had more than recovered its lost ground, and was conducted on more practical and economical lines. From that date to about 1882 it was the staple export industry of the colony, reaching its maximum in 1875, when almost 1,000,000 cwt. of coffee were exported. About 1870 the plants began to be noticeably attacked by a fungus blight—*Hemileia vastatrix*, the coffee leaf disease—which spread steadily and irresistibly over the vast sheet of coffee plantation in the mountains, and was disregarded until· too late, if indeed any practicable measures could have been adopted against it at any time in its history. By 1880 the industry, though still considerable, was in a parlous condition, and the planters in great distress, but with the most commendable pluck they set themselves to redeem their fallen fortunes, aided by the efforts of the Botanical Department of the Government. Cinchona trees—the source of the valuable alkaloid quinine—introduced by Government years before, but disregarded so long as coffee was profitable, were now the salvation of the island. Large areas were planted with this product, and at first large profits were realised, but soon overproduction rapidly brought down the price of quinine, to the incalculable benefit of sufferers all over the world, but to the ruin of the profitableness of the Ceylon bark industry—a ruin consummated by the attacks of a canker disease, and the competition of better barks from Java. The gap, however, was bridged, and by the time that cinchona had passed its zenith, it was clear that tea was the industry of the future, and large areas were being planted up in it, while an export was already commencing, Ceylon tea being favourably received upon the markets of Europe. The rise of the tea industry has been phenomenal, and it is not safe to assume that it has even yet reached its maximum. The height of the tea boom was perhaps in 1896, and during the last few years very little further extension of area has gone on, while the new industry of Pará rubber growing has sprung up, and already (December, 1920) no less than about 397,000 acres are planted in this product, which has proved to be extremely remunerative.

Not only have these larger industries sprung up, but also considerable industries in other things, as for instance cocoa and cardamoms, while the area under coconuts has continually spread, until now it is the largest area under any one product in the island.

A somewhat similar history has to be related of Java. Sugar is the largest planting industry there, occupying about a million acres, but Java has also got almost entire command of the cinchona trade, grows large quantities of good coffee, pepper, tea, and many other things, and is now getting quite a hold upon the new industry of rubber.

The West Indies, more particularly the British islands, suffered so much from the collapse of their slave-supported industry in sugar, and their adherence to old fashioned methods of preparation (as described under sugar in Part II), that they were for a very long time considerably under a cloud, and only of recent years is this beginning to lift, largely in consequence of the successful work done by the Imperial Department of Agriculture. Lately they have established a large and prosperous industry in cotton, while in many of the islands cocoa or fruit has largely taken the place of sugar, and other minor things are also cultivated.

India has large and prosperous industries in tea in Assam and other parts, in coffee in southern India, and had until lately a large indigo trade, but this is tending to disappear under the competition of the artificial dye.

The Federated Malay States had once a considerable industry in coffee, but this has gradually died out, and now the country is mainly devoted to the growth of rubber, while in the Straits Settlements pepper and other things are also cultivated, and in both countries there is a large area under sugar and coconuts.

West Africa is now being opened up and rendered more healthy, and already large industries in cacao and cotton are established there.

Turning now to the colonies of other nations, the Americans are establishing considerable fruit industries in Porto Rico, and hemp and other things in the Philippines; Germany had a large planting community, attending to fibres, rubber, etc., in East Africa, to cacao and rubber in West Africa and Samoa; France has planters of tea and rubber in Indo-China, of cacao and rubber in Africa; and even Italy is beginning to plant in Erythraea.

In the independent countries of the tropics, a considerable amount of planting also goes on. The largest planting industry of all is probably that of coffee in southern Brazil, whilst there are also large areas in that country devoted to sugar, tobacco, cacao, cotton, etc. There are very large areas under rubber in Mexico, bananas in Costa Rica, sugar in Cuba, coffee in Central America and Venezuela, cacao in Ecuador, and so on.

We may now go on to briefly consider the general methods of opening an estate. The land having been chosen, the first work is usually to clear it, it being most often, perhaps, covered with forest. The aid of the natives of the country is called in to do this, and they are usually clever at it. The trees are all cut on the same side, and then the fall is started, and often takes place over a large area together, the trees falling in much the same direction. They are then left on the ground to dry, and presently burnt, either just as they lie, or after a certain amount of piling by aid of elephants or otherwise.

The plants which are to go upon the ground are meanwhile raised in nurseries, and when the land is sufficiently clear are planted out in holes made among the stumps and filled with good soil. In a few years, except at very high elevations, decay and white ants will remove all trace of the former timber.

At this stage coolie labour of some regularity has to be provided for, and this often, especially in the case of thinly peopled countries, means importing it; in this case, at any rate, the coolies have to be provided with lines, as their single-roomed dwellings are often called. Most commonly, perhaps, the coolies are imported under advances of money made to pay for the cost of passage, etc., and these advances are repaid to the planter out of their pay.

The bungalow for the superintendent, the coolie lines, and any other buildings required at once have also to be put up in the early stages of planting an estate. After this, there is usually a period of greater or less length, varying from six months in cotton to three years in tea, and five or six in rubber, before any actual return can be looked for (unless quick growing catch crops are cultivated), so that it is obvious that considerable capital is required for planting. In rubber, for example, it is estimated that some £60 per acre must be spent before any return can be looked for.

When a few planters have established themselves in any locality, the next step is usually the formation of a Planters' Association. Ceylon has the best organised associations, there being one in each of about thirty districts, while in Kandy there is a general combined association, with over 1000 members. These associations make it their business to discuss and call attention to the wants of their members, as regards roads, drains, medical attention, sanitation, hospitals, and what not, and to press these matters upon the attention of the Government through the central association. In a prosperous colony like Ceylon, where in one way and another the planting industry provides the bulk of the revenue, such recommendations have much weight with the Government.

In Java, the associations are of planters of one product, as of cinchona, tea, or coffee. This, while very good for the single products, is perhaps not so good for the planting industry in general, for the conflicting claims of the different industries are not so easy to adjust.

Having in the consideration of peasant agriculture dealt with the idea that the country was to be entirely self-supporting, growing all that it required, and consuming all that it grew, we may now proceed to consider the other extreme, that of a country in which all, or practically all, the land is the property of, and worked by, large capitalist owners, the bulk of the population consisting of paid labourers upon these properties. This state of affairs may be seen in parts of Brazil, Ceylon, India, and Java, where the whole district is practically owned by a few individuals or companies, and the population consists of coolie labourers, with the few overseers, shopkeepers, and others necessary. Excepting that in modern times the labourers are free, the general economic condition may be compared with that of the older slave-labour period. Such a country is often very prosperous, but its prosperity rests upon an unstable basis, for as a rule there is in such cases but little diversity of industries, and all the eggs are in one basket. Such a state of affairs has usually come about, where a country or district has been found to be eminently suited to some one industry, into which there has then been a rush, other industries being neglected in favour of the one which pays best, as is inevitable. Such cases have been or are the old cotton industry of slavery days in the southern United States, the sugar industry of the West Indies, the coffee industry of Ceylon, and now to a less marked degree the tea industry of that colony.

In such a state of matters, the local market is usually a very small one, the industry depends upon external markets, and there is a large export trade. The success of the industry is also as a rule dependent upon a large supply of cheap labour. A survey of the tropical countries which export large quantities of produce shows that the export has a direct relation to the abundance and cheapness of the labour supply, and countries which have not abundant local labour must import it if they are to take much part in trade. Some approximate figures, given years ago by Mr Ireland in the *Times*, illustrate this. Of the countries in which there is a pressure of population, Java exports produce to the value of 10s. per head per annum, Barbados 95s. Of the countries employing imported labour, Hawaii exports 520s. per head, the Federated Malay States, 170s., British Guiana, 120s., while of the independent tropical States, Brazil exports 30s. per head, Siam, 10s.

With such an agricultural industry, the country or district may be as much in a state of exploitation as if it were dependent upon mining, if not more so. During its most prosperous periods, the profits are to a greater or less extent taken out of the country by the planters, the imported coolies, the foreign money-lenders, and others. The finest soils and the best forests are liable to ruthless destruction if the Government be not strong enough to resist popular clamour for the opening of fresh land in time of great prosperity of particular industries.

The prosperity of such large industries largely depends on cheap labour and new land, and sooner or later over-production, attacks of disease such as always tend to work havoc upon large areas devoted to one crop, the opening up of new land in the same or other countries, or the competition of countries with cheaper labour or better methods, brings depression, if not even total collapse. Well-known instances are (1) coffee in Ceylon, whose failure and disappearance were due in the first place

to disease, and in the second to the competition of Brazil;
(2) cinchona in Ceylon, which failed owing to over-production
and the competition of Java, the latter country adopting
scientific treatment for the continual improvement of the
barks; (3) sugar in the West Indies, whose depression and
almost complete collapse were due to loss of the cheap slave
labour in the first instance and afterwards to the competition
of beet sugar (bounty-aided), to better methods, newer land,
and cheaper labour in other countries.

If the staple industry collapse, widespread disaster follows
in a country so organised. Coolies and others are thrown out
of work, and often have no land of their own to support themselves upon, the subsidiary trades of transport, supply of clothing,
etc., suffer, the Government revenue decreases, and everything
becomes more or less disorganised, with risk of famine, rioting,
or other troubles.

It would be wrong, however, to suggest that such a state
of affairs must necessarily occur in a country organised on the
system we are considering. Disease may be taken in time,
natural advantages of soil or climate, or labour, or of suitability
of the country to a particular crop, may be so great as to allow
no chance of profitable competition to rival countries, planters
may be enterprising and progressive, and the kind of crop, its
quality and yield, the methods used in cultivating and preparing
it for market, and other features, may be continually improved
by aid of science, to such an extent as to keep the country
ahead of its rivals. It seems improbable, for instance, that
Java will be ousted from her position of supremacy in cinchona
cultivation, or India and Ceylon in tea.

It would be equally wrong to infer that under this system
the country itself, even if its planters and its labourers be both
foreign (as is largely the case in Ceylon), is not enriched. All
kinds of subsidiary trades flourish upon the planting industry,
the planters and the coolies spend large sums in the country,
the revenue is large, and consequently the Government can do
much for the opening up of the country by roads, railways,
bridges, and other transport facilities, for education, sanitation,
etc. In spite of the collapse of coffee, Ceylon has been much

richer for its planting enterprises. Further, though at first the planters and capitalists engaged in the planting industry may be all foreign, sooner or later a number of natives are also found to engage in the same industry, and their savings and profits are not taken out of the country like those of the foreign planters. This, for instance, has occurred to a large extent in Ceylon, where there are now a large number of native capitalists, large and small, engaged in the tea, coconut, and other industries.

Evidently, therefore, we require to arrive at some mean or compromise between these two extremes. Nearly all those who have had to deal with the agricultural problems of such countries as Ceylon or the West Indies, have pronounced in favour of diversification of agricultural industries, or in other words, the encouragement of the cultivation of "new products," i.e., products not as yet cultivated in the country. I propose to enlarge the significance of this expression, and to say that the best course to adopt is *to encourage the diversification of agriculture*, so that not only shall the country grow many products and so not place all its eggs in one basket, but that it shall have as many kinds of agriculture as possible, from the largest capitalist organisation, working on the very large scale with hired labour and machinery, down to the smallest and simplest forms of villagers' cultivation, carried on upon small blocks of land by the labour simply of the owner and his family.

.At present there is plenty of room in most tropical countries for every form of agriculture, so that there is no need to calculate with great exactness, or consider whether one form is becoming too dominant. Until the various countries are much more fully opened up and populated, it would seem most advisable to encourage both forms of agriculture, capitalist and peasant, to the utmost. But there are a few points to which attention is necessary from the first. For instance, in any given district, unless it is very conspicuously suited to one kind of agriculture only, or to one product only, like a district irrigated for rice, too large an area should not be allowed to become devoted to one form of agriculture only. If a large area is taken up for planting, sufficient area should be reserved for small holders within a moderate distance, so that in the future there may be village labour obtainable upon the large estates, as in Java. On the other hand, the planting estates should not be too much cut up by small holdings between them, for there is much more risk of theft, greater expense in making boundaries, and far more trouble in keeping the cultivation free of weeds when it is surrounded by native holdings.

Similarly, allowance must be made for the little towns and hamlets of shops, small factories, etc., which must necessarily grow up when the country is largely opened up for agriculture. These will of course tend to lie chiefly along the main channels of communication, such as trunk roads, rivers, etc. A large part of the frontages to such roads, etc., might therefore be reserved with advantage for sale as sites of shops, etc. If the road reservations advocated in a previous chapter be decided upon, land for the agricultural settlement of ordinary villagers may well be sold along them, reserving frontage on the trunk roads for sale at higher rates for the special purposes mentioned. The ordinary cultivator will be every bit as well suited on land on the side roads, and it is waste of good sites to let him take them up at low rates along the fine main roads. He should not be too far away from these main roads, but there need be no difficulty in this if the road reservations be made, as suggested.

CHAPTER VII

THE AGRICULTURAL NEEDS OF THE PLANTING ENTERPRISE. SUMMARY OF PART III

WE may consider the more specially agricultural needs of capitalist enterprise in the same order as those of peasant industries, to the discussion of which reference may be made for further details. Thus the work of introducing new products, and new kinds of those already grown, and that of breeding new and improved kinds, is as desirable for the planting enterprise as for village agriculture. At the same time, it is well to point out for the second time that enterprise of the kind now under consideration tends to run in grooves, the product that offers greatest attraction being alone taken up, as was lately the case with rubber in very many tropical countries.

To introduce a "new product" is a great deal more easily said than done. In the earlier days of tropical planting, there were still many products which were as yet only produced from wild plants, or cultivated only by the backward native races of tropical and subtropical countries. These, taken up by Europeans, with capital, virgin soil, good methods, economical working, and careful preparation for market, in many cases rapidly drove the older product of the jungle or of village agriculture to a great extent out of the markets. Ceylon affords excellent illustrations, in the successive rise of her industries of coffee, cinchona, cacao, cardamoms, tea, and lastly india-rubber. Now, however, the day of this kind of success is probably largely over. Almost all products which have any large trade are now being cultivated in some part of the tropics by European, American, or Chinese planters, and to find new ones capable of forming the basis of large and profitable industries is no easy matter. It is better to make the best of those we have than to be continually looking out for new ones to take their place. Before a new industry can be established, thorough tests have to be made of its suitability to the climate and soil, and its cheapness and efficiency as compared with rival countries practising it.

As regards methods of cultivation, while there is no doubt less to learn than in the case of village agriculture, there is great room for improvement. To take the case of machinery for cultivation, it would be hard to find a soil more suited to the use of light machines than that of the coast districts in many tropical countries. Already machinery is coming in in many places. High cultivation, the use of green manuring, and prevention of wash, at present rendered difficult by lack of labour, might all be rendered possible by careful study of the problems involved, and the invention of light and simple machinery for the different purposes.

All the methods of cultivation want careful study in experimental gardens, and thorough testing against the existing methods of other countries, and against suggested improved methods. There is much to learn in tillage, in actual cultivation of the crop, propagation, selection of seeds, manuring, weeding, pruning, catch-cropping, mixture of crops, rotation of crops, and other matters. All these are best studied at first with the aid of Experiment Stations, and with free discussion, but it is important to get the planters themselves to develop an "experimental" habit of mind, and start experiments themselves to test and extend the results obtained in the Experiment Stations. Cooperative experimental work has proved of great value to agriculture in Canada, the United States, and elsewhere.

The next point for consideration is the prevention of disease, and the introduction of better methods of treatment, and of sound plant sanitation generally. When a crop is cultivated over a large piece of land, unbroken by other crops, any disease that breaks out upon it is far more liable to spread rapidly and get out of hand than in the case of mixed cultivation or of little patches of different crops. This liability to epidemics of disease is one of the most serious dangers confronting large agricultural enterprises. The most famous instance in the tropics is of course the ruin of the coffee industry of Ceylon by the attacks of the leaf-disease fungus and the coffee-scale insect.

One great difficulty in the way of dealing with such outbreaks in good time is the unwillingness of estate owners to confess that their property is attacked by disease. This is natural enough; such a statement lowers the value of the property in the share market. But there is no doubt that in countries like Ceylon this difficulty has been much lessened of late years, and that planters—like the fruit-growers of the western United States—have largely realised that the policy of concealment is a mistake, and that it is better to call in help at the very first appearance of trouble. Applications for such help to the Government officers who deal with disease are of course regarded as private matters, while at the same time the feeling of the public continually grows in favour of such action. Greater confidence in the safety of crops from devastating pests or diseases is naturally felt by agriculturists when they feel assured that most people who notice outbreaks will at once report them to responsible officers, who will do all that can be done to assist the adoption of proper treatment at the earliest possible time.

At the same time, experience in all advanced agricultural countries shows that even when the majority are content to treat disease promptly, and have realised that this is the most profitable course, there always remain some who will do nothing, and whose cultivations thus form a hotbed of disease to re-infect those of their neighbours. For them—as in matters of public health and prevention of epidemic and infectious diseases—legislation is necessary and just, and they must be compelled to deal with insanitary conditions, as soon as public opinion is ripe for so dealing with them. Ceylon now has a Pests Ordinance in operation, under which Government can proclaim any pest, with the measures required for its treatment, call upon people to adopt these, and punish them for non-compliance.

Lastly, there remains to be considered the question of improvement of methods of preparing produce for market. In general, of course, estate products are the best prepared in the country, but the competition of other countries has to be met, and these are continually improving their methods. Continual investigation of methods with a view to their improvement must be the watchword of all progressive industries. Work of this kind can best be done upon a large Experiment Station, and if in connection with cooperative experimental work among planters, so much the better. Arrangements are already in force with the Imperial Institute and other authorities in England whereby reports can be obtained upon the quality and value of products sent to Europe.

To sum up, the needs of estate agriculture are much the same as those of village agriculture, excepting as regards labour. Leaving out of account these primary questions of labour, transportation, drainage, etc., the chief needs of this form of enterprise would seem to be those which can be best met by the formation of a scientific Department of Agriculture, which should include the necessary staff of expert advisers in matters of disease prevention, etc., a system of Experiment Stations for thorough trial of new products, new methods, new machinery, new ways of preparing crops for market, and so on. Though ignorance may often prove an obstacle to progress in this form of enterprise, it is more easily removed than in the case of the villager by lectures, leaflets and other publications, demonstrations at Experiment Stations and on estates, and other ways. Progress is little likely to be checked to any serious extent at this period of planting history by the other obstacles which are so formidable in the case of the villagers. Competition will almost ensure progress, but the great thing is to systematise this, and this is best done with the help of a technical department which shall keep abreast of the progress being made in all forms of agriculture throughout the world.

To recapitulate Part III of the book, then, it is evident that with the opening up of a country agricultural progress— using the term as implying the opening up of new land, the introduction and successful cultivation of new crops, the extension and improvement of old ones, the improvement of methods of cultivation and of preparation of produce, greater economy and efficiency all round, and greater stability of agricultural industries and freedom from epidemic diseases or other crises—becomes possible, and we have to consider how best to further it. Both estate and peasant agriculture should be fostered, the former especially in a thinly peopled country as its extension helps to open up and populate the country very much more rapidly. The needs of both these forms of agriculture are very similar, or at least can be fairly well harmonised. The country must be made as attractive to the agricultural capitalist and to the labourer and peasant as is possible. To do this the first great essentials are the settlement of the questions of land and its availability (i.e., roads, drainage, etc.), finance, and labour for large estates. Without assurance of satisfactory treatment of these points, capital will go elsewhere for investment, unless there is some industry so attractive as to overcome even these disadvantages. The questions of easy acquisition of land, road frontage, drainage, canals, etc., are of equal importance to both forms of agriculture, and finance is also vital. Large capitalist enterprises may well be left to attend to this matter themselves, but some system of cheaply financing small enterprises, and thus helping the villagers to escape the burden of heavy debt and high rates of interest, preferably by mutual cooperation, should receive early consideration in every tropical country.

To raise the standard of agriculture throughout the country we must also raise the standard of living; these two are in intimate relation to one another. The villager will not grow larger or better crops, or improve his agriculture unless he has an immediate local market, sufficiently remunerative to tempt him to grow for it, and sufficiently certain and permanent to give him reasonable security against future loss. One important factor in attaining these various ends we have seen to be the intermingling of village and estate agriculture in suitable blocks, one block comprising the one form only, the next the other. Combined with this practice, which will give the villager object lessons in his own district, is the principle that the peasant should be encouraged to grow the "estate" crops, and those which he best understands and prefers, while the estates should be subsidised to whatever extent is actually necessary to induce them to buy the peasants' produce at fixed rates.

The further points to be attended to if agriculture is to progress are technical, and it is pretty evident that to attend properly to these a technical and scientific Department of Agriculture is required. All crops grown in the country require careful study with regard to the varieties grown, the methods of cultivation used, the liability to disease, the preparation of the product for market, the prices obtained, and so on. In all these points improvement is possible and necessary, by the introduction of new crops from abroad, by the introduction of new kinds of the already existing crops, by the breeding of new varieties better suited to local conditions, by the improvement of local methods, tools, machinery, use of manure, mixture and rotation of crops, by better and more prompt treatment of disease, by improvement of methods of preparation of produce, by cheapening of cost of production and transport, and in many other ways.

The great obstacles in the way of this improvement are ignorance, poverty, indolence, and conservatism. Education must therefore be an important factor. Gardening at school should be encouraged, on the lines already indicated, and later definite peripatetic agricultural teaching must be tried, perhaps through the medium of the officers engaged in carrying out sanitary enactments. The operation of these enactments affords an excellent peg on which to hang future attempts at the amelioration of local agriculture.

PART IV

AGRICULTURAL ORGANISATION AND POLICY

CHAPTER I

ORGANISATION OF AGRICULTURE

THE duty of the Government of a country is obviously to encourage agriculture to the utmost, and to make it as attractive as other pursuits, both to the capitalist and to the peasant or labourer. What is wanted is a genuine and steadfast encouragement of agriculture, a removal of difficulties from its path, and the adoption of such a policy, and such an attitude towards it and those who pursue it, as will make it reasonably certain that it shall afford as good prospects as any other form of enterprise to the planter, peasant, or labourer.

To ensure the end in view it is no use nibbling at the numerous fringes of the problem. A definite policy must be adopted, and the efforts of all the various departments of Government and other organisations directed steadily and resolutely to the carrying out of this policy. The essentially important points to be aimed at must be carefully distinguished from the less essential, and effort directed towards them. And not towards one or two of them only, but towards all at once. There must be full and complete concentration and continuity of effort towards the same end.

Perhaps the greatest weakness in the present state of affairs in many tropical countries is this very lack of concentration of effort and of a definite policy on the part of the Government[1]. Everyone, from the highest to the lowest, is anxious to

---

[1] This was written in 1908, and things have changed greatly since that date, but is left as of historic interest.

do something for the advancement of the agricultural progress of the country, and many have done great things for it. The weak point is lack of concentration and of continuity. In many countries there is no agricultural department or organisation, whose special business is to attend to agricultural matters or policy. Each officer of Government has his own views as to what is required, and in each position which he may occupy—and, as a rule, his occupation is but for a very few years at most—he puts these views into operation so far as his time, the availability of funds, and the instructions or criticisms of his superior officers will allow. The next occupant of his post probably has entirely different views, and the net result of this kind of thing is but little. Roads and railways and other public works, again, are carried out without special reference to the future of agriculture in the country; agricultural finance, drainage, and other matters of vital importance are left more or less neglected; and so on.

A general consideration of the history of most tropical countries shows that a steady and satisfactory progress is best ensured when there is a definite department of the Government concerned with the particular matter in hand. Agricultural progress has been but slow, and due more to private enterprise or to great natural advantages than to any effort of Governments. Agriculture is daily becoming more scientific, and a Department of Agriculture is an evident necessity of the case, just as there is a Department of Public Works, of Forests, or of Mining. The poorer agriculturist cannot afford the experiments necessary for progress, were he even qualified to make them.

Nothing will make agriculture progress rapidly, or make it sufficiently attractive, but a concentration of effort of all departments or organisations concerned, with a definite policy on the part of the supreme Government. All effort possible should be concentrated on agriculture with the object of making a " boom " in it. There is often a feeling that this is undesirable, that the first success may be followed by collapse, but if behind the advertisement there be a solid basis for prosperity, there is no reason why there should not be rapid and permanent progress, like that of Ceylon in tea. It is natural that any industry which proves profitable should be somewhat overdone, but this will adjust itself. The proper course is to aim at making a boom in all forms of agriculture; when the rush shows signs of being too great, there will be time enough to put on the drag, if necessary.

It is clear, from what has been said above, that practically all departments of Government are largely concerned in agricultural progress. It follows therefore, that a Department of Agriculture *may* have a very wide scope; in fact, if it is to concern itself with the control of all work bearing on agriculture, it must obviously be almost synonymous with the Government itself. This would seem both impracticable and inadvisable; the weakness in the agricultural organisation of many eastern colonies seems to lie in the attempt to include too much in the Agricultural Department. Probably the best course at present is to have a department concerned with all the technical work of agriculture, such as the introduction and trial of crops, methods, machinery, etc., the study and prevention of disease, and all other scientific help to agriculture that may be needed, and for the head of that department to be the chief adviser of the Government in all matters of agricultural policy, the Government controlling all departments to a common end. Thus road-provision or drainage should be carried out by the Public Works or Irrigation departments, impelled thereto by the Government after consideration of the recommendations of the head of the Agricultural department. The latter department, again, is helpless to do much with the villager in a district where the Government officer in charge may be opposed to the ideas which it is wished to carry out, but the Government can insist upon a definite and continuous policy.

So many interests are concerned in agriculture, that it is desirable that they should be represented in some way in the councils of the agricultural department, so that their recommendations, opinions, and wishes may receive full consideration before any important matter of policy is pressed upon Government by the head of the department. This is probably best to be effected by the formation of an advisory Board of Agriculture, upon which such departments of Government as Public Works, Irrigation, Forests, and Land should be represented, as well as the planting, village, labour, and other interests.

In brief, then, perhaps the most satisfactory solution of the problem is the establishment of a technical Department of Agriculture, under a Director, who shall be assisted by a thoroughly representative Advisory-Board of Agriculture. The Director should be mainly responsible for the agricultural policy of the Government, and its adviser in all matters concerned with agriculture ; a definite agricultural policy should be adopted by the Government, and steadfastly and thoroughly carried out for a long period of time, all departments and other agencies concerned being resolutely guided and directed to the one end in view. In the next chapter suggestions will be given as to the policy to be followed. They form a connected scheme, and bear on all the chief points which seem to require attention. They should be considered as a whole, and every possible agency be put in motion towards the common end, if satisfactory progress is to be made.

It is of course not absolutely necessary for the organisation for the purpose of improving agriculture to be a Government institution, but in the tropics it is probably better that it should, as the natives of tropical countries look to Government for all help and progress. An Agricultural Society, as exists in Jamaica, Ceylon, Madras, etc., may often be the means of very considerable aid to native agriculture, but it requires skilled technical help and advice to draw upon, and these, in the places named, are provided by Government departments.

NOTE.—Since the above was written, progress in the directions indicated has been very marked, and most of the tropical colonies and more progressive countries are now provided with departments of agriculture, and sometimes with definite policies as well.

CHAPTER II

AGRICULTURAL POLICY

It is obvious that the same line of policy cannot be, and ought not to be, followed in every country, on account of the extreme variety in the local conditions. The suggestions that follow are therefore of the most general description, and it is for local authorities to decide which are the most applicable to their own state of affairs. At the same time, it must be borne in mind that for rapid and steady progress, it is necessary to attend to all the most important lines. There should be complete concentration of effort upon agricultural progress. For example, it is of very little use settling the conditions of land without also attending to those of finance or transport.

We may put these suggestions into a tabular form thus:

Make agriculture in general more attractive as compared with other pursuits.

Make the land fully available, by providing roads, drains, etc., at first of course simply as reservations; start with the best land. Settle the forest and other reserves once for all.

Attract population into the country, capitalist, peasant, and labouring, by good advertisement with rigid adhesion to the truth.

Break up the land, if there be in the country many races and many types of agriculture, into sections, divided by roads, and reserved for one only of these races or types. For instance, one section may be reserved for estate agriculture, one for Tamils, one for Chinamen, one for Javanese, in an eastern country; one for estates, one for negroes, one for coolies, in a western. Of course existing density of population is largely the determining factor in the application of this rule.

Encourage the local people to earn money by working on the estates owned by capitalists.

Encourage the use of machinery to reduce the demand for hand labour, and to make work more cheap and efficient.

Arrange matters of finance, i.e. money-lending, seed or manure supply, etc., for the poorer cultivators.

Encourage the peasantry in growing "export" crops, i.e. crops for sale. Whether they are sold or used inside or outside the country does not matter, provided that it has some export trade, but the peasant cannot buy unless he sells, and he now requires to buy from other countries.

Open markets for these export crops, e.g. local markets, or markets at estate factories (by subsidy if necessary), or arrange for cooperative sale at a distance, in larger markets than exist at the villager's door.

Arrange education at local schools to have more bearing upon agriculture. For the younger children open school gardens with nature study lessons; for older children tinge these lessons more and more with agriculture, chiefly general points, such as rotation of crops, etc. For boys of 16 or over start regular agricultural colleges, with plenty of outdoor practical work.

Arrange for local shows and other stimuli to progress. If the country be a little advanced, start local agricultural societies wherever possible.

Introduce legislation for dealing with the treatment of outbreaks of disease among cultivated crops.

Open a department of agriculture to attend to technical matters of progress, and make its head the chief adviser of Government upon agricultural affairs. The department should more specially attend to introduction of new and better kinds of plants, breeding of improved local races, the attacks of disease, experiments with cultivated crops, methods of growth, rotation of crops, harvesting, curing, and marketing, experiments with machinery, whether

new, or improvements upon local machines, and other
similar technical work.

Finally, the Government should adopt a fixed policy and
carry it out steadfastly, at any rate for a considerable
number of years.

In carrying out such a policy, the watchword must be
efficiency, in the true sense of the word. Attention must be
directed mainly to the essential points, letting the details be
filled in later. Every department, every organisation, and every
individual concerned should attend to that for which it or he
is best fitted, and do it to the best purpose, and all efforts must
be co-ordinated to the common end. The land should be used
for those crops to which it is best suited, the people for those
cultivations which they best understand and can practise, the
cultivations chiefly encouraged should be those offering the best
chance of profit and the most safe and steady market, and so on.

An agricultural policy, concerned as it is intimately with
all the habits, customs, preferences, prejudices, and ignorances
of tropical and conservative peoples, should be directed to the
lines of least resistance. The natural trend of things should
be carefully watched, the preferences of the people noticed,
their customs respected, and the agricultural policy directed
along such lines as will take advantage of these facts, not in
such a way as to run counter to them—e.g., in places where the
people would rather grow other crops to which the land is
better suited, or to which their habits incline them, or which
yield greater profit with less labour, the cultivation of rice
should not be forced upon them.

It is of the very highest importance that effort for agricultural
progress should not be scattered, spasmodic, or discontinuous.
The efforts of all concerned should be directed to one end, concentrated upon the immediate problems in hand, and carried on
steadfastly for long periods of time. It is useless to try to go
too fast, and to expect immediate results is more sanguine than
wise or reasonable.

People in a tropical country naturally tend to look to the
Government for all help and progress. It is better to teach

them to help themselves, and to help them to do so, though it must be admitted that at present there is little prospect of any voluntary effort producing much result, and consequently for many years to come. the work of progress will fall to the Government and to a small section of the agricultural community.

We must now proceed to deal with some more concrete points in the policy to be pursued, our aim being in every case to pick out the essential point, and to direct attention mainly to that.

The ideal set before us being to obtain a fairly dense population of all kinds, engaged in all the different forms of agricultural enterprise, it is evident that for any rapid progress in a thinly peopled country it is necessary to attract people from abroad to engage in agriculture, and so far as possible to persuade them to settle. To do this the country must be made more attractive to them—be they capitalists, peasants, or labourers—than the other countries with which it has to compete. All should be equally welcome who are of good stock and character and willing to take their part in building up the country. Afterwards, when a rush has (perhaps) been established, discrimination may be used if thought advisable, and the less desirable races kept out.

In the same way, all forms of agriculture, and those who wish to engage in them, should be equally encouraged, except those which are mere exploitation, such as chena or ladang cultivation, or tapioca without intermingling or rotation. If any one form of agricultural enterprise is to be encouraged more than another, it should be the capitalist or planting industry. The capitalist, large or small, is not obliged to make any given country the scene of his work; he can choose his country, and there are many in which planting has already proved successful. He brings money into the country, opens up large areas, creates work and trade. Two or three large planting enterprises will do more to open up and enrich the country than thousands of villagers can do.

As Sir Frank Swettenham has pointed out, there is at times a tendency among Government officers to look askance at Europeans anxious to engage in planting enterprises, as if they were trying simply to exploit the country for their own benefit. This is a very one-sided view of the matter. The native of a thinly peopled country, if given a chance, is a worse exploiter than any other, with his chena cultivation, his tapioca fields, or what not. Of course the investor from abroad is not there from philanthropic motives; he hopes to "make his fortune." He does not want to cut himself off from his country and friends, and to risk health, life, and money in a strange land and in an enervating climate for a return similar to that which he could get at home. In making his own fortune—if indeed he ever does make it—he makes prosperity and wealth for many of the natives of the country, and for those who have worked for him. He should receive every encouragement, and all obstacles which would tend to drive him to other countries, or check his success in his adopted country, should as far as possible be removed.

Every encouragement can be given to all kinds of agriculture, without causing mere exploitation of the country. The more that genuine agriculture is encouraged, the less will be the risk of such exploitation, and the desire to carry it on. Exploitation pure and simple, be it chena cultivation, tapioca cultivation on extensive areas without proper provision for continuous occupation and cultivation of the land, or the system of moving on to new land when the old becomes weedy, so popular with the natives of some thinly peopled countries, should be checked with the strong hand. Misfortune, inseparable from all enterprise, may at times involve abandonment of land, but no cultivation which is carried on with the deliberate intention of exhausting and then abandoning the land should be allowed.

The way to make the country attractive to outside capital, population, and labour, is obviously to remove the various hindrances, discouragements, and disadvantages under which agriculture suffers, to encourage it in every possible way, and provide it with the necessary practical and technical help, and to advertise the country and its agricultural attractiveness as widely as possible in those regions from which capitalists, peasants, or labourers are to be attracted. But in advertising—whatever methods be adopted—the greatest care must be taken that exaggeration and inaccuracy be avoided, so that no one shall be disappointed on arrival to find that things are not as described.

Every effort should be made to advertise the country to the capitalist who may invest in agriculture—to let him know that there he can grow such and such crops to profit, that he can get land at reasonable prices. with good soil, good facilities for drainage and transportation, and a good labour supply. One of the first things, for instance, which should be put in hand, in a thinly or moderately peopled country, is a kind of agricultural handbook, with good maps showing the available land, types of soil, road and drain reservations, elevations, and other practical information, and with practical details in the text as to land available, method of getting it, cost, labour, rules as to opening and keeping in cultivation, crops for which it is suitable, cost of opening land in such crops, yield and value of crop, cost of cultivation, profitableness, and so on, as well as the necessary details as to climate, cost of living, etc. Such a handbook should be constantly revised, and should be distributed in all quarters whence capital is likely to flow. Its price should be as low as possible, and extensive free gifts should be made to all public libraries, journals, chambers of commerce, planters' associations in other countries, and similar institutions.

Other advertising literature should be prepared to appeal to the peasant and the labourer, and written in suitable simple language. The very greatest care should be taken to avoid inaccuracy or exaggeration, and attention should be paid to suitable illustration. The peasant should be informed that he can get land on easy terms, in sections inhabited by people of his own nationality and caste, that it will grow such and such crops to profit, that good markets, financial help (by credit societies, or otherwise), facilities for drainage and transport, and other advantages, are obtainable, under a secure and just Government. His position as regards taxation and other civic duties and liabilities should also be made very clear. The labourer should have the conditions of labour made clear, the rate of pay, the cost of food and clothing; he should know that he can get good work, good treatment, good pay, and that he will be encouraged to settle down at the end of his term of work, upon land reserved for people of his own race and caste, to be granted upon such and such terms, that he can grow such and such crops, obtain good markets, and so on.

One great advertisement must also be remembered—the standard of quality of exported articles of agricultural produce. It is of the highest importance to get a good name from the start, and keep it, if necessary by the making of laws for inspection at the ports and refusal of exit to inferior articles.

To pass on now to the removal of obstacles from the path of agricultural progress, and the making of agriculture as attractive as other occupations. This is evidently closely bound up with the first consideration. The various disadvantages, under which agriculture and those who pursue it suffer, have been fully dealt with above, and it will suffice to put them together in brief outline.

In the first place, the best agricultural land of the country should be picked out, and the chief attention devoted to that until progress becomes rapid and population large. The man who buys land for agricultural purposes should be able to buy it in such shape and so located that he is in no way dependent upon the acts, sufferance or indolence of his neighbours, or upon the circumstances of the surrounding land, for the carrying out of his enterprises. In other words, he should have independent access to public roads and public drainage facilities, wherever his land may lie; no land should be sold which does not conform to these conditions. This is of the very highest importance for any future agricultural progress or prosperity.

This work has comparatively little to do with a Department of Agriculture; it is simply a preliminary to any real progressive agriculture in the country. In the present virgin condition of so much of most tropical countries, this kind of work is easily carried out; in this respect they have an enormous advantage over most eastern countries, where every inch of land is often fully occupied, and the making of roads or drainage canals consequently a troublesome and expensive process. It is of the very highest importance to agricultural progress, and to the prosperity of the country, that it be thoroughly provided with transport facilities; there should be at least as complete a network of roads as in such a country as England, so that every little patch of land may have its own frontage. Similarly with drains; everyone who has not natural drains should have a frontage on a public drainage canal, or reservation for such a canal. Of course, rail may replace road.

The Forest Department should be called upon to settle the forest reserves, in order that the danger of floods and silting may be as far as possible guarded against, and that agriculturists may know at an early date that such and such lands are not to be available for agriculture, however desirable for that object.

The limits of existing villages, estates, forest reserves, settlements of all the different races in the country, and of all alienated lands should be at once determined, beginning in the richer soils. The departments of Public Works, Survey, and any other concerned, should then be called upon to lay out the road reservations, again beginning in the districts most suitable for agriculture. These reservations should form a complete network, and in each mesh of the network the area included should not as a rule exceed about a square mile. In places where the country is flat or nearly so, and quite unoccupied, the roads may best be parallel, demarcating the country into squares, as in the western United States, but in hilly districts they will have to be laid out as best suits the engineering necessities of the case. In districts again where there is already much settlement, the roads should be made to separate the different races, or different types of agriculture there existing—e.g., to cut out one section including only natives from another devoted to planting industry, and from a third in which there is a small colony of some immigrant race.

As has already been pointed out, the road reservations need only be marked upon the map at first, in unoccupied country; the great thing is to have a map of the country with all the roads clearly marked, so that purchasers of land may know that they will abut upon a road, and that when their land is opened up, the road will be cleared also. The terms upon which roads will be made, and how far away from the nearest "made" road land will be sold, are mere details for subsequent settlement. The important thing is to make the reservations while the country is virgin.

Drainage in flat lands is another matter which must be provided for by the Government, and at the same time that the road reservations are marked out, the drains should be demarcated also. As far as practicable, the roads and drains should be side by side, and arrangements should be made for the future use of the drains as canals, with the necessary passing places, and docks at the more important centres. As with the roads, the drains need at first only be marked upon the map, but when any land is sold, the necessary drain should be cut to it through the drainage reservations. This should be done by the Government, and a small drainage rate charged, if necessary.

By the carrying out of these two very important measures, the land will thus be broken up into "sections" averaging about a square mile each, divided by roads (made or demarcated), and in coastal or other very flat districts also by drains (made or demarcated). The Land offices have now to deal with their very important share in agricultural progress Intending purchasers will know that whatever land they buy has both drainage and transport frontages, and that the necessary communications will be made by Government to the already existing made roads and made drains, within a settled period.

The most important work of the land offices, from the point of view of agricultural progress, is the intermingling of the different races, and of the different types of agricultural enterprises. This is rendered very simple by the system of "sections" already indicated. Each section, or at any rate each larger sub-division of a section, should be reserved for one race or caste, or for one type of agriculture. Reservations being thus marked on the map, the roads and drains are then made as required. In the sections reserved for peasant agriculture, further reservations may be made for roads and drains to reach the central parts.

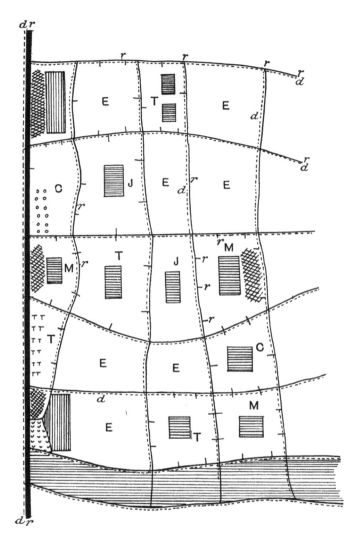

XXIV. The plan shows a small portion of flat coast country laid out as suggested. It is supposed to be in the Federated Malay States. The stout black line along the left is a coast road with a drain beside it and the shadings represent existing agriculture, the rest being untouched land. *E* is estate agriculture, *M, J, C, T,* blocks occupied by Malays, Javanese, Chinese, and Tamils. *rr* represent reservations for roads, *dd* for drains. Each section is reserved for the nationality or type of agriculture shown by the letter in it. The short lines projecting from the road reservation lines represent the beginnings of roads into the sections for peasant agriculture. The shaded belt at the bottom represents a swamp.

This intermixture of races and types of agriculture is of the greatest importance to the progress of agriculture in the country. It helps and stimulates the villager by example and rivalry; it assists to raise the general standard of living, and so to improve the market for produce and provide better local demand; it helps to check the spread of disease among cultivated plants; it provides village labour at easy distance from the planting estates, and provides opportunities of earning money by external work to the inhabitants of the village sections.

Not only should the Land offices attend to this breaking up of the land into sections inhabited by different kinds of people and different types of agriculture, but they should also endeavour, when it is reasonably practicable, to prevent too much of any one district becoming taken up with one cultivation only. Thus if one estate section is entirely rubber, they should try to get the next one, if suitable for it, taken up for sugar, or for coconuts. Not only will disease be less liable to spread rapidly over large areas, but the labour difficulty will be less acute, the different products in a district perhaps not all requiring their greatest labour supply at the same time, as would be the case if all the estates were in one product.

By selling all land with road frontage, the frontages on the great trunk roads, and at the corners where four roads meet, need no longer be allowed to go at low rates; they may be charged for according to their value as building sites for shops, etc.

The next important point is the labour question. Without a good, reliable, and reasonably cheap labour supply, capitalists will not invest in agricultural enterprises. The introduction of labourers into the country, if not already there, must be made a special object of endeavour. Every possible attraction should be held out, and difficulties and inconveniences removed. Let coolies be well treated, sufficiently well paid, have the voyage made as comfortable as possible, and be free from extortion or ill-treatment on the way; let special terms be offered to induce them to settle in sections of land reserved for one race or caste and under their own headmen; and let these facts be freely advertised. Actual raising of the rate of pay should only be a last resource, when the cost of living, the advances, etc., have been reduced to a minimum, and all other inducements offered that are possible.

The removal of the next important hindrance from the path, the poverty of the small cultivator, which prevents his being able to adopt improvements or try experiments with new crops, will in many countries require the aid of the Financial department of Government. It was suggested above that some system of Cooperative Credit Societies be established in the villages, with unlimited liability and Government audit, each society being confined to one village or "section." The same problem must also be attacked from the other end by some arrangement for providing a good market for the villagers' crops; local markets should be opened, and they should be encouraged to grow the same crops as the neighbouring estates, and the latter be subsidised, when necessary, to induce them to undertake to buy the village produce at fixed rates, with payment in cash.

Another department whose share in the work of agricultural progress is a very important one, is the Department of Public Instruction. Education is among the most important agencies in raising the general standard of living, making the people more receptive towards new ideas, and stimulating progress. It should be generously provided and for all nationalities alike, and every effort should be made to prevent its becoming, as is so often the tendency with tropical peoples, a mere matter of book learning and passing examinations. School gardens, with their accompanying lessons in nature study, elementary horticulture, etc., should be made an important feature in the regular curriculum, at least in all those schools where the masters are found capable and willing in regard to such work. Actual technical instruction in agriculture may come later.

Other departments of Government are also at times able to help in agricultural progress—e.g., the Railways by granting lower rates, the Public Health by special attention to unhealthy but otherwise favourable districts, especially in regard to the sanitary conditions for coolies, and so on.

Last, but not least, there remains the Administration, the work of the district officers and similar officials, who control the headmen, and exercise enormous influence among the natives of all races. As has already been pointed out, these officers can do a great deal for or against agricultural progress; in fact, when one of them is opposed to any scheme, it is practically idle to expect anything to come of it in his district. For this reason, and because these officers being so constantly removed from place to place, continuity of effort is impaired, it is absolutely necessary that the Government have a definite agricultural policy, and see that it is carried out by its subordinates.

In regard to village and native agriculture generally, the policy should be to lead rather than to drive, though the latter may be employed at times with advantage—e.g., in dealing with outbreaks of disease. The villager should be shown where his advantage lies, and encouraged to grow those things that he prefers, that he understands, and for which he has a good market. Special attention should be devoted to the removal of hindrances from his path—e.g., in the matter of roads, drainage, finance, markets and education. His standard of living should be raised by intermingling of races and of types of agriculture, and the same process will provide him with example, with object lessons, and with better markets. It is better in general to aim at increasing his efficiency than the amount of work he does. He should be taught that agriculture is honourable as well as profitable. Some system of bestowal of honours or rank upon those who have done much for agriculture might well be adopted, and local shows also should be encouraged, rather than large public shows, at which most of the rewards are liable to go to others than the real makers or growers of the exhibits.

It may make matters more clear, if we put the problem in the form of a rough diagram, as is done on the following page. Every tropical country tends to settle down to a certain "agricultural equilibrium," generally very low, and the object must be to raise this. We have indicated this by the use of levels.

14—2

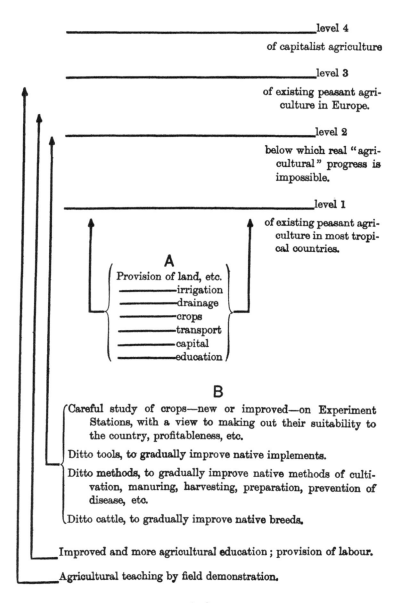

_____level 4

of capitalist agriculture

_____level 3

of existing peasant agri-
culture in Europe.

_____level 2

below which real "agri-
cultural" progress is
impossible.

_____level 1

of existing peasant agri-
culture in most tropi-
cal countries.

A

Provision of land, etc.
————————irrigation
————————drainage
————————crops
————————transport
————————capital
————————education

B

Careful study of crops—new or improved—on Experiment
Stations, with a view to making out their suitability to
the country, profitableness, etc.

Ditto tools, to gradually improve native implements.

Ditto methods, to gradually improve native methods of cultivation, manuring, harvesting, preparation, prevention of
disease, etc.

Ditto cattle, to gradually improve native breeds.

Improved and more agricultural education ; provision of labour.

Agricultural teaching by field demonstration.

And so on.

If, as in most tropical countries, the average level of agriculture is level 1, then all the factors A must be first attended to. In Ceylon, for instance, capital is the weak point, in other countries it may be land, or education. But it must be clearly understood that *all* must be attended to, to raise the level to 2. After that, the factors B come in and of course an Agricultural Department may be working at B while the Government attends to A. It must be specially noted that what is wanted for the progress of agriculture at level 1 is on the whole quite different from what is wanted at level 4. This is an important consideration that tends to be lost sight of, now that there is a rush into making departments of agriculture. So far as they are technical they can only help people above level 2, except in the item of provision of crops, which was the work of the older Botanic Gardens.

Speaking generally, the weakest point in the chain of factors for the improvement of peasant agriculture, in most tropical countries, is the provision of *capital*. It is not intended to imply that enough education is provided, or that the land is made sufficiently available by transport facilities, irrigation, drainage, or what not, but simply that in the present condition of affairs in most tropical countries there is little possibility of further progress in peasant agriculture without the provision of capital. The question of agricultural progress may be closely compared to the physiological process of growth in a plant. If an ample supply of heat and moisture be maintained, then increase of growth will stop, when the supply of food is not kept up to the standard of the other two factors. If this supply be greatly increased, the next factor to break down and stop increasing growth may be the temperature or the moisture. Blackman[1] in dealing with this subject expresses it thus: "When a process is conditioned as to its rapidity by a number of separate factors, the rate of the process is limited by the pace of the slowest factor." This slowest factor is called the limiting factor, and in our opinion it is most commonly supply of capital that is the limiting factor in agricultural progress in the tropics at the present time, and until this

[1] *l.c.* p. 4.

factor is strengthened no amount of improvement in education, transport, or other of the factors will produce any result in quickening the rate of progress. The extraordinarily rapid spread of cooperative credit societies in India goes to show how desirable such things are at present, and our experience of Ceylon and the Malay States indicates that in these at any rate the want is much the same.

In the wet equatorial countries the bulk of the crops, other than rice, tend to be perennials, thus needing more capital than annuals, and thus encouraging capitalist[1] enterprise to a greater extent than peasant. The general tendency of the opening up that is going on, whether in European colonies or in self-governed countries like Brazil, is also to encourage capitalist as against peasant enterprise, and the endeavour of governments should be to encourage both equally; while the capitalist is helped by improvement of crops, methods, etc., the peasant should be helped in matters of finance, education, and the other factors given in the table under A.

It must further be recognised that the introduction of any improvement, whether in the factors A or the factors B of the diagram, benefits at first only a few, who thus gain, leaving the rest to be compelled to follow by the instinct of self-preservation. The general effect, therefore, and one which on the face of it looks desirable, is to lengthen out the column of agriculturists from a shape like a $\wedge$ to one more like a λ. The base remains much as at the beginning, but pressure is a little relieved above and this is perhaps a benefit to all concerned. The relative distances of top and bottom, however, will remain all but unaltered, and real improvement in conditions must be work of very great slowness. If anything the top tends continually to go ahead faster than the bottom, so that the effect of improvement is on the whole deleterious to the latter   But evolution seems to be an absolute necessity, and all we can do is therefore to do our best for those at the bottom, though the conversation of some who are pushing the establishment

[1] By capitalist in this book is simply meant one who has a balance to the good, however small, instead of being in debt to the usurer.

of departments of agriculture would lead one to suppose that a millennium was at hand.

In former times, little was done for agriculture, and the natural rate of progress was exceedingly slow. But with the more humanitarian ideas of government that have come into vogue during the last hundred years, this has been altered. By attention to questions of land and its availability, transport, and education, agricultural progress has been accelerated, to the point in very many cases where capital has become the limiting factor, and if this be not in turn attended to, progress must go on at the old rate, and all that has been done will count for little; whereas if it be properly cared for, progress may go on as before till some other factor becomes limiting. The essential for the best government of an agricultural people is consequently to recognise early the factor that is about to limit progress, and attend chiefly to that. Unless *all* the factors are kept up to proper condition progress will be almost negligible, but at any one time one alone is probably most in need of attention.

The same rule applies to the progress of agriculture under the later factors B. In the first place, it must be pointed out that the incoming of B does not eliminate the necessity for attention to A; the latter must also be kept up to the mark, though all but the last two of them may in time reach a point of practical perfection. But with regard to B proper, it must again be recognised that all parts of the problem hang together and must be attended to at the same time. If cattle are to be improved, their food supply, and the tools they are to use, must be improved also. If better quality of fruit is to be produced, manure must be used, and a market found for the new produce; and so on.

In conclusion, therefore, it is evident that in settling the policy to be pursued in any given country, there are many and complex problems to be considered. For example, a country like India may need comparatively little export trade, as she can grow·nearly everything that she requires within her own borders, and the quality of her exports is not in general very high, whereas a country like Brazil, though even larger, and possessing as great a variety of climates, may need to export a good deal, in order to pay for the many products of the colder countries that she requires for her generally higher state of civilisation. An island like Montserrat (p. 145) may require the encouragement of capitalist industry, a country like Brazil that of peasant agriculture. A country like Ceylon may require the extension of existing crops, one like Brazil the introduction of as many new ones as possible. One country may need the proper settlement of conditions of transport, another the proper provision of capital or of markets, for the progress of peasant agriculture. Yet another may need a proper labour supply to encourage capitalist agriculture: and so on. Our endeavour in this book has been to set forth the whole problem as clearly as may be, leaving those interested in any particular country to decide the exact policy required there.

CHAPTER III

DEPARTMENTS OF AGRICULTURE

AGRICULTURE has become so technical, and accurate scientific experiments upon cultivation, manuring, preparation of crops, rotation of crops, plant-breeding, etc., so absolutely necessary to its progress in most countries, that a scientific department, or some other organisation which is prepared to keep up a scientific staff and meet the cost of such work, must be established in every progressive tropical country.

The department should not try to include too much. The Government is the body to direct upon agricultural progress all the departments concerned, whether with regard to land, roads, drains, finance, education, or what not. The agricultural department should concern itself primarily with the technical improvement of agriculture, and only in watching and criticising with the work of other organisations.

Such a department wants a trained scientific head, technically acquainted with the work that must go on in his department, but if he is to be largely concerned with accounts, or with other organisations, civilian help is desirable also. His department should be established, if possible, as far as headquarters are concerned, at some cooler station than is afforded by the plains in the tropics, for better work can then be done, under better conditions, by the scientific staff. At the same time, they must not be placed in a station too different from the ordinary agricultural conditions of the country, so far as outdoor experimental work is concerned.

Experiments with the different cultivated crops of the country must be carried out upon a special Experiment Station, and if this can be upon a large enough scale to enable its crops to be sold in the open market, under some name which will conceal their origin, a much better commercial test will be obtained. This is the system which was first adopted in Ceylon, and is now being imitated elsewhere. Experiments with machinery can also be tried there.

Introduction of new and better plants from abroad requires the aid of a Botanic Garden and Herbarium, and of a botanist upon the staff. Plant breeding work, which bids fair to be one of the most important duties of such a department, can be carried on in the Botanic Garden, or upon the Experiment Station.

The aid of an Entomologist and of a Mycologist may be necessary for the study of the local diseases, and the investigation of methods of treatment.

A Chemist is one of the most important officers of such an institution, to analyse soils, manures, etc., control experiments upon manuring, rotation of crops, and so on, and should be assisted by a Bacteriologist.

A Veterinary Surgeon is required to attend to stock improvement, breeding, diseases, etc.

If agricultural colleges are to be started (in general best after boys have been gradually trained up through the school gardens), the staff of such a department should be able to do much of the teaching required, and the colleges should be situated near to the Experiment Stations.

Such a department will obviously require a somewhat expensive equipment in the matter of laboratories, library, and so on.

Lastly, the Board of Agriculture may be mentioned. It should be advisory, not controlling, and should include representatives of all important departments, interests, and organisations connected with agriculture, such as land, public works, administration, the mercantile, planting, and peasant interests, and so on.

Such being a brief outline of the necessities at the headquarters of such a department, we have now to consider how to bring home to the agricultural population the results of all the work.

The department must obviously publish a journal, or, as is done in Ceylon, circulars, i.e. occasional publications dealing only with one item of work. This form of publication has the great advantage that nothing need be published until it has been thoroughly worked up, that the publication can be large or small, and that it can be used to save correspondence, a circular (marked or unmarked) being sent as a complete or partial answer to a letter.

The journal must evidently be in English, or other European language, in most tropical countries, and something must also be published in the vernacular for the benefit of the majority of the population, who will not understand it. As such people will not as a rule read long articles, perhaps the best form for such publication to take is that of short leaflets, which can be distributed by any organisation available for the purpose. It is worth noting that even for the best educated and most progressive part of the community, the publications should be as short as possible. It is better to give a short article, and repeat it later under another title, and in other words, than to give so long a one that it is not properly read or assimilated.

By the publication of a journal, by the visits of the planters to the Botanic Gardens and the Experiment Stations, or to the Mycologist and Entomologist, and by the establishment among them of cooperative experiments, the planting or capitalist community will probably be sufficiently served, for they can write about anything upon which they desire fuller information, and can visit the departmental libraries, museums, etc.

The next question is, how to get at the peasant class, the poorer villagers, and labourers. This is a difficult problem. Perhaps one of the best ways of reaching them is through the administrative officers of Government, who should have trained agricultural instructors under them. The work to be done by these instructors should be planned out by the Government, or by their administrative superior, in consultation with the head of the agricultural department, but they should not be responsible to the latter department. This department should inspect and criticise their work, and report to the administrative officer concerned.

Another good way of getting at the rather better-to-do class is through agricultural societies, which may be entirely voluntary or attached to some Government department, preferably the agricultural or the administrative. These societies may issue leaflets, manage small experimental gardens, hold meetings for discussion of agricultural topics, organise local finance, markets, etc., press for improvement of local transport facilities, and so on. Such agricultural societies are doing good work in Jamaica, Ceylon, South India and other places.

INDEX

For EU product safety concerns, contact us at Calle de José Abascal, 56–1°, 28003 Madrid, Spain or eugpsr@cambridge.org.

www.ingramcontent.com/pod-product-compliance
Ingram Content Group UK Ltd.
Pitfield, Milton Keynes, MK11 3LW, UK
UKHW010346140625
459647UK00010B/853